Beckett

Unofficial Guide To

Pokémon

PRICE GUiDE

BECKETT®

B

MEDIA

Beckett Media • 4635 McEwen Road • Dallas, Texas 75244
972-991-6657 • www.beckettpokemon.com

Contents

3 Professor Oak's Trivia
More perplexing puzzles from our Pokémon professor!

4 Side By Side, it's Pichu and Pichu!
A look back at the Pichu Brothers

8 Top 20 Pokemon Cards of All Time!
Do you have any of these in your collection?

14 Complete Guide to Pokémon Monsters
From #1 to #493, we caught them all for you to see!

212 Pokémon® Price Guide
A comprehensive guide to all Pokémon® cards

Chief Executive Officer Peter Gudmundsson

Founder & Advisor Dr. James Beckett III

Chief Operating Officer Margaret Steele

Associate Publisher Tracy Hackler

Chief Financial Officer Jennifer LePage

VP Sales & Marketing Mike Obert

Editorial Director Doug Kale

Assistant Editor Rebecca Bundy

Contributing Writers Alex Lucard

Art Director Eric Knagg

Designers Jeff Bauzon, Cathy Hutzler, Bill Bridgeforth

Production Manager Pete Adauto

Production Daniel Moscoso

Marketing Director Jenifer Grellhesl

Product Sales Sonya Lewis (Manager)

Published by Beckett Media LP

4635 McEwen Road

Dallas, TX 75244

972 - 991- 6657

World Wide Web Home Page: www.beckett.com/pokemon

An Apprise Media Company

Chief Executive Officer Charles G. McCurdy

Senior Vice President Michael Behringer

By Alex Lucard

PROFESSOR OAK'S TRIVIA

MORE PERPLEXING PUZZLES FROM OUR POKÉMON PROFESSOR!

Welcome Professor Oak's Trivia! How well do you know Pokémon? Lets see. Take my ten question trivia test.

1. In the anime, what is May's first Pokémon?

2. *In Pokémon Mysterious Dungeon*, what are the three Pokémon you can only have as your starter if you choose to play as a girl?

3. What does Bonsly evolve into?

4. With the *Pokémon Diamond & Pearl* TCG set, how many holographic cards are there?

5. The 10th Pokémon movie, which was just released in Japan, focuses on which three Pokémon?

6. When we first meet Jessie and James in the anime, who are their original three Pokémon?

7. What special item doubles a Pikachu's Special Attack skill?

8. How many Pokémon are there currently?

9. Which system is the video game version of the Pokémon TCG for?

10. Which of the following is not an evolution for Magnemite: Magneton, Magnavox, or Magnezone? ❖

EXTRA CREDIT:

In the original *Pokémon Stadium* for the Nintendo 64, there are nine mini games you could play. Can you name three of them?

1. TORCHIC 2. CHIKORITA, SKITTY AND EEVEE 3. SUDOWOODO 4. 17 5. DIALGA, PALKIA AND DARKRAI 6. EKANS, KOFFING AND MEOWTH 7. A LIGHT BALL 8. 493 9. GAME BOY (YOU CAN ALSO SAY GAME BOY POCKET OR GAME BOY COLOR) 10. MAGNAVOX EXTRA CREDIT: MAGIKARP SPLASH, CLEFAIRY SAYS, RUN RATTATA RUN, SNORE WAR, THUNDERING DYNAMO, SUSHI-GO-ROUND, EKANS HOOP HURL, ROCK HARDEN AND DIGI DIGI DIGI

Side By Side, It's Pichu and Pichu!

A look back at the Pichu Brothers

By Alex Lucard

With the coming of *Pokémon Gold and Silver*, we were given the baby form of Pikachu in Pichu. Like all things Pikachu, Pichu quickly captured the hearts of Pokéfans everywhere and it wasn't long until Pichu started appearing in animated form, most notably as the Pichu Brothers.

The Pichu Brothers are a rascally pair of wild Pokémon that were originally intended for a one shot animated short, but they became so popular that they ended up as recurring characters, similar to Jigglypuff. Let's take a look back at this dynamic duo and the shorts they've appeared in.

www.pokemon2002.jp

ピカ★ピカ星空キャンプ

全国東宝系大ヒット上映中！

© Nintendo · CREATURES · GAMEFREAK · TV TOKYO · SHO-PRO · JR KIKAKU ©2002 ピカチュウプロジェクト

Pichu's Debut

On April 11th, 2001, *Pokémon: the Third Movie* was unveiled to US audiences. Before the movie started, audiences watched a short animated Pikachu cartoon entitled "Pikachu and Pichu." This would be the debut of the Pichu Brothers. Like all Pikachu shorts before the movies, the human characters from the anime are absent. In this cartoon, Pikachu sees one of the Pichu Brothers in the building across from him. This Pichu makes rude faces at him and Pikachu returns the favor. Later, while on top of the building, Pikachu is playing with the other Pokémon belonging to Misty, Brock and Ash when he again encounters the same Pichu. Pichu again makes lewd gestures towards Pikachu and then the second Pichu comes out to see what is going on. With this, the establishment of the Brothers is complete.

The rest of the cartoon revolves around the Pichu Brothers getting into trouble and Pikachu having to help them out. The Pichu Brothers nearly fall off of a building and tick off a Houndour that chases them all around the city. In the end, the Houndour and the Pichu Brothers put aside their differences to keep a Pokémon playground from being destroyed by their battling. Pikachu has to say goodbye to his new friends in the Pichu Brothers so that he can get back to Ash. However, this would not be the last time we'd see the Pichu Brothers

PIKACHU RECORDS

We Want More Pichu!

The most interesting thing about this cartoon is that it establishes that Pichu have powerful electric attacks, but that they are too young and undeveloped to control their power. Thus, their own electric attacks damage themselves as well as their opponents. This does not transfer over to the Pokémon video games, as there, Pichu can use electric attacks with impunity. Oddly enough, this aspect from this 10 minute Pokémon short was carried over to *Super Smash Brothers Melee* where Pichu is an unlockable character. He takes a slight bit of damage from his own electric attacks and he is very light, but he's the fastest character in the game!

The Pichu Brothers would appear later that year around Christmas time in the anthology "Pikachu's

Winter Vacation 2001." They only appear in the last of the three cartoons that make up this collection in a short called "We the Pichu Brothers." In this cartoon, the Pichu Brothers are having an argument and they end up using electric attacks on each other. As noted in their first appearance, their own electric attacks hurt themselves when they use them, so both brothers end up knocking each other out. One of the brothers ends up falling off a slide onto a skateboard. The skateboard takes off from the impact... and then rolls down a hill. The older of the Pichu Brothers is out cold still, so their friend Wooper tries to follow the skateboard, which ends up going through heavy traffic.

The cartoon then revolves around the elder Pichu Brother and his friends Teddiursa, Magby and Smoochum searching for Wooper and the younger Pichu. Escapades include the younger Pichu being carried off by hellium filled baloons, the entire group of Pokémon angering the same Houndour they annoyed in the cartoon "Pikachu and Pichu" and a wild brawl breaks out between the Pichu Brothers and Azumarill, Smoochum and Magby. The end result of the Ice, Fire, and Water attack is a slide made out of ice that all of the Pokémon decide to play together on instead of fighting. It's a cute little story and we end up seeing this same collection of Pokémon in the fourth Pichu Brothers cartoon, but we've still got the third one to look at first!

More Pichu on Film

Debuting before the feature film *Pokémon Heroes* was the Pichu Brothers' third animated short entitled "Camp Pikachu!" This short cartoon takes place in the Johto region and opens with the Pichu Brothers stowing away on a train. Thanks to a mishap with a Skarmory and a mailbag, the Pichu Brothers are knocked off the train and sent sailing through the air. They end up colliding with a Wynaut who is sitting in a tree and all three plummet to the earth! Not to worry though, because as luck would have it, all three land right on Misty's Psyduck. Ash's Pikachu happens along with some of the other main Pokémon from the cartoon series and he instantly recognizes these two Pichu as the ones he met before. Piakchu and friends invite the Pichu Brothers and the Wynaut to forage for food with them and play some games.

Not much really happens in this cartoon. It's just a chance for animators to show Pokémon playing together in cute ways, like Sudowoodo playing tricks on Wynaut and the Pichu Brothers and Totodile inventing a game that ends with a cameo of Team Rocket's Meowth and Wobuffet blasting off. Later that night a Duskull, who is a friend of the Wynaut, drops by and the two

of them, along with one of the Pichu Brothers, end up playing practical jokes on the other Pokémon, especially on the other Pichu Brother. They have a few other adventures, but in the end, the Pichu Brothers make it back on board the train and wave goodbye to their friends.

Pichu's Got Game

The final short the Pichu Brothers appeared in wasn't just a cartoon; it was a video game as well! "Pichu Bros: Party Panic" was a cartoon divided into multiple

parts throughout the video game *Pokémon Channel*. You had to complete certain tasks to finish the cartoon and once it was done you could watch it in English, in Japanese, or even with commentary from the actress who plays Misty in the Japanese language of the Pokémon anime series! An even bigger reward for completing the cartoon was available to people who lived in Europe or Japan. Once the cartoon was complete, you could unlock a downloadable JIRACHI for your copies of *Pokémon Ruby/Sapphire*. Lucky them!

This cartoon is best known for two things. The first is the very catchy song "Side by Side, it's Pichu and Pichu," which the name of this article is taken from. The second is that this cartoon incorporates the original tech demo for the Nintendo GameCube called "Meowth's Party," which is a 3-D CGI segment featuring several dozen Pokémon having fun, singing and dancing.

Those Playful Pichu Brothers

"Pichu Bros: Party Panic" takes place once again in Johto, and in the same playground the first two Pichu Brothers cartoons occurred in. The cartoon begins with Meowth, Wobuffet, a Cubone and the Squirtle Squad on a high building looking out over a city at night. Meowth declares he is going to throw the greatest

 text along edge:
©2008 Pokémon, ©1997-2008 Nintendo, Creatures, GAME FREAK, TV Tokyo, ShoPro, JR Kikaku. Pokémon properties are trademarks of Nintendo.

shindig in Pokémon history. The cartoon then cuts to the main Pokémon of the cartoon, the Pichu Brothers, racing through town and having fun, along with shots of the supporting Pokémon in Teddiursa, Magby, Wooper and Smoochum.

All six Pokémon end up back at their playground and Smoochum tells them about how all the other Pokémon they have seen have moon shaped pieces of papers and seem really excited and happy. The friends decide they want to know what's going on so they run out looking for clues. Eventually the group find an Aipom and a Smeargle who are play sword fighting with their pieces of paper. The Pichu Brothers ask what they are for and Aipom reveals that there's going to be a big invitation only party with lots of yummy fruit for all of the guests. The young Pokémon get excited and Smeargle draws them the location of where the party will be (by the clock tower), so Magby suggests they head over there right now!

Unfortunately, when they get there, the Squirtle Squad blocks them from entering and Cubone comes out to let the Pichu Brothers and friends know they need an invitation to get in. None of them have any though! This makes all the young Pokémon very sad. As luck would have it, one of the Pichu Brothers notices an invitation floating through the air carried by the wind. All the friends decide to chase after it in hopes of getting a taste of all that food.

The group ends up getting split up by various incidents until only the Pichu Brothers are left. They are just about to get the invitation... when they land on top of the same poor Houndour they have harassed in previous cartoons. Needless to say, the Houndour ends up pursuing them and thus the quest for the flying

invite is put on hold.

While the Pichu Brothers are running for their lives, Smoochum runs into a crying Oddish. Smoochum learns the invitation they were after belonged to this very Oddish, who is very sad that she lost her chance to go to the party. At the same time, the Pichu Brothers manage to get away from the Houndour by going up an elevator. At the top of the building, the Brothers take a sigh of relief when the invitation smacks one right in the face! Both Pichu are overjoyed at this remarkable coincidence. Everyone but Smoochum reunites back at the clubhouse and when the Pichu Brothers reveal they have the invitation, they all celebrate. Until Smoochum enters with the Oddish and explains that it's really her invitation. The younger Pichu doesn't want to give the invite back to Oddish, but the older scolds it for being greedy and told it to do the right thing. Oddish gets its invite back and is super happy, but the clubhouse gang is sadder than ever, because they had tasted success and had to give it up.

Before despair sets in, an Azumarril visits them and gives them their invitations. It turns out they were just the last stop on the guest list! Everyone gets to go to the party, has a great time, gets a lot of food to eat, and there is even a fireworks display at the end which sends poor old Meowth blasting off again.

These are the four main appearances of the Pichu Brothers At this point it's not a matter of if they will appear in another cartoon short, it's just a question of when we will get to see them next. With these two brothers being as popular as they are, it's only a matter of time. ❖

TOP 20 Pokémon Cards of All Time!

Do you have any of these cards in your collection?

We've compiled a list of the 20 most valuable Pokémon cards from all of the regular-issued card sets. This list includes cards dating back to the first Base set released in 1999. The original Charizard card from that 1st Edition Base set recently climbed back up to the $100 price range. Here's a look at all of those hot cards.

Charizard ex
160 HP

STAGE 2
Evolves from Charmeleon
When Pokémon has been Knocked Out, your opponent takes 2 Prize cards.

Illus. Hironobu Sugiyama

Poké-BODY Energy Flame
All Energy attached to Charizard ex are 🔥 Energy instead of its usual type.

⚪⚪⚪⚪ **Slash** 50

🔥🔥🔥🔥🔥 **Burn Down** 200
Discard 5 🔥 Energy attached to Charizard ex. This attack's damage isn't affected by Weakness, Resistance, Poké-Powers, Poké-Bodies, and any other effects on the Defending Pokémon.

weakness ⚪🔥   resistance   retreat cost ⚪⚪

©2004 Pokémon/Nintendo

Charizard ex (holo) (R)
EX FireRed LeafGreen
Price Range: $60.00 - $100.00

STAGE 2   Evolves from Charmeleon   Put Charizard on the Stage 1 card

Charizard
120 HP 🔥

Flame Pokémon. Length: 5' 7", Weight: 200 lbs.

Pokémon Power: Energy Burn As often as you like during your turn (before your attack), you may turn all Energy attached to Charizard into 🔥 Energy for the rest of the turn. This power can't be used if Charizard is Asleep, Confused, or Paralyzed.

🔥🔥🔥🔥 **Fire Spin** Discard 2 Energy cards attached to Charizard in order to use this attack. **100**

weakness 💧   resistance ⚪ -30   retreat cost ⚪⚪⚪

Spits fire that is hot enough to melt boulders. Known to unintentionally cause forest fires. LV. 76 #6

Illus. Mitsuhiro Arita © 1995, 96, 98, 99 Nintendo, Creatures, GAMEFREAK. © 1999 Wizards. 4/102 ★

Charizard (holo) (R)
Base Set 1st Edition
Price Range: $50.00 - $100.00

Lugia ex
100 HP ⚪

BASIC
When Pokémon ex has been Knocked Out, your opponent takes 2 Prize cards.

Illus. Hikaru Koike

Poké-BODY Silver Sparkle
If Lugia ex is your Active Pokémon and is damaged by an opponent's attack (even if Lugia ex is Knocked Out), flip a coin. If heads, choose an Energy card attached to the Attacking Pokémon and return it to your opponent's hand.

🔥💧⚡ **Elemental Blast** 200
Discard a 🔥 Energy, 💧 Energy, and ⚡ Energy attached to Lugia ex.

weakness   resistance -30   retreat cost ⚪

©2005 Pokémon/Nintendo   105/115

Lugia ex (holo) (R)
EX Unseen Forces
Price Range: $40.00 - $68.00

TRAINER
Supporter

TV Reporter

You can play only one Supporter card each turn. When you play this card, put it next to your Active Pokémon. When your turn ends, discard this card.

Draw 3 cards. Then discard any 1 card from your hand.

Illus. Ken Sugimori

©2003 Pokémon/Nintendo   88/97 ◆

TV Reporter (Rev. Foil)
EX Dragon
Price Range: $30.00 - $60.00

5 Charizard DS (holo) (R)
EX Dragon Frontiers
Price Range: $35.00 - $50.00

6 Wailord ex (holo) (R)
EX Sandstorm
Price Range: $30.00 - $50.00

7 Rayquaza (holo) (R)
EX Deoxys
Price Range: $25.00 - $50.00

8 Latios star (holo) (R)
EX Deoxys
Price Range: $30.00 - $45.00

Charizard 120 HP

STAGE 2 *Evolves from Charmeleon*

Collect Fire 30
Flip a coin. If heads, search your discard pile for 2 Energy cards and attach them to Charizard (1 if there is only 1).

Flame Pillar 60
You may discard a Energy card attached to Charizard. If you do, choose 1 of your opponent's Benched Pokémon and do 30 damage to that Pokémon. (Don't apply Weakness and Resistance for Benched Pokémon.)

Gyarados δ DELTA SPECIES 80 HP

BASIC
You can't have more than 1 Pokémon ☆ in your deck.

Spiral Growth 20
Flip a coin until you get tails. For each heads, search your discard pile for a basic Energy card and attach it to Gyarados ☆.

All-out Blast 50+
Discard cards from the top of your deck until you have 1 card left. This attack does 50 damage plus 20 more damage for each Energy card you discarded in this way.

9 Charizard (holo) (R)
EX Dragon
Price Range: $25.00 - $42.00

10 Gyarados (shining holo) (R)
EX Holon Phantoms
Price Range: $22.00 - $40.00

Mew ex 90 HP

BASIC
When Pokémon-ex has been Knocked Out, your opponent takes 2 Prize cards.

POKé-BODY Versatile
Mew ex can use the attacks of all Pokémon in play as its own. (You still need the necessary Energy to use each attack.)

Power Move
Search your deck for an Energy card and attach it to Mew ex. Shuffle your deck afterward. Then, you may switch Mew ex with 1 of your Benched Pokémon.

Charizard 110 HP
STAGE 2 *Evolves from Charmeleon Put Charizard on the Stage 1 card*
Stage 2 Pokémon

POKé-BODY Crystal Type
Whenever you attach a basic Energy card from your hand to Charizard, Charizard's type (color) becomes the same as that type of Energy until the end of the turn.

Fireblast 40
Discard an Energy card attached to Charizard.

Dragon Tail 50x
Flip 2 coins. This attack does 50 damage times the number of heads.

11 Mew ex (holo) (R)
EX Legend Maker
Price Range: $20.00 - $40.00

12 Charizard (holo) (R)
Skyridge
Price Range: $20.00- $40.00

Latias ☆ — 80 HP

BASIC

Healing Light — 10
Remove 1 damage counter from each of your Pokémon (including Latias ☆).

Shooting Star — 50+
If the Defending Pokémon is Pokémon-ex, discard all Energy cards attached to Latias ☆ and this attack does 50 damage plus 100 more damage.

Flygon ex — 150 HP

STAGE 2 — Evolves from Vibrava

When Pokémon-ex has been Knocked Out, your opponent takes 2 Prize cards.

Poké-POWER Emerge Charge
Once during your turn, when you play Flygon ex from your hand to evolve 1 of your Pokémon, you may search your discard pile for up to 2 Energy cards and attach them to Flygon ex.

Reactive Blast — 40+
You may discard any number of React Energy cards attached to Flygon ex. If you do, this attack does 40 damage plus 30 more damage for each React Energy card you discarded.

Dragon Claw — 100

13
Latias star (holo) (R)
EX Deoxys
Price Range: $18.00 - $40.00

14
Flygon ex (holo) (R)
EX Legend Maker
Price Range: $20.00 - $36.00

STAGE 2 — Evolves from Wartortle — Put Blastoise on the Stage 1 card

Blastoise — 100 HP

Shellfish Pokémon. Length: 5' 3", Weight: 189 lbs.
Pokémon Power: Rain Dance As often as you like during your turn (before your attack), you may attach 1 Energy card to 1 of your Pokémon. (This doesn't use up your 1 Energy card attachment for the turn.) This power can't be used if Blastoise is Asleep, Confused, or Paralyzed.

Hydro Pump Does 40 damage plus 10 more damage for each Energy attached to Blastoise but not used to pay for this attack's Energy cost. Extra Energy after the 2nd doesn't count. — 40+

A brutal Pokémon with pressurized water jets on its shell. They are used for high-speed tackles. LV.52 #9
Illus. Ken Sugimori ©1995, 96, 98, 99 Nintendo, Creatures, GAMEFREAK. ©1999 Wizards. 2/102 ★

Empoleon Lv. X — HP 140

LEVEL-UP — Put onto Empoleon

Poké-BODY Supreme Command
Once during your turn (before your attack), you may choose up to 2 cards from your opponent's hand without looking and put them face down next to the Defending Pokémon. (These cards are not in play or in your opponent's hand.) At the end of your opponent's next turn, return those cards to your opponent's hand. This power can't be used if Empoleon is affected by a Special Condition.

Hydro Impact
Choose 1 of your opponent's Pokémon. This attack does 80 damage to that Pokémon. (Don't apply Weakness and Resistance for Benched Pokémon.) Empoleon can't attack during your next turn.

Put this card onto your Active Empoleon. Empoleon LV. X can use any attack, Poké-Power, or Poké-Body from its previous Level.
Illus. Shizurow
©2007 Pokémon / Nintendo. 120/130

15
Blastoise (holo) (R)
Base 1st Edition
Price Range: $20.00 - $35.00

16
Empoleon Lv. X (holo) (R)
Diamond & Pearl
Price Range: $20.00 - $35.00

Infernape Lv. X

120 HP

LEVEL-UP Put onto Infernape

Poké-POWER Burning Head

Once during your turn (before your attack), you may look at the top 3 cards of your deck, choose 1 of them, and put it into your hand. Discard the other 2 cards. This power can't be used if Infernape is affected by a Special Condition.

🔥🔥 Flare Up 150

Search your discard pile for 8 🔥 Energy cards, show them to your opponent, and shuffle them into your deck. (This attack does nothing if you don't have 8 🔥 Energy cards in your discard pile.)

Put this card onto your Active Infernape. Infernape LV. X can use any attack, Poké-Power, or Poké-Body from its previous Level.

Illus. Shizurow

©2007 Pokémon

Celebi ex

70 HP

BASIC

When Pokémon ex has been Knocked Out, your opponent takes 2 Prize cards.

Spiral Leaf

Flip a coin. If heads, put 1 damage counter on each of your opponent's Pokémon. If tails, remove 1 damage counter from each of your Pokémon.

Time Trap 30

Flip a coin. If heads, look at the top 4 cards of your opponent's deck, and put them back on top of your opponent's deck in any order. If tails, look at the top 4 cards of your deck, and put them back on top of your deck in any order.

©2005 Pokémon / Nintendo 112/115

 17 Infernape Lv. X (holo) (R)
Diamond & Pearl
Price Range: $20.00 - $35.00

18 Celebi ex (holo) (SCR)
EX Unseen Forces
Price Range: $20.00 - $35.00

Pikachu ☆

60 HP

BASIC

You can't have more than 1 Pokémon ☆ in your deck.

Thundershock 10

Flip a coin. If heads, the Defending Pokémon is now Paralyzed.

Spring Back 20+

If your opponent has only 1 Prize card left, this attack does 20 damage plus 50 more damage.

©2006 Pokémon / Nintendo 104/110

Torterra Lv. X

HP 160

LEVEL-UP Put onto Torterra

Poké-POWER Forest Murmurs

Once during your turn (before your attack), if you have more Prize cards left than your opponent, you may choose 1 of your opponent's Benched Pokémon and switch it with 1 of the Defending Pokémon. This power can't be used if Torterra is affected by a Special Condition.

🍃🍃🍃 Vigorous Dash 100

Does 30 damage to 1 of your opponent's Benched Pokémon. (Don't apply Weakness and Resistance for Benched Pokémon.) Torterra does 30 damage to itself.

Put this card onto your Active Torterra. Torterra LV. X can use any attack, Poké-Power, or Poké-Body from its previous Level.

Illus. Shizurow

©2007 Pokémon / Nintendo 122/130

 19 Pikachu star (shining holo) (R)
EX Holon Phantoms
Price Range: $20.00 - $35.00

20 Toterra Lv. X (holo) (R)
Diamond & Pearl
Price Range: $18.00 - $33.00

Complete Guide to Pokémon Monsters

From #1 to #493, we caught them all for you to see!

#001 Bulbasaur

Type: Grass/Poison

Evolution: Evolves into Ivysaur

Description: The seed on Bulbasaur's back continues to grow when sunlight hits it. Eventually, it will sprout a flower when Bulbasaur evolves into Ivysaur.

Cool Card: EX Crystal Guardians #46

Price Range: .10 - .20

#002 Ivysaur

Type: Grass/Poison

Evolution: Evolves from Ivysaur and into Venusaur

Description: This little guy is a real toughie! His speed and special attacks are much stronger than Bulbasaur.

Cool Card: EX Crystal Guardians #35

Price Range: .20 - .50

#003 Venusaur

Type: Grass/Poison

Evolution: Evolves from Ivysaur

Description: This is one mean blue and green grass-powered fighting machine! You don't want to mess with this 221 pound Pokémon!

Cool Card: Expedition #30

Price Range: 2.00 – 4.00

#004 Charmander

Cool Card: EX Crystal Guardians #49

Price Range: .10 - .20

Type: Fire

Evolution: Evolves into Charmeleon

Description: This cute little guy carries a flame on the tip of his tail. However, don't make him angry because his flame will burn quickly and brightly!

#005 Charmeleon

Cool Card: EX Crystal Guardians #29

Price Range: .20 - .50

Type: Fire

Evolution: Evolves from Charmander and into Charizard

Description: This Pokémon becomes agitated very quickly. When in battle, this guy brings out his razor sharp claws and whips his fiery tail around.

#006 Charizard

Type: Fire/Flying

Evolution: Evolves from Charmeleon

Description: When he spits fire it's hot enough to melt almost anything. When Charizard becomes upset the flame on his tail turns a whitish-blue color!

Cool Card: EX Dragon Frontiers #100

Price Range: 35.00 – 50.00

#007 Squirtle

Type: Water

Evolution: Evolves into Wartortle

Description: Awww…don't you just want to take him home with you? This little fellow can shoot water at prey while in the water.

Cool Card: Team Rocket #68

Price Range: .10 - .25

#008 Wartortle

Type: Water

Evolution: Evolves from Squirtle and into Blastoise

Description: What a tough guy! He will take on anyone despite his 3"3" size. It's been said that this Pokémon's tail turns dark when it gets older.

Cool Card: EX Crystal Guardians #42

Price Range: .20 - .50

#009 Blastoise

Type: Water

Evolution: Evolves from Wartortle

Description: Those water jets on Blastoise's shell are so powerful they can break through thick steel. Wowser! One of his best attacks is called Hydro Pump.

Cool Card: EX Crystal Guardians #2

Price Range: 4.00 – 12.00

#010 Caterpie

Type: Bug

Evolution: Evolves into Metapod

Description: Don't annoy this little Pokémon or it will release a horrible stench from the antenna on its head. It's also crafty enough to camouflage itself among leaves.

Cool Card: Expedition #96

Price Range: .10 - .20

#011 Metapod

Type: Bug

Evolution: Evolves from Caterpie and into Butterfree

Description: Unfortunately the Metapod, like a cocoon, doesn't do very much. Its main attack is to Harden its shell. This protects it against certain attacks.

Cool Card: Neo Discovery #42

Price Range: .20 - .50

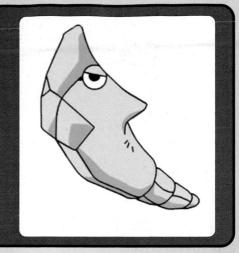

#012 Butterfree

Type: Bug/Flying

Evolution: Evolves from Metapod

Description: This Pokémon's wings are covered with a poisonous powder that repels water and can poison any opponent.

Cool Card: Expedition #38

Price Range: .50 – 1.00

#013 Weedle

Type: Bug/Poison

Evolution: Evolves into Kakuna

Description: This cute little Pokémon may look harmless, but beware of the stinger on its head. This stinger gives off a very strong poison to protect itself.

Cool Card: EX Delta Species #87

Price Range: .10 - .20

#014 Kakuna

Type: Bug/Poison

Evolution: Evolves from Weedle and into Beedrill

Description: Like the Metapod, the Kakuna Hardens its shell to protect itself. However, it does have a stinger that can shoot out and poison its enemy.

Cool Card: Skyridge #70

Price Range: .10 - .20

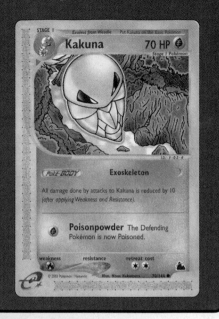

#015 Beedrill

Type: Bug/Poison

Evolution: Evolves from Kakuna

Description: The Beedrill can fly high and fast and uses its large poisonous stingers on its forelegs and tail to defeat its enemy or prey.

Cool Card: Base Set 1st Ed. #17

Price Range: 1.00 – 2.00

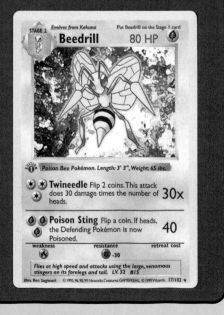

#016 Pidgey

Type: Normal/Flying

Evolution: Evolves into Pidgeotto

Description: This docile Pokémon can kick up sand to protect itself. It can also flap its wings fast enough to cause a dust cloud.

Cool Card: Base Set 1st Ed. #57

Price Range: .30 - .75

#017 Pidgeotto

Type: Normal/Flying

Evolution: Evolves from Pidgey and into Pidgeot

Description: It has superb vision and can dive bomb and catch its prey with its well-developed claws. It can also peck at its enemy.

Cool Card: EX FireRed LeafGreen #45

Price Range: .20 - .50

#018 Pidgeot

Type: Normal/Flying

Evolution: Evolves from Pidgeotto

Description: This Pokémon can fly at speeds of Mach 2 in search of prey. It sometimes spreads its wings to frighten its enemies.

Cool Card: Expedition #59

Price Range: .50 – 1.00

#019 Rattata

Type: Normal

Evolution: Evolves into Raticate

Description: This little scavenger will settle down in areas where food is plentiful. It has a quick bite and its fang can chew on almost anything.

Cool Card: Team Rocket #66

Price Range: .10 - .25

#020 Raticate

Type: Normal

Evolution: Evolves from Rattata

Description: With webbed hind legs, this Pokémon can swim through large rivers. Its sharp fangs can gnaw through concrete buildings.

Cool Card: Base Set 1st Ed. #40

Price Range: .50 – 1.00

#021 Spearow

Type: Normal/Flying

Evolution: Evolves into Fearow

Description: This bird Pokémon can fly high and fast to protect its territory. It can also pluck insects from tall grass.

Cool Card: Gym Heroes #52

Price Range: .20 - .50

#022 Fearow

Type: Normal/Flying

Evolution: Evolves from Spearow

Description: It attacks with its long beak and can pluck small insect hiding underground. It can also fly very quickly into the sky when it senses danger.

Cool Card: EX Crystal Guardians #18

Price Range: .50 – 1.00

#023 Ekans

Type: Poison

Evolution: Evolves into Arbok

Description: Spell this Pokémon's name backwards and you get snake. It moves silently to jump on bird eggs and can swallow its prey whole. They hide in grass.

Cool Card: EX Team Rocket Returns #55

Price Range: .10 - .20

#024 Arbok

Type: Poison

Evolution: Evolves from Ekans

Description: This cobra-like Pokémon has warning markings on its body to puzzle its prey. The vengeful creature never gives up the chase once it targets its prey.

Cool Card: EX Dragon Frontiers #13

Price Range: .50 – 1.00

#025 Pikachu

Type: Electric

Evolution: Evolves from Pichu and into Raichu

Description: Pikachu is the most famous Pokémon of all. It raises its tail to monitor the surrounding area. It can also release electrical energy stored in its cheeks.

Cool Card: Base Set 1st Ed. #58

Price Range: 2.00 – 4.00

#026 Raichu

Type: Electric

Evolution: Evolves from Pikachu

Description: When this Pokémon builds up enough energy, it glows in the dark. It can also gather more electricity from the atmosphere when its cheek pouches run empty.

Cool Card: Fossil #29

Price Range: .50 – 1.00

#027 Sandshrew

Type: Ground

Evolution: Evolves into Sandslash

Description: The Sandshrew loves to burrow deep underground in places far from water. It also has the ability to roll itself into a ball for protection.

Cool Card: Legendary #91

Price Range: .10 - .20

#028 Sandslash

Type: Ground

Evolution: Evolves from Sandshrew

Description: It can kick up a dust storm to blind its enemy. Sandslash can also roll up into a spiny ball to attack. Enemies should stay clear from its sharp claws.

Cool Card: Gym Heroes #23

Price Range: .50 – 1.00

#029 Nidoran♀

Type: Poison

Evolution: Evolves into Nidorina

Description: The female Nidoran have smaller horns. However, they do secret poisonous venom. They're usually very docile.

Cool Card: EX Dragon Frontiers #56

Price Range: .10 - .20

#030 Nidorina

Type: Poison

Evolution: Evolves from Nidoran♀ and into Nidoqueen

Description: Like the Nidoran♀, this Pokémon is also docile. It likes to use attacks such as clawing and biting. When threatened, it can also raise the barbs on its back.

Cool Card: Skyridge #83

Price Range: .10 - .20

#031 Nidoqueen

Type: Poison/Ground

Evolution: Evolves from Nidorina

Description: The scales on this Pokémon's body provide strong protection against attacks. One of its best attacks is Body Slam.

Cool Card: Legendary #32

Price Range: .50 – 1.00

#032 Nidoran♂

Type: Poison

Evolution: Evolves into Nidorino

Description: This little fellow can raise its ears to check its surroundings. But when in danger it will attack its enemy with a poisonous sting.

Cool Card: Aquapolis #96

Price Range: .10 - .20

#033 Nidorino

Type: Poison

Evolution: Evolves from Nidoran♂ and into Nidoking

Description: This is an aggressive Pokémon that is easily agitated. The horn on its head contains a powerful poison that it can inject its enemies with. Look out!

Cool Card: EX Dragon Frontiers #35

Price Range: .20 - .50

#034 Nidoking

Type: Poison/Ground

Evolution: Evolves from Nidorino

Description: Don't mess with Nidoking! He is a strong Pokémon with a powerful tail that can smash almost anything. The horns on his body are also very hard.

Cool Card: Aquapolis #24

Price Range: .50 – 1.00

#035 Clefairy

Type: Normal

Evolution: Evolves from Cleffa and into Clefable

Description: This cute and magical Pokémon is rarely seen by anyone. It stores moonlight in the wings on its back and floats in midair.

Cool Card: Diamond and Pearl #77

Price Range: .10 - .20

#036 Clefable

Type: Normal

Evolution: Evolves from Clefairy

Description: The Clefable is also rarely seen and will run and hide the moment it sees people. With its super-sonic hearing, the Clefable can hear sounds from very far away.

Cool Card: Diamond and Pearl #22

Price Range: .50 – 1.00

#037 Vulpix

Type: Fire

Evolution: Evolves into Ninetales

Description: Don't you just want to pet this little Pokémon on its head? It's so cute! The Vulpix is born with one tail. As it gets older it will keep growing new tails until it reaches nine.

Cool Card: Gym Challenge #37

Price Range: .20 - .50

#038 Ninetales

Type: Fire

Evolution: Evolves from Vulpix

Description: According to legends, nine noble saints were united and rein-carnated into Ninetales. The energy in its tails can keep this Pokémon alive for 1000 years.

Cool Card: Expedition #57

Price Range: .50 – 1.00

#039 Jigglypuff

Type: Normal

Evolution: Evolves from Igglybuff and into Wigglytuff

Description: This wide-eyed Pokémon has the ability to put enemies to sleep with its mysteriously soothing melody. Start running if its eyes light up.

Cool Card: EX Team Magma vs. Team Aqua #41

Price Range: .10 - .20

#040 Wigglytuff

Type: Normal

Evolution: Evolves from Jigglypuff

Description: This happy-go-lucky little creature had a body that's soft and rubbery. However, don't make it angry. It can inflate quickly and attack an enemy with Body Slam.

Cool Card: EX Crystal Guardians #13

Price Range: 3.00 – 6.00

#041 Zubat

Type: Poison/Flying

Evolution: Evolves into Golbat

Description: The Zubat emits ultra-sonic sounds from its mouth to survey the surrounding areas. It usually hangs from the ceilings of abandoned buildings and caves.

Cool Card: Gym Heroes #24

Price Range: .50 – 1.00

#042 Golbat

Type: Poison/Flying

Evolution: Evolves from Zubat and into Crobat

Description: This Pokémon uses its sharp vampire-like fangs to bite and suck blood. It can drink more than 10 ounces at a time.

Cool Card: Team Rocket #24

Price Range: .50 – 1.00

#043 Oddish

Type: Grass/Poison

Evolution: Evolves into Gloom

Description: The Oddish is a strange little Pokémon. It wanders around at night planting seeds in various places. When it bathes in the moonlight it begins to grow.

Cool Card: Gym Heroes #47

Price Range: .20 - .50

#044 Gloom

Type: Grass/Poison

Evolution: Evolves from Oddish and into Vileplume or Bellossom

Description: This Pokémon drools a very sticky syrup from its mouth. A Gloom drips this gooey substance to attract its prey, but when you get close it really stinks.

Cool Card: Team Rocket 1st Ed. #36

Price Range: .20 - .50

#045 Vileplume

Type: Grass/Poison

Evolution: Evolves from Gloom

Description: The Vileplume's head is so big and heavy it can barely hold it straight up. When it shakes those big petals it releases a poisonous pollen.

Cool Card: Aquapolis #43

Price Range: .50 – 1.00

#046 Paras

Type: Bug/Grass

Evolution: Evolves into Parasect

Description: It likes to burrow underground and eat tree roots. The mushrooms on its back take in all of this Pokémon's nutrients. One of its attacks is called Stun Spore.

Cool Card: Neo Revelation #47

Price Range: .10 - .25

#047 Parasect

Type: Bug/Grass

Evolution: Evolves from Paras

Description: Parasect like to stay in dark and damp places. The larger the mushroom on its back grows, the stronger the mushroom spores it sends out.

Cool Card: Aquapolis #27

Price Range: .50 – 1.00

#048 Venonat

Type: Bug/Poison

Evolution: Evolves into Venomoth

Description: This Pokémon likes to eat small bugs at night and is attracted by night lights. It also oozes poison all over its body.

Cool Card: Neo Destiny #90

Price Range: .10 - .20

#049 Venomoth

Type: Bug/Poison

Evolution: Evolves from Venonat

Description: The Venomoth has large wings that, when flapped quickly, can release a poisonous powder. This poison can cause paralysis.

Cool Card: Gym Heroes 1st Ed. #34
Price Range: .50 – 1.00

#050 Diglett

Type: Ground

Evolution: Evolves into Dugtrio

Description: This little fellow lives underground and feeds on plant roots. It will only pop its head out of the ground when the sun isn't bright.

Cool Card: Skyridge #50
Price Range: .10 - .20

#051 Dugtrio

Type: Ground

Evolution: Evolves from Diglett

Description: This is a team of Diglett triplets. They sometimes cause earthquakes when they burrow 60 miles underground.

Cool Card: Expedition #44

Price Range: .50 – 1.00

#052 Meowth

Type: Normal

Evolution: Evolves into Persian

Description: He was one of the first talking Pokémon. Meowth is fascinated by round shiny objects and likes to pick them up. He's a part of Team Rocket's team.

Cool Card: Legendary #53

Price Range: .20 - .50

#053 Persian

Type: Normal

Evolution: Evolves from Meowth

Description: This Pokémon is said to have amazing fur and walks with elegance. The red gem on its forehead can glow at any time. It can also tear apart its prey.

Cool Card: EX Unseen Forces #116

Price Range: 4.00 – 10.00

#054 Psyduck

Type: Water

Evolution: Evolves into Golduck

Description: The Psyduck has mystical powers and always has a puzzled look on its face. When facing its enemies, it can also use psychokinetics.

Cool Card: Team Rocket 1st Ed. #65

Price Range: .10 - .25

#055 Golduck

Type: Water

Evolution: Evolves from Psyduck

Description: The Golduck, which is slimmer and has longer limbs than Psyduck, swims gracefully in lakes. The bead on its forehead glows when it uses telekinetic powers.

Cool Card: Fossil #35

Price Range: .30 - .75

#056 Mankey

Type: Fighting

Evolution: Evolves into Primeape

Description: These little Pokémon get angry very quickly. Plus, they like to gather in groups and attack for no reason. Stay away from these guys!

Cool Card: EX FireRed LeafGreen #38

Price Range: .20 - .50

#057 Primeape

Type: Fighting

Evolution: Evolves from Mankey

Description: Caution! Don't ever stare at this Pokémon. If you do, it will get angry and chase you. Some of this Pokémon's attacks include Rage and Screech.

Cool Card: Aquapolis #29

Price Range: .50 – 1.00

#058 Growlithe

Type: Fire

Evolution: Evolves into Arcanine

Description: Pokémon fans love this little critter because it's so friendly and loyal. Growlithe are very protective of their territory and are fearless when standing up against foes.

Cool Card: Gym Heroes #35

Price Range: .20 - .50

#059 Arcanine

Type: Fire

Evolution: Evolves from Growlithe

Description: This Pokémon is legendary in China. It is considered very beautiful and graceful. It's been said that people are also enchanted by its grand mane.

Cool Card: Base Set 1st Ed. #23

Price Range: .50 – 1.00

#060 Poliwag

Type: Water

Evolution: Evolves into Poliwhirl

Description: It enjoys swimming instead of walking with its newly formed legs. Depending on the areas where Poliwag live, their belly swirls face different directions.

Cool Card: Base Set 1st Ed. #59

Price Range: .30 - .75

#061 Poliwhirl

Type: Water

Evolution: Evolves from Poliwag and into Poliwrath or Politoed

Description: This Pokémon can live in or out of water and it continually sweats to keep its body slimy. Staring at its belly swirl will make you sleepy.

Cool Card: Base Set 1st Ed. #38

Price Range: .50 – 1.00

#062 Poliwrath

Type: Water/Fighting

Evolution: Evolves from Poliwhirl

Description: The Poliwrath is an excellent swimmer and mainly lives on dry land. Some of its attacks include Doubleslap and Body Slam.

Cool Card: Expedition #60

Price Range: .50 – 1.00

#063 Abra

Type: Psychic

Evolution: Evolves into Kadabra

Description: When it senses danger, it can teleport itself to a safe area. This Psychic Pokémon can read minds and sleeps 18 hours a day.

Cool Card: Base Set 1st Ed. #43

Price Range: .30 - .75

#064 Kadabra

Cool Card: Legendary #49

Price Range: .20 - .50

Type: Psychic

Evolution: Evolves from Abra and into Alakazam

Description: This Pokémon possesses very strong spiritual power. It can make clocks run backwards and cause machines to malfunction at any time.

#065 Alakazam

Cool Card: EX Crystal Guardians #99

Price Range: 15.00 – 25.00

Type: Psychic

Evolution: Evolves from Kadabra

Description: This is one of the smartest Pokémon on the planet. It's so smart, its brain can outperform a super-computer. Its IQ is said to be around 5000!

#066 Machop

Type: Fighting

Evolution: Evolves into Machoke

Description: Machop enjoys training in martial arts and building its muscles. To make itself stronger, it enjoys lifting boulders.

Cool Card: Diamond and Pearl #86

Price Range: .10 - .20

#067 Machoke

Type: Fighting

Evolution: Evolves from Machop and into Machamp

Description: The Machoke has to wear a special belt to regulate its powerful energy. The muscles on its body become thicker and stronger after every battle.

Cool Card: Diamond and Pearl #53

Price Range: .20 - .50

#068 Machamp

Type: Fighting

Evolution: Evolves from Machoke

Description: Watch out for Machamp! This guy can use all four of its muscular arms to send its opponent flying into the sky. It can throw many punches at a time.

Cool Card: Diamond and Pearl #31

Price Range: .50 – 1.00

#069 Bellsprout

Type: Grass/Poison

Evolution: Evolves into Weepinbell

Description: This carnivorous Pokémon can move its vines very quickly to catch its prey. It loves to eat bugs and devours them whole.

Cool Card: Aquapolis #68

Price Range: .10 - .20

#070 Weepinbell

Type: Grass/Poison

Evolution: Evolves from Bellsprout and into Victreebel

Description: This big-mouthed plant can spit out poisonous powder whenever it wants. It can also slice up its prey with its razor-sharp leaves.

Cool Card: Gym Heroes 1st Ed. #48

Price Range: .20 - .50

#071 Victreebel

Type: Grass/Poison

Evolution: Evolves from Weepinbell

Description: This Pokémon loves to lure in prey with its aromatic honey. Once caught, the prey is then melted by the acid in a Victreebel's stomach.

Cool Card: Aquapolis #42

Price Range: .50 – 1.00

#072 Tentacool

Type: Water/Poison

Evolution: Evolves into Tentacruel

Description: Tentacool are usually found drifting in the waves of shallow seas. It has toxic feelers that can stab anything that it touches.

Cool Card: Gym Heroes #32

Price Range: 50 – 1.00

#073 Tentacruel

Type: Water/Poison

Evolution: Evolves from Tentacool

Description: This guy is bigger and scarier that its pre-evolved form. It has 80 tentacles and can absorb lots of water. It likes to entangle its prey.

Cool Card: Aquapolis #38

Price Range: .50 – 1.00

#074 Geodude

Type: Rock/Ground

Evolution: Evolves into Graveler

Description: A Geodude can use its arms to climb steep mountains. But watch out! It will also swing its mighty fists when it's angered.

Cool Card: Expedition #110

Price Range: .10 - .20

#075 Graveler

Type: Rock/Ground

Evolution: Evolves from Geodude and into Golem

Description: This big rock formation can roll over any obstacle or change direction whenever it wants. Remember to steer clear of this Pokémon's path.

Cool Card: Legendary #44

Price Range: .20 - .50

#076 Golem

Type: Rock/Ground

Evolution: Evolves from Graveler

Description: The Golem has a boulder-like body that can withstand dynamite blasts. It likes to use explosive jumps to move itself from mountain to mountain.

Cool Card: Expedition #49

Price Range: .50 – 1.00

#077 Ponyta

Type: Fire

Evolution: Evolves into Rapidash

Description: A Ponyta is a very high jumper. It likes to practice jumping over high-growing grass. But be careful of its hooves, as they are harder than diamonds.

Cool Card: Diamond and Pearl #94

Price Range: .10 - .20

#078 Rapidash

Type: Fire

Evolution: Evolves from Ponyta

Description: This Pokémon is so fast it can top speeds of 150 MPH. This Pokémon is very competitive and likes to chase anything that moves fast.

Cool Card: Diamond and Pearl #59

Price Range: .20 - .50

#079 Slowpoke

Type: Water/Psychic

Evolution: Evolves into Slowbro or Slowking

Description: This guy is one of the slowest moving Pokémon around. It likes to lie near water and a sweet sap will sometimes leak from its tail.

Cool Card: Aquapolis #108

Price Range: .10 - .20

#080 Slowbro

Type: Water/Psychic

Evolution: Evolves from Slowpoke

Description: Did you know that a Shellder is latched onto the tip of a Slowbro's tail? Yup! It stays on the tail because of the tasty flavor that oozes out.

Cool Card: Aquapolis #33

Price Range: .50 – 1.00

#081 Magnemite

Type: Electric/Steel

Evolution: Evolves into Magneton

Description: This is one amazing-looking Pokémon. Did you know that it uses anti-gravity to keep itself suspended in the air? It also emits electricity from the magnets on its body.

Cool Card: Diamond and Pearl #87

Price Range: .10 - .20

#082 Magneton

Type: Electric/Steel

Evolution: Evolves from Magnemite and into Magnezone

Description: This is what happens when three Magnemites get linked together. Magneton cause strange magnetic storms that can disrupt radio waves.

Cool Card: Diamond and Pearl #54

Price Range: .20 - .50

#083 Farfetch'd

Type: Normal/Flying

Evolution: None

Description: Very few of these Pokémon have ever been seen. They like to carry around stalks of green onions and use them as weapons.

Cool Card: EX FireRed LeafGreen #23

Price Range: 2.00 – 4.00

#084 Doduo

Type: Normal/Flying

Evolution: Evolves into Dodrio

Description: This two-headed bird has very short wings and large feet. It likes to race through grassy plains leaving giant footprints wherever it goes.

Cool Card: Base Set 1st Ed. #48

Price Range: .30 - .75

Basic Pokémon

Doduo   50 HP

Twin Bird Pokémon. Length: 4' 7", Weight: 86 lbs.

Fury Attack Flip 2 coins. This attack does 10 damage times the number of heads.   **10x**

weakness   resistance   retreat cost

-30

A bird that makes up for its poor flying with its fast foot speed. Leaves giant footprints. LV. 10 #84

Illus. Mitsuhiro Arita   ©1995, 96, 98, 99 Nintendo, Creatures, GAMEFREAK. ©1999 Wizards.   48/102

#085 Dodrio

Type: Normal/Flying

Evolution: Evolves from Doduo

Description: The Dodrio can make complex plans with its three brains. If an enemy takes it eyes off of one of the three heads, it'll get pecked at.

Cool Card: Jungle #34

Price Range: .30 - .75

STAGE 1   Evolves from Doduo   Put Dodrio on the Basic Pokémon

Dodrio   70 HP

Triplebird Pokémon. Length: 5' 11", Weight: 188 lbs.

Pokémon Power: Retreat Aid As long as Dodrio is Benched, pay ⟨⟩ less to retreat your Active Pokémon.

Rage Does 10 damage plus 10 more damage for each damage counter on Dodrio.   **10+**

weakness   resistance   retreat cost

-30

Uses its three brains to execute complex plans. While two heads sleep, one head stays awake. LV. 28 #85

Illus. Mitsuhiro Arita   ©1995, 96, 98 Nintendo, Creatures, GAMEFREAK. ©1999 Wizards.   34/64

#086 Seel

Type: Water

Evolution: Evolves into Dewgong

Description: This Pokémon likes to hang out in the coldest regions of Seafoam and Cinnabar Islands. The horn on its head is used for breaking through ice.

Cool Card: Base Set 1st Ed. #41

Price Range: .50 – 1.00

#087 Dewgong

Type: Water/Ice

Evolution: Evolves from Seel

Description: A Dewgong can swim steadily at 8 knots in the coldest waters. It likes to hunt for food at night when it's very cold.

Cool Card: EX Dragon Frontiers #15

Price Range: .50 – 1.00

#088 Grimer

Type: Poison

Evolution: Evolves into Muk

Description: This Pokémon loves to get dirty and smells horrible. It thrives on polluted sludge and gives off all sorts of bad poisons.

Cool Card: Team Rocket #57

Price Range: .10 - .25

#089 Muk

Type: Poison

Evolution: Evolves from Grimer

Description: Covered in filthy sludge, a Muk leaves toxic poisons behind wherever it goes. Touching this Pokémon can cause a high fever.

Cool Card: Gym Challenge 1st Ed. #26

Price Range: .50 – 1.00

#090 Shellder

Type: Water

Evolution: Evolves into Cloyster

Description: This Water Pokémon has a hard shell that can repel any type of attack. It's surprisingly fast and can swim backwards.

Cool Card: Gym Heroes 1st Ed. #89

Price Range: .10 - .25

#091 Cloyster

Type: Water/Ice

Evolution: Evolves from Shellder

Description: It can shoot spikes from the top of its shell when fighting. Its shell is harder than diamonds. It weighs almost 300 pounds.

Cool Card: EX Dragon Frontiers #14

Price Range: .50 – 1.00

#092 Gastly

Type: Ghost/Poison

Evolution: Evolves into Haunter

Description: Because this Pokémon's body is made up of gases, it can seep into any place it desires. It can weaken its prey by sending poisonous gas through their skin.

Cool Card: Diamond and Pearl #82

Price Range: .10 - .20

#093 Haunter

Type: Ghost/Poison

Evolution: Evolves from Gastly and into Gengar

Description: With a tongue made of gas, it can lick the life out of its victim. It likes to hide in dark places while planning its next move on an unsuspecting guest.

Cool Card: Diamond and Pearl #50

Price Range: .20 - .50

#094 Gengar

Type: Ghost/Poison

Evolution: Evolves from Haunter

Description: What a devilish grin he has, right? If you stand too close to a Gengar, you'll feel a sudden chill. Beware! He may try to lay a curse on you.

Cool Card: Diamond and Pearl #27

Price Range: .50 – 1.00

#095 Onix

Type: Rock/Ground

Evolution: Evolves into Steelix

Description: This monster's 463 pound body is made up of a black stone that's as hard as a diamond. It can burrow through the ground at 50 MPH.

Cool Card: Diamond and Pearl #92

Price Range: .10 - .20

#096 Drowzee

Type: Psychic

Evolution: Evolves into Hypno

Description: When this Pokémon twitches its nose, it knows another creature is sleeping nearby. It likes to eat dreams and can get sick eating bad dreams.

Cool Card: EX Delta Species #67

Price Range: .10 - .20

#097 Hypno

Type: Psychic

Evolution: Evolves from Drowzee

Description: Hypno always holds a pendulum to try and put its victims to sleep. If you lock eyes with a Hypno, it can put you under hypnosis.

Cool Card: Aquapolis #16

Price Range: .50 – 1.00

#098 Krabby

Type: Water

Evolution: Evolves into Kingler

Description: Krabby has pincers that are strong, but they can break off during a battle. Fortunately for them, their pincers can grow back fast. It can also sense when danger is approaching.

Cool Card: EX Crystal Guardians #54

Price Range: .10 - .20

#099 Kingler

Type: Water

Evolution: Evolves from Krabby

Description: The Kingler's large pincer has the crushing power of 10,000 HP. When it doesn't use its large claw in battle it gets in its way of fighting.

Cool Card: EX Crystal Guardians #22

Price Range: .50 – 1.00

#100 Voltorb

Type: Electric

Evolution: Evolves into Electrode

Description: This Pokémon moves around by rolling and can self-destruct at a moment's notice. It sometimes camouflages itself as a Poké Ball.

Cool Card: Base Set 1st Ed. #67

Price Range: 1.00 – 3.00

#101 Electrode

Type: Electric

Evolution: Evolves from Voltorb

Description: This round Pokémon can store lots of energy in its body. It likes to amuse itself by exploding. It often explodes for no reason.

Cool Card: EX FireRed LeafGreen #107

Price Range: 7.00 – 14.00

#102 Exeggcute

Type: Grass/Psychic

Evolution: Evolves into Exeggutor

Description: They need to have six heads clustered together in order to keep their balance. Each head uses telepathy to talk to each other.

Cool Card: EX FireRed LeafGreen #33

Price Range: .20 - .50

#103 Exeggutor

Type: Grass/Psychic

Evolution: Evolves from Exeggcute

Description: This walking tree-like Pokémon can grow many heads. When the heads fall off, they group together to form Exeggcute. It also uses telepathy.

Cool Card: Legendary #23

Price Range: .50 – 1.00

#104 Cubone

Type: Ground

Evolution: Evolves into Marowak

Description: The skull on its head is of its deceased mother. It's never removed this skull helmet and no one has ever seen its face. It sometimes emits a mournful sound.

Cool Card: EX Team Magma vs. Team Aqua #40
Price Range: .10 - .20

Cubone   50 HP

BASIC

Bone Attack   20
Flip a coin. If tails, this attack does nothing.

#105 Marowak

Type: Ground

Evolution: Evolves from Cubone

Description: It likes to carry a bone and uses it like a boomerang to hit its enemy. No one knows where it collects these bones.

Cool Card: EX Team Rocket Returns #7
Price Range: 3.00 - 6.00

Dark Marowak   70 HP

STAGE 1   Evolves from Cubone   This Pokémon is both ● ● type.

Brick Smash   30
This attack's damage isn't affected by Resistance, Poké-Powers, Poké-Bodies, or any other effects on the Defending Pokémon.

Hard Bone   70
Discard a Basic Pokémon or Evolution card from your hand or this attack does nothing.

#106 Hitmonlee

Type: Fighting
Evolution: Evolves from Tyrogue
Description: This Pokémon, known as the Kick Master, can stretch its legs at its opponent and kick them repeatedly. The sole on their feet is as hard as a diamond.

Cool Card: Unseen Forces #25
Price Range: .50 – 1.00

#107 Hitmonchan

Type: Fighting
Evolution: Evolves from Tyrogue
Description: It's a pure punching machine. Hitmonchan can punch its way through concrete at high speeds. Don't ever stand in the way of this Pokémon.

Cool Card: EX Team Rocket Returns #98
Price Range: 6.00 – 12.00

#108 Lickitung

Type: Normal
Evolution: Evolves into Lickilicky
Description: This Pokémon's tongue is almost seven feet long. It can leave a trial of gooey saliva that will stick to anything. It also uses its tongue to clean its body.

Cool Card: EX Dragon Frontiers #19
Price Range: .50 – 1.00

#109 Koffing

Type: Poison
Evolution: Evolves into Weezing
Description: Koffing is loaded with toxic gases, which can explode without warning. The gases can also give people the sniffles, coughs and teary eyes.

Cool Card: Gym Challenge 1st Ed. #79
Price Range: .10 - .25

#110 Weezing

Type: Poison
Evolution: Evolves from Koffing
Description: When two Koffing fuse together, they become Weezing. It can then grow larger by absorbing dust, germs and poisonous gases.

Cool Card: Gym Challenge 1st Ed. #50
Price Range: .20 - .50

#111 Rhyhorn

Type: Ground/Rock

Evolution: Evolves into Rhydon

Description: This Pokémon can destroy all obstacles in its path. Its bones are 1000 times harder than human bones. It also has a one track mind.

Cool Card: Diamond and Pearl #95

Price Range: .10 - .20

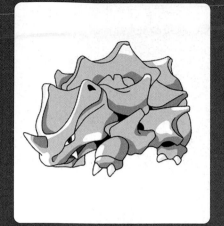

#112 Rhydon

Type: Ground/Rock

Evolution: Evolves from Rhyhorn and into Rhyperior

Description: It armor-like skin can withstand molten lava of 3,600 degrees. The drill-like horn on its head can shatter almost any diamond.

Cool Card: Diamond and Pearl #60

Price Range: .20 - .50

#113 Chansey

Type: Normal

Evolution: Evolves from Happiny and into Blissey

Description: This gentle and kind-hearted Pokémon will give an injured Pokémon some of its nutritious eggs to make it feel better. It's very hard to capture.

Cool Card: EX Unseen Forces #20

Price Range: .50 – 1.00

#114 Tangela

Type: Grass

Evolution: Evolves into Tangrowth

Description: This vine-filled Pokémon looks like a pile of spaghetti gone wild. The vines on its body are always growing and like to jiggle.

Cool Card: Base Set 1st Ed. #66

Price Range: .30 - .75

#115 Kangaskhan

Type: Normal

Evolution: None

Description: It protects its young and sleeps standing up to avoid crushing it. It never gives up a battle no matter how badly it's hurt.

Cool Card: Jungle #5

Price Range: 3.00 – 6.00

#116 Horsea

Type: Water
Evolution: Evolves into Seadra
Description: Horsea uses its mouth to spray water at its enemy. If a larger enemy approaches, it can use its dorsal fin to quickly swim away.

Cool Card: EX Dragon Frontiers #31
Price Range: .20 - .50

#117 Seadra

Type: Water
Evolution: Evolves from Horsea
Description: This Pokémon can swim backwards fast when in a battle. It sometimes uses its poisonous spikes to ward off its enemies.

Cool Card: EX Dragon Frontiers #22
Price Range: .50 – 1.00

#118 Goldeen

Type: Water
Evolution: Evolves into Seaking
Description: It swims upstream in large groups to lay its eggs. It's also a strong swimmer and can swim in streams at the rate of five knots.

Cool Card: Diamond and Pearl #84
Price Range: .10 - .20

#119 Seaking

Type: Water

Evolution: Evolves from Goldeen

Description: It can carve out a boulder in a stream using the horn on its head. The Seaking will patrol the areas around its nest to protect its offspring.

Cool Card: Diamond and Pearl #62

Price Range: .20 - .50

#120 Staryu

Type: Water

Evolution: Evolves into Starmie

Description: The center of its body flickers when it sees the stars at night twinkling. If a part of it ever gets chopped off it can grow that section back.

Cool Card: Skyridge #103

Price Range: .10 - .20

#121 Starmie

Type: Water/Psychic
Evolution: Evolves from Staryu
Description: Starmie can glow in the seven different colors of the rainbow. The center core of its body sends out electric waves into space.

Cool Card: Skyridge #30
Price Range: .50 – 1.00

#122 Mr. Mime

Type: Psychic
Evolution: Evolves from Mime Jr.
Description: Never interrupt it when its miming or it will slap you silly. It has a special power on its fingertips to create an invisible wall out of thin air.

Cool Card: Jungle #22
Price Range: 1.00 – 3.00

#123 Scyther

Type: Bug/Flying
Evolution: Evolves into Scizor
Description: This Pokémon moves so fast it creates a blur. It likes to hide in high grass to protect itself. It can also slice its prey with its scythes.

Cool Card: EX Team Rocket Returns #102
Price Range: 6.00 – 12.00

#124 Jynx

Type: Ice/Psychic

Evolution: Evolves from Smoochum

Description: It moves to a rhythm of its own and can cause people to dance in unison with it. It can also use dancing to communicate.

Cool Card: EX Dragon Frontiers #17
Price Range: .50 – 1.00

#125 Electabuzz

Type: Electric

Evolution: Evolves from Elekid and into Electivire

Description: Electabuzz constantly discharges large amounts of electricity and likes to hang out near power plants. If you get close to one it will make your hair stand up.

Cool Card: Diamond and Pearl #81
Price Range: .10 - .20

#126 Magmar

Type: Fire

Evolution: Evolves from Magby and into Magmortar

Description: This is one hot Pokémon. He was born in an active volcano and his body is always soaked in flames. It can heal itself with lava.

Cool Card: EX Legend Maker #21

Price Range: .50 – 1.00

#127 Pinsir

Type: Bug

Evolution: None

Description: A Pinsir can grip its prey with its large pincers and swing it around. It likes to sleep in trees or near roots where it keeps hidden.

Cool Card: EX Legend Maker #24

Price Range: .50 – 1.00

#128 Tauros

Type: Normal

Evolution: None

Description: Don't stand in the way of this Pokémon. It will charge you and can whip you with one of its long tails. Tauros fight each other by locking horns.

Cool Card: Jungle #47

Price Range: .30 - .75

#129 Magikarp

Type: Water

Evolution: Evolves into Gyarados

Description: This Pokémon is very unreliable. They can be found swimming in seas, lakes and rivers. They can jump high, but never more than seven feet.

Cool Card: Gym Challenge 1st Ed. #73

Price Range: .10 - .25

#130 Gyarados

Type: Water/Flying

Evolution: Evolves from Magikarp

Description: Gyarados are rarely seen in the wild and are capable of destroying large cities when they're in a rage. They can stay enraged until they destroy everything near them.

Cool Card: Gym Challenge 1st Ed. #5

Price Range: 3.00 – 6.00

#131 Lapras

Type: Water/Ice

Evolution: None

Description: This is one of the gentlest Pokémon around. It can carry people on its back from one side of a lake or ocean to the other. They rarely fight too.

Cool Card: EX Ruby and Sapphire #99

Price Range: 4.00 – 10.00

#132 Ditto

Type: Normal

Evolution: None

Description: This is a clever Pokémon. It can transform into almost a perfect copy of its opponent. If you make it laugh, it can't hold its disguise.

Cool Card: Fossil #18

Price Range: .50 – 1.00

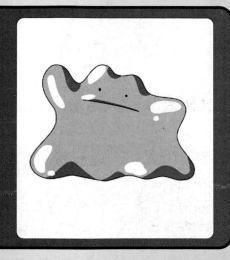

#133 Eevee

Type: Normal

Evolution: Evolves into Vaporeon, Jolteon, Flareon, Espeon, Umbreon, Leafeon or Glaceon

Description: This cute little guy has an irregular DNA structure. Its evolutions are dependant on several different factors, including what time of day it is, where it's trained, and what it's holding. It can adapt to any environment.

Cool Card: EX Sandstorm #63

Price Range: .10 - .20

#134 Vaporeon

Type: Water

Evolution: Evolves from Eevee

Description: They live near water and look invisible once they hit the water. Their cells can blend perfectly with water. When their fins vibrate, it's going to rain.

Cool Card: Jungle 1st Ed. #12

Price Range: 3.00 – 6.00

#135 Jolteon

Type: Electric

Evolution: Evolves from Eevee

Description: This Pokémon has an electrifying personality. However, when it becomes sad or angry it charges up with lots of electrical power.

Cool Card: Skyridge #13

Price Range: .50 – 1.00

#136 Flareon

Type: Fire
Evolution: Evolves from Eevee
Description: Flareon can blow 3,000 degree fire from its body at any time. It fluffs out its furry collar to cool down its body temperature.

Cool Card: Legendary #48
Price Range: .20 - .50

#137 Porygon

Type: Normal
Evolution: Evolves into Porygon2
Description: This is an artificial Pokémon that is capable of flying into space. It doesn't breathe and therefore can live in any environment.

Cool Card: EX FireRed LeafGreen #47
Price Range: .20 - .50

#138 Omanyte

Type: Rock/Water
Evolution: Evolves into Omastar
Description: This Pokémon, which had been extinct for many years, was recently genetically resurrected from fossils. It used to swim on the sea floor eating plankton.

Cool Card: Legendary #57
Price Range: .20 - .50

#139 Omastar

Type: Rock/Water

Evolution: Evolves from Omanyte

Description: This is a prehistoric Pokémon that became extinct because its shell became too heavy to move around. When it wraps around its prey it never lets go.

Cool Card: EX Sandstorm #19

Price Range: .50 – 1.00

#140 Kabuto

Type: Rock/Water

Evolution: Evolves into Kabutops

Description: This is another ancient Pokémon that was recently resurrected from fossils. It lived about 300 million years ago.

Cool Card: Legendary #48

Price Range: .20 – .50

#141 Kabutops

Type: Rock/Water
Evolution: Evolves from Kabuto
Description: This guy has very sharp claws and has a sleek body that is perfect for fast swimming. It can tuck in its limbs to become more compact when swimming.

Cool Card: EX Sandstorm #97
Price Range: 6.00 - 13.00

#142 Aerodactyl

Type: Rock/Flying
Evolution: None
Description: This prehistoric Pokémon was recently resurrected by taking its DNA found in a piece of amber. It used to fly in the sky while shrieking high-pitched cries.

Cool Card: Skyridge #1
Price Range: .50 – 1.00

#143 Snorlax

Type: Normal
Evolution: Evolves from Munchlax
Description: I guess you can say this is one of the laziest Pokémon you'll ever encounter. It can eat anything even if the food is rotten.

Cool Card: Diamond and Pearl #37
Price Range: .50 – 1.00

#144 Articuno

Type: Ice/Flying

Evolution: None

Description: This legendary bird Pokémon can turn water into ice and takes moisture from the air and turns it into snow. One of its best attacks is Blizzard.

Cool Card: Fossil #17

Price Range: .50 – 1.00

#145 Zapdos

Type: Electric/Flying

Evolution: None

Description: Zapdos is a legendary bird Pokémon that can send enormous bolts of lightning from nearby clouds. When it flaps its wings, thunderstorms appear.

Cool Card: Aquapolis #44

Price Range: .50 – 1.00

#146 Moltres

Type: Fire/Flying
Evolution: None
Description: This is another legendary Pokémon that is quite powerful. When it flaps its flaming wings it can turn the sky red. It can scatter embers with its wings.

Cool Card: EX FireRed LeafGreen #115
Price Range: 7.00 – 14.00

#147 Dratini

Type: Dragon
Evolution: Evolves into Dragonair
Description: This mythical Pokémon was recently caught by a fisherman. When it sheds its skin it means it's starting to grow.

Cool Card: Gym Heroes #42
Price Range: .20 - .50

#148 Dragonair

Type: Dragon
Evolution: Evolves from Dratini and into Dragonite
Description: It has the ability to change climate conditions when it emits a gentle aura from its body. One of its attacks is the Hyper Beam.

Cool Card: Neo Destiny #22
Price Range: .50 – 1.00

#149 Dragonite

Type: Dragon/Flying

Evolution: Evolves from Dragonair

Description: Dragonite like to fly over seas looking to help people who are in danger. This Pokémon is rarely seen.

Cool Card: Fossil #4

Price Range: 2.00 – 4.00

#150 Mewtwo

Type: Psychic

Evolution: None

Description: This Pokémon was created by scientists by splicing DNA genes similar to Mew's. It likes to rest quietly in a cave. It was created for battling.

Cool Card: EX Ruby and Sapphire #101

Price Range: 5.00 – 10.00

#151 Mew

Type: Psychic

Evolution: None

Description: Mew is one of the rarest Pokémon around. It only appears to people who are pure of heart and have a strong desire to see it. It can also learn any move.

Cool Card: EX Dragon Frontiers #101
Price Range: 20.00 – 30.00

#152 Chikorita

Type: Grass

Evolution: Evolves into Bayleef

Description: The leaf on its head is very aromatic and can check the humidity and temperature outside. It also likes to soak up the sun's rays.

Cool Card: Expedition #100
Price Range: .10 - .20

#153 Bayleef

Type: Grass

Evolution: Evolves from Chikorita and into Meganium

Description: This Pokémon's leaves give off a spicy aroma. The scent that these leaves give off causes anyone that smells them to become very energetic.

Cool Card: EX Dragon Frontiers #26
Price Range: .20 - .50

#154 Meganium

Type: Grass

Evolution: Evolves from Bayleef

Description: The scent that comes from the petals of this Pokémon contains a substance that calms aggressive behavior. It can also revive dead grass and plants.

Cool Card: EX Dragon Frontiers #4

Price Range: 3.00 – 6.00

#155 Cyndaquil

Type: Fire

Evolution: Evolves into Quilava

Description: This Pokémon is usually very timid and tends to stay hunched over. If it gets angry it shoots flames out of its back. The flames scare away foes.

Cool Card: EX Dragon Frontiers #45

Price Range: .10 - .20

#156 Quilava

Type: Fire
Evolution: Evolves from Cyndaquil and into Typhlosion
Description: When this Pokémon turns its back it means that it's ready to attack with the fire from its back. Its fur is nonflammable.

Cool Card: Expedition #91
Price Range: .20 - .50

#157 Typhlosion

Type: Fire
Evolution: Evolves from Quilava
Description: When this Pokémon becomes enraged, anything that touches it will go up in flames. When it rubs its fur together it can cause huge explosions.

Cool Card: EX Sandstorm #00
Price Range: 5.00 – 15.00

#158 Totodile

Type: Water
Evolution: Evolves into Croconaw
Description: Even though this Pokémon is small, it's rough and tough. Its well-developed jaws are powerful enough to crush anything.

Cool Card: Neo Destiny #85
Price Range: .10 - .20

#159 Croconaw

Type: Water

Evolution: Evolves from Totodile and into Feraligatr

Description: It has 48 fangs in its mouth. If it loses one of its fangs, it will grow right back. If a Croconaw clamps down on its prey it has no hope of escape.

Cool Card: EX Dragon Frontiers #27
Price Range: .20 - .50

#160 Feraligatr

Type: Water

Evolution: Evolves from Croconaw

Description: This big guy can move fast in and out of water. It can savagely rip apart its victim. The hind legs on this Pokémon are also very strong.

Cool Card: Expedition #47
Price Range: .50 – 1.00

#161 Sentret

Type: Normal
Evolution: Evolves into Furret
Description: This Pokémon stands on its tail to get a better view of its surroundings. When danger is near it screeches and pounds its tail on the ground.

Cool Card: EX Legend Maker #62
Price Range: .10 - .20

#162 Furret

Type: Normal
Evolution: Evolves from Sentret
Description: It creates nests that only its sleek body can fit into. It likes to hunt for Rattata. They weigh about 72 pounds.

Cool Card: Aquapolis #48
Price Range: .20 - .50

#163 Hoothoot

Type: Normal/Flying
Evolution: Evolves into Noctowl
Description: This Pokémon usually stands on one foot and likes to hoot around the same time every day. It can keep perfect time just like a clock.

Cool Card: Diamond and Pearl #85
Price Range: .10 - .20

#164 Noctowl

Type: Normal/Flying

Evolution: Evolves from Hoothoot

Description: The Noctowl can turn its head 180 degrees to sharpen its intellectual powers. It can sneak up on prey without being detected.

Cool Card: Diamond and Pearl #34

Price Range: .50 – 1.00

#165 Ledyba

Type: Bug/Flying

Evolution: Evolves into Ledian

Description: These Pokémon tend to stay in groups. If it gets cold out, they cluster together to keep each other warm. They secrete a fluid on their feet.

Cool Card: EX Dragon Frontiers #53

Price Range: .10 – .20

#166 Ledian

Type: Bug/Flying
Evolution: Evolves from Ledyba
Description: When stars begin to flicker in the night sky, Ledian will start to scatter a glowing powder. They like to sleep in a big leaf during daytime hours.

Cool Card: Skyridge #15
Price Range: .50 – 1.00

#167 Spinarak

Type: Bug/Poison
Evolution: Evolves into Ariados
Description: It spins a web to catch its prey using a very durable thread. They usually stay motionless until it gets dark.

Cool Card: Aquapolis #62
Price Range: .20 - .50

#168 Ariados

Type: Bug/Poison
Evolution: Evolves from Spinarak
Description: An Ariados can spin string from both the front and back of its body. It likes to wander at night in search of food. One of its attacks is called Screech.

Cool Card: Aquapolis #3
Price Range: .50 – 1.00

#169 Crobat

Type: Poison/Flying

Evolution: Evolves from Golbat

Description: The wings on its legs help the Crobat to fly very fast, but sometimes it has a hard time stopping. These Pokémon weight about 165 pounds.

Cool Card: Skyridge #6

Price Range: .50 – 1.00

#170 Chinchou

Type: Water/Electric

Evolution: Evolves into Lanturn

Description: This Pokémon has the power to shoot positive and negative electricity between the two antennae on its head. The antennae evolved from a fin.

Cool Card: Aquapolis #71

Price Range: .10 - .20

#171 Lanturn

Type: Water/Electric
Evolution: Evolves from Chinchou
Description: Lanturn can light up an area of the sea from a depth of over three miles. It uses the bright lights on its body to also lure in prey.

Cool Card: Aquapolis #20
Price Range: .50 – 1.00

#172 Pichu

Type: Electric
Evolution: Evolves into Pikachu
Description: Although it's not skilled at storing electricity, it can send out a jolt when amused or startled. One of its attacks is called Sweet Kiss.

Cool Card: Expedition #50
Price Range: .50 – 1.00

#173 Cleffa

Type: Normal
Evolution: Evolves into Clefairy
Description: When people see meteors in the sky, the sightings of Cleffa begin the increase. They're only a foot high and weigh seven pounds.

Cool Card: Diamond and Pearl #78
Price Range: .10 - .20

#174 Igglybuff

Type: Normal

Evolution: Evolves into Jigglypuff

Description: This little Pokémon has a very soft body that is extremely flexible. It can also roll and bounce all over the place.

Cool Card: EX Crystal Guardian #21

Price Range: .50 – 1.00

#175 Togepi

Type: Normal

Evolution: Evolves into Togetic

Description: Like a battery, Togepi gather up the positive and happy energy around them and store them in their bodies. They, like their evolution form, are extremely happy.

Cool Card: EX Dragon Frontiers #41

Price Range: .20 - .50

#176 Togetic

Type: Normal/Flying
Evolution: Evolves from Togepi and into Togekiss
Description: Togetic are rumored to seek out trainers with a pure heart, and then grant them constant happiness. Though they can't fly with their wings, they're adept at levitating!

Cool Card: Aquapolis #39
Price Range: .50 – 1.00

#177 Natu

Type: Psychic/Flying
Evolution: Evolves into Xatu
Description: Their inability to fly with their small wings makes Natu expert jumpers and climbers. If you stare at one, they won't stop staring until you look away!

Cool Card: Neo Genesis #67
Price Range: .10 - .25

#178 Xatu

Type: Psychic/Flying
Evolution: Evolves from Natu
Description: Worshipped by some as prophets, none really know why a Xatu will stare at the sun all day in meditation, nor if they're actually able to see into the future.

Cool Card: EX Dragon Frontiers #25
Price Range: .50 – 1.00

#179 Mareep

Type: Electric

Evolution: Evolves into Flaaffy

Description: Mareep use their fluffy wool to generate static electricity and then store it within their body. The more energy they have stored, the brighter the bulb on their tail becomes.

Cool Card: EX Dragon #64

Price Range: .10 - .20

#180 Flaaffy

Type: Electric

Evolution: Evolves from Mareep and into Ampharos

Description: These adorable Pokémon use the wool upon their bodies to quickly build up static electricity, which can be hurled at an enemy should they get too close!

Cool Card: EX Dragon Frontiers #30

Price Range: .20 - .50

#181 Ampharos

Type: Electric

Evolution: Evolves from Flaafy

Description: Ampharos give off so much light, they can actually be seen from space! Ampharos also used to be used to send signals between people a great distance away.

Cool Card: EX Dragon #89

Price Range: 4.00 – 8.00

#182 Bellossom

Type: Grass

Evolution: Evolves from Gloom

Description: It's hard to imagine that such a beautiful, fragrant Pokémon could evolve from the pungent-smelling Gloom. At night, Bellossom's flowers close up.

Cool Card: Aquapolis #5

Price Range: .50 – 1.00

#183 Marill

Type: Water

Evolution: Evolves from Azurill and into Azumarill

Description: The tail on this mouse-like Pokémon is extremely long and stretchy. When fishing from a stream, Marill wrap their tails around a nearby tree to keep from falling in.

Cool Card: Diamond and Pearl #88

Price Range: .10 - .20

#184 Azumarill

Type: Water

Evolution: Evolves from Marill

Description: Born as the perfect lifeguard, Azumarill can create air bubbles and then float them out to anyone who might be drowning.

Cool Card: Diamond and Pearl #18

Price Range: .50 – 1.00

#185 Sudowoodo

Type: Rock

Evolution: Evolves from Bonsly

Description: Sudowoodo use their resemblance to trees to hide themselves from enemies. During the winter, however, they stand out like sore thumbs due to the fact that their 'leaves' don't drop!

Cool Card: Aquapolis #36

Price Range: .50 – 1.00

#186 Politoed

Type: Water
Evolution: Evolves from Poliwhirl
Description: Politoed are considered the "kings" of their evolutionary siblings since they're the only ones that become full frogs. The longer the hair on their head is, the more revered they are.

Cool Card: Neo Discovery #27
Price Range: .50 – 1.00

#187 Hoppip

Type: Grass/Flying
Evolution: Evolves into Skiploom
Description: Light as a puffball, Hoppip's drift and float along low breezes. If they sense a powerful wind heading their way, they link their leaves with each other to keep from being blown away.

Cool Card: Neo Genesis #61
Price Range: .10 - .25

#188 Skiploom

Type: Grass/Flying
Evolution: Evolves from Hoppip and into Jumpluff
Description: The vibrant flower atop Skiploom's head blooms whenever the temperature rises above 64 degrees F. The hotter it gets, the more the flower blooms, so they're also great thermometers!

Cool Card: Aquapolis #60
Price Range: .20 - .50

#189 Jumpluff

Type: Grass/Flying

Evolution: Evolves from Skiploom

Description: Jumpluff are avid explorers, using their puffy extremities to float around the world on warm winds. They'll drop down onto the ground if the air becomes too cold.

Cool Card: Aquapolis #17

Price Range: .50 – 1.00

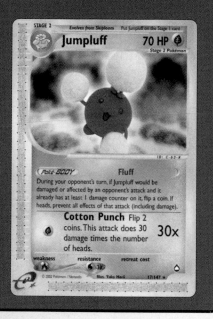

#190 Aipom

Type: Normal

Evolution: Evolves into Ambipom

Description: Aipom have extremely developed tails, especially the hand-like part at the end of them. Due to this, their real arms are rather useless.

Cool Card: Aquapolis #67

Price Range: .10 - .20

#191 Sunkern

Type: Grass
Evolution: Evolves into Sunflora
Description: These weak, defenseless Pokémon focus their entire existence on evolving! Sunkern don't move, their diets consisting of only the dew collected on their leaves and the ground around them.

Cool Card: Skyridge #106
Price Range: .10 - .20

#192 Sunflora

Type: Grass
Evolution: Evolves from Sunkern
Description: The happy Sunflora absorb sunlight and convert it into nutrients. They're quite active during the day when it's warm, but stop moving once the sun goes down.

Cool Card: EX Unseen Forces #16
Price Range: 3.00 – 5.00

#193 Yanma

Type: Bug/Flying
Evolution: Evolves into Yanmega
Description: With the ability to see 360 degrees around it and stop in mid-flight at a moment's notice, the Yanma is an excellent flying Pokémon to have on any team!

Cool Card: EX Team Rocket Returns #28
Price Range: .50 – 1.00

#194 Wooper

Type: Water/Ground

Evolution: Evolves into Quagsire

Description: These cute little Pokémon rarely leave the water, but when they do, they cover themselves in a thin coat of mucus that'll harm any that touch it.

Cool Card: EX Dragon Frontiers #71

Price Range: .10 - .20

#195 Quagsire

Type: Water/Ground

Evolution: Evolves from Wooper

Description: Their carefree and lazy nature makes them seem stupid. And it might be true; it's not uncommon for a Quagsire to pull a fisherman from its boat as it tries to swallow the hook and fishing pole!

Cool Card: EX Dragon Frontiers #21

Price Range: .50 - 1.00

#196 Espeon

Type: Psychic

Evolution: Evolves from Eevee

Description: Beautiful and extremely loyal, Espeon have precognitive powers thanks to their sensitive hairs and tail. Many think they developed them in order to better protect their trainer.

Cool Card: EX Unseen Forces #102

Price Range: 12.00 – 22.00

#197 Umbreon

Type: Dark

Evolution: Evolves from Eevee

Description: Umbreon evolve from Eevee when exposed to lots of moonlight. They love to wait patiently in the shadows for prey, and the yellow rings on their bodies glow just as they're about to attack.

Cool Card: EX Unseen Forces #112

Price Range: 12.00 – 20.00

#198 Murkrow

Type: Dark/Flying

Evolution: Evolves into Honchkrow

Description: Reputed as omens of ill or evil, the Murkrow doesn't exactly fall into the category of horribly misunderstood. It defeats enemies by getting them hopelessly lost, and loves to steal shiny objects, even rings off of the owner's fingers!

Cool Card: Unseen Forces #30

Price Range: .50 – 1.00

#199 Slowking

Type: Water/Psychic

Evolution: Evolves from Slowpoke

Description: Slowking's are rather intelligent Pokémon that spend their days puzzling over the mysteries of the world. If the Shellder comes off of their head, though, they forget everything they've learned!

Cool Card: Aquapolis #34

Price Range: .50 – 1.00

#200 Misdreavus

Type: Ghost

Evolution: Evolves into Mismagius

Description: Misdreavus scare enemies with its mournful, eerie sobs. The jewels around its neck also absorb the fear of enemies and allies alike, changing it into nutrients that keep it healthy.

Cool Card: Diamond and Pearl #91

Price Range: .10 - .20

#201 Unown

Type: Psychic
Evolution: None
Description: These unusual Pokémon are shaped like an ancient alphabet, though it's unknown which came first: the Pokémon, or the language. They have many shapes, one for each letter in the alphabet.

Cool Card: Neo Discovery #33
Price Range: .50 – 1.00

#202 Wobbuffet

Type: Psychic
Evolution: Evolves from Wynaut
Description: Generally in battle, the Wobbuffet is totally passive and lets opponents hit it as much as they'd like. Injure its tail, however, and you'll have some major problems on your hands!

Cool Card: Diamond and Pearl #41
Price Range: .50 – 1.00

#203 Girafarig

Type: Normal/Psychic
Evolution: None
Description: Girafarig tails actually have a small brain hidden behind their creepy, smirking grin. Though it's too small for them to think with, it doesn't have to sleep and keeps watch over the Girafarig 24 hours a day.

Cool Card: EX Legend Maker #16
Price Range: .50 – 1.00

#204 Pineco

Type: Bug

Evolution: Evolves into Forretress

Description: Pineco hang from trees waiting for prey. If someone disturbs the tree they're on while eating, they'll drop down and explode on the unsuspecting intruder!

Cool Card: EX Dragon #71

Price Range: .10 - .20

#205 Forretress

Type: Bug/Steel

Evolution: Evolves from Pineco

Description: One can only wonder what's inside a Forretress's shell, since the innards are only exposed for a split second when catching and pulling in prey!

Cool Card: Skyridge #9

Price Range: .50 – 1.00

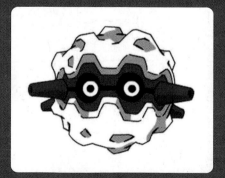

#206 Dunsparce

Type: Normal
Evolution: None
Description: Dunsparce's tail helps them burrow (backwards!) into the ground where they can rest safely. When moving about, their tiny wings glide them silently along nearby breezes.

Cool Card: EX Legend Maker #31
Price Range: .20 - .50

#207 Gligar

Type: Ground/Flying
Evolution: Evolves into Gliscor
Description: Their large wings let Gligar fly noiselessly through the air, thus giving them an advantage over prey since they can get in a sneak attack!

Cool Card: EX Dragon Frontiers #16
Price Range: .50 – 1.00

#208 Steelix

Type: Steel/Ground
Evolution: Evolves from Onix
Description: Steelix prefer to live deep underground, but if an enemy should challenge one, it'll use its claws and pinchers to hang onto an enemy while injecting it with a nasty toxin.

Cool Card: Diamond and Pearl #38
Price Range: .50 – 1.00

#209 Snubbull

Type: Normal

Evolution: Evolves into Granbull

Description: Their fangs and scary faces hide the fact that Snubbull's are not only cowards, but would prefer to make friends with other Pokémon than fight them!

Cool Card: Skyridge #101

Price Range: .10 - .20

#210 Granbull

Type: Normal

Evolution: Evolves from Snubbull

Description: Granbull's horns might seem intimidating, but they're really kind Pokémon that are careful not to bite anyone without a good reason.

Cool Card: Neo Genesis 1st Ed. #37

Price Range: .20 - .50

#211 Qwilfish

Type: Water/Poison

Evolution: None

Description: Though a fish, Qwilfish are actually not good swimmers. By sucking large amounts of water into their bodies, they use the pressure to shoot toxic quills at enemies!

Cool Card: EX Team Rocket Returns #27

Price Range: .50 – 1.00

#212 Scizor

Type: Bug/Steel

Evolution: Evolves from Scyther

Description: Scizor's body is as hard as steel, making it virtually impossible to harm with normal attacks! It uses its wings to regulate its body temperature.

Cool Card: EX Unseen Forces #108

Price Range: 15.00 – 20.00

#213 Shuckle

Type: Bug/Rock

Evolution: None

Description: Turtle-like in appearance, Shuckle like to pull their bodies inside of their shells and live off of the berries they have stored there.

Cool Card: EX Unseen Forces #47

Price Range: .20 - .50

#214 Heracross

Type: Bug/Fighting

Evolution: None

Description: Heracross use their entire bodies in battle; by rooting themselves, they can get the best angle to fling an enemy away with their horns!

Cool Card: Diamond and Pearl #28

Price Range: .50 – 1.00

#215 Sneasel

Type: Dark/Ice

Evolution: Evolves into Weavile

Description: This Pokémon uses its claws to climb trees and gather fruits and eggs that have been left unguarded by the parents.

Cool Card: Diamond and Pearl #100

Price Range: .10 - .20

#216 Teddiursa

Type: Normal
Evolution: Evolves into Ursaring
Description: Teddiursa gather fruits and nuts, though their diets mostly comprise of the honey that forms on their paws. When the crescent moon on their heads become full, they're ready to evolve!

Cool Card: Skyridge #109
Price Range: .10 - .20

#217 Ursaring

Type: Normal
Evolution: Evolves from Teddiursa
Description: Contrary to its massive and deadly appearance, Ursaring are foragers and prefer vegetables and truffles to meat. They only live in the forest and can be exceptionally gentle.

Cool Card: Neo Destiny #21
Price Range: .50 – 1.00

#218 Slugma

Type: Fire
Evolution: Evolves into Magcargo
Description: Instead of blood, lava circulates throughout a Slugma's body and carries nutrients and oxygen to the necessary body parts.

Cool Card: EX Deoxys #75
Price Range: .10 - .20

#219 Magcargo

Type: Fire/Rock

Evolution: Evolves from Slugma

Description: These Pokémon are walking furnaces; their body temperatures average 18,000 degrees F! Raindrops evaporate on contact, surrounding Magcargo in a dense fog.

Cool Card: Neo Revelation 1st Ed. #33
Price Range: .20 - .50

#220 Swinub

Type: Ice/Ground

Evolution: Evolves into Piloswine

Description: Swinub's delicate nose allows it to sniff out and dig up delicious food, its favorite being a particular mushroom that only grows under dead grass.

Cool Card: Skyridge #107
Price Range: .10 - .20

#221 Piloswine

Type: Ice/Ground

Evolution: Evolves from Swinub and into Mamoswine

Description: These wooly Pokémon absolutely love the cold! Their thick fur keeps them warm in the chilly arctic regions and they use their horns to dig food out of the frozen ground.

Cool Card: Skyridge #24

Price Range: .50 – 1.00

#222 Corsola

Type: Water/Rock

Evolution: None

Description: Corsola gather in large groups and offer the perfect hiding spot for smaller fish. They prefer warm waters, so they'll migrate every year to keep from freezing.

Cool Card: EX Unseen Forces #37

Price Range: .20 - .50

#223 Remoraid

Type: Water

Evolution: Evolves into Octillery

Description: By gathering up water into their bodies, Remoraid can shoot down flying Pokémon once they focus that water into a strong, powerful stream of water!

Cool Card: Aquapolis #105

Price Range: .10 - .20

#224 Octillery

Type: Water

Evolution: Evolves from Remoraid

Description: Octillery capture their prey with their tentacles and wait until they're immobilized before delivering the finishing blow. If a foe is too strong, they spit ink into the water and escape.

Cool Card: Neo Destiny 1st Ed. #62

Price Range: .10 - .20

#225 Delibird

Type: Ice/Flying

Evolution: None

Description: These Pokémon wander around gathering up food and storing it in their tails. Their kindness is the stuff of legends, as they're known to save lost adventurers by sharing their food with them!

Cool Card: EX Team Rocket Returns #21

Price Range: .50 – 1.00

#226 Mantine

Type: Water/Flying
Evolution: Evolves from Mantyke
Description: Mantine swim around in packs without a care in the world. Their kind natures extend to the Remoraid, who attach themselves to their massive wings and feed off of food that floats by.

Cool Card: EX Dragon Frontiers #20
Price Range: .50 – 1.00

#227 Skarmory

Type: Steel/Flying
Evolution: None
Description: Skarmory's sharp and beautiful wings are easily damaged in battle. Once a year though, they shed their tattered wings and grow new ones!

Cool Card: EX Power Keepers #98
Price Range: 8.00 – 16.00

#228 Houndour

Type: Dark/Fire
Evolution: Evolves into Houndoom
Description: Fast and cunning, Houndour hunt in packs and use a unique system of barks and yips to not only scare prey into a corner, but to coordinate attack plans with each other.

Cool Card: Neo Discovery #24
Price Range: .50 – 1.00

#229 Houndoom

Type: Dark/Fire

Evolution: Evolves from Houndour

Description: Houndoom prefer to live in packs and fight amongst themselves in order to establish dominance and pick a leader.

Cool Card: Neo Revelation 1st Ed. #8

Price Range: 3.00 – 6.00

#230 Kingdra

Type: Water/Dragon

Evolution: Evolves from Seadra

Description: Kingdra love to sleep at the bottom of the ocean where the pressure is so intense that nothing else can live there. When they surface looking for prey, they cause massive whirlpools!

Cool Card: Aquapolis #19

Price Range: .50 – 1.00

#231 Phanpy

Type: Ground
Evolution: Evolves into Donphan
Description: Phanpy love water, especially since their long noses make it easy to spray water either on themselves or at others if they're in a playful mood.

Cool Card: EX Ruby and Sapphire #62
Price Range: .10 - .20

#232 Donphan

Type: Ground
Evolution: Evolves from Phanpy
Description: As beasts of burden, the Donphan can clear away rock and mudslides. In battle, their tough bodies can crush any opponent in their path!

Cool Card: Aquapolis #7
Price Range: .50 – 1.00

#233 Porygon2

Type: Normal
Evolution: Evolves from Porygon and into Porygon-Z
Description: This adorable man-made Pokémon was created with artificial intelligence, allowing it to adapt and learn new things.

Cool Card: EX Delta Species #25
Price Range: .50 – 1.00

#234 Stantler

Type: Normal

Evolution: None

Description: The small balls on a Stantler's horns serve several purposes: they allow the Pokémon to create illusions, can be used as sleeping aids when shed in the winter, and make the horns look like giant eyes!

Cool Card: Neo Genesis 1st Ed. #76

Price Range: .10 - .25

#235 Smeargle

Type: Normal

Evolution: None

Description: Every Smeargle secretes a unique color from the end of their tails. Much like a painter, they use their tails like paintbrushes to mark their territory with distinctive designs.

Cool Card: EX Dragon Frontiers #39

Price Range: .20 - .50

#236 Tyrogue

Type: Fighting
Evolution: Evolves into Hitmonlee, Hitmonchan or Hitmontop
Description: This train-happy Pokémon gets stressed out if it's not training every day, so make sure to set up a rigid training program if you decide to train one!

Cool Card: EX Unseen Forces #33
Price Range: .50 – 1.00

#237 Hitmontop

Type: Fighting
Evolution: Evolves from Tyrogue
Description: Utilizing a perfect balance between offense and defense, the Hitmontop spins around on its head while delivering nasty kicks in rapid succession!

Cool Card: Neo Discovery #22
Price Range: .50 – 1.00

#238 Smoochum

Type: Ice/Psychic
Evolution: Evolves into Jynx
Description: Smoochum actually move faster when spinning around than when walking normally, though they trip a lot. They check their appearance often to make sure they don't have dirt on their faces from tripping so much.

Cool Card: EX Unseen Forces #31
Price Range: .50 – 1.00

#239 Elekid

Type: Electric

Evolution: Evolves into Electrabuzz

Description: Elekid build up electricity in their bodies by swinging their arms around. Make sure to keep them away from metal though; even a single touch will discharge every last volt of gathered energy!

Cool Card: Diamond and Pearl #48

Price Range: .20 - .50

#240 Magby

Type: Fire

Evolution: Evolves into Magmar

Description: These Pokémon adore hot locations, generally in or around volcanoes. A perceptive trainer can tell how a Magby is doing by observing the state of the flames that shoot out from their mouth!

Cool Card: Neo Genesis 1st Ed. #23

Price Range: .50 – 1.00

#241 Miltank

Type: Normal
Evolution: None
Description: Need a sweet pick-me-up? Miltank create up to 5 gallons of sweet milk a day, which can either be turned into yogurt or sipped from a cup.

Cool Card: EX Unseen Forces #42
Price Range: .20 - .50

#242 Blissey

Type: Normal
Evolution: Evolves from Chansey
Description: Blissey's unique fur allows it to sense when people are sad. It'll rush off and give them an egg of condolence that, when eaten, will instantly make someone feel better!

Cool Card: EX Unseen Forces #101
Price Range: 10.00 – 15.00

#243 Raikou

Type: Electric
Evolution: None
Description: One of three legendary Johto region Pokémon, Raikou stores an incredible amount of electricity in his body, which when released causes the ground to tremble as if struck by lightning.

Cool Card: EX Deoxys #108
Price Range: 7.00 – 14.00

#244 Entei

Type: Fire

Evolution: None

Description: One of three legendary Johto region Pokémon, Entei embodies passion, flames and lava, and his bark can cause nearby volcanoes to erupt!

Cool Card: Aquapolis #10

Price Range: 2.00 – 4.00

#245 Suicune

Type: Water

Evolution: None

Description: One of three legendary Johto region Pokémon, Suicune can move at the speed of light, call forth cool winds from the north, and purify any source of water.

Cool Card: EX Team Magma vs. Team Aqua #94

Price Range: 10.00 – 18.00

#246 Larvitar

Type: Rock/Ground
Evolution: Evolves into Pupitar
Description: Larvitar love eating soil. In fact, they're born underground and must eat all of the soil above them just to escape and see their parents' faces!

Cool Card: EX Dragon Frontiers #52
Price Range: .10 - .20

#247 Pupitar

Type: Rock/Ground
Evolution: Evolves from Larvitar and into Tyranitar
Description: Pupitar move around by expelling gas from their bodies to propel them forward. Their bodies are also incredibly durable.

Cool Card: Aquapolis #56
Price Range: .20 - .50

#248 Tyranitar

Type: Dark/Rock
Evolution: Evolves from Pupitar
Description: Preferring to make its home in rocky mountainsides, the monstrously strong Tyranitar are always on the prowl for other Pokémon to challenge.

Cool Card: EX Dragon Frontiers #99
Price Range: 15.00 – 25.00

#249 Lugia

Type: Psychic/Flying

Evolution: None

Description: Lugia prefers to live quietly at the bottom of the ocean, since a single gentle beat of its wings can tear homes off of their foundation!

Cool Card: Aquapolis #149

Price Range: 10.00 – 20.00

#250 Ho-oh

Type: Fire/Flying

Evolution: None

Description: Rumored to live at the base of a rainbow, the Ho-oh's bright plumes shift between seven different colors depending on how the light hits its feathers!

Cool Card: Neo Revelation 1st Ed. #18

Price Range: .50 – 1.00

#251 Celebi

Type: Grass/Psychic
Evolution: None
Description: This adorable legendary Pokémon comes from the future. It's thought that as long as Celebi is around, a bright future awaits everyone. Celebi is also one of a very few Pokémon that doesn't naturally appear in any of the games!

Cool Card: EX Crystal Guardians #100
Price Range: 23.00 – 35.00

#252 Treecko

Type: Grass
Evolution: Evolves into Grovyle
Description: This cool little lizard is extremely brave and unwavering, even in the face of adversaries much larger than itself.

Cool Card: EX Crystal Guardians #68
Price Range: .10 - .20

#253 Grovyle

Type: Grass
Evolution: Evolves from Treecko and into Sceptile
Description: The leaf-like wings on the Grovyle make it adapt to jumping and gliding from branch to branch. Make no mistake: if there's a tree around, you won't be able to catch one!

Cool Card: EX Crystal Guardians #19
Price Range: .50 – 1.00

#254 Sceptile

Type: Grass

Evolution: Evolves from Grovyle

Description: The seeds on Sceptile's back are full of nutrients that revitalize trees. They love to care for trees in the forest and are rarely found elsewhere.

Cool Card: EX Crystal Guardians #96
Price Range: 15.00 – 20.00

#255 Torchic

Type: Fire

Evolution: Evolves into Combusken

Description: Feeling a little cold at night? Just pull your trusty Torchic into your arms and give this feathery cutie a squeeze; it'll warm you right up!

Cool Card: EX Power Keepers #67
Price Range: .10 - .20

#256 Combusken

Type: Fire/Fighting
Evolution: Evolves from Torchic and into Blaziken
Description: This is not a Pokémon you want to mess with. Along with a fiery hot breath, Combusken's got some fast moves and a cry that's extremely loud and distracting.

Cool Card: EX Crystal Guardians #16
Price Range: .50 – 1.00

#257 Blaziken

Type: Fire/Fighting
Evolution: Evolves from Combusken
Description: Able to leap over buildings in a single bound, Blaziken can also utilize its terribly strong legs and blazing punches in battle.

Cool Card: EX Team Magma vs. Team Aqua #89
Price Range: 20.00 – 30.00

#258 Mudkip

Type: Water
Evolution: Evolves into Marshtomp
Description: Mudkip use the bright orange gills on their cheeks to breathe under water. They may look small and weak, but they can crush rocks bigger than themselves!

Cool Card: EX Ruby and Sapphire #59
Price Range: .10 - .20

#259 Marshtomp

Type: Water/Ground
Evolution: Evolves from Mudkip and into Swampert
Description: This Pokémon's hind legs are incredibly adapt at letting it run over mud without slipping. It's actually more at home in mud than it is in water.

Cool Card: EX Ruby and Sapphire #40
Price Range: .20 - .50

#260 Swampert

Type: Water/Ground
Evolution: Evolves from Marshtomp
Description: Swampert's massive fins allow it to sense subtle shifts in tides and winds, allowing it to predict when a storm's coming.

Cool Card: EX Crystal Guardians #98
Price Range: 12.00 – 20.00

#261 Poochyena

Type: Dark
Evolution: Evolves into Mightyena
Description: Poochyena's make the perfect pet for kids who don't like their peas, since it'll basically eat anything given to it (that's edible, that is).

Cool Card: EX Ruby and Sapphire #064
Price Range: .10 - .20

#262 Mightyena

Type: Dark
Evolution: Evolves from Poochyena
Description: These Pokémon travel in packs and will only follow a trainer that possesses superior battle skills.

Cool Card: EX Holon Phantoms #101
Price Range: 7.00 – 15.00

#263 Zigzagoon

Type: Normal
Evolution: Evolves into Linoone
Description: Zigzagoon's use their hard, bristly back fur to mark their territory when rubbing up against trees. If it senses danger, it may play dead to avoid being eaten!

Cool Card: EX Ruby and Sapphire #79
Price Range: .10 - .20

#264 Linoone

Type: Normal

Evolution: Evolves from Zigzagoon

Description: Due to their superior speed (they've been known to top 60 mph!), a Linoone will charge straight at its foe in battle. Just don't expect them to be able to turn on a dime.

Cool Card: EX Sandstorm #44

Price Range: .20 - .50

#265 Wurmple

Type: Bug

Evolution: Evolves into Silcoon or Cascoon

Description: Since this little guy is a favorite treat of the Swellow, it's learned to use the sharp spikes on its tail for self-defense, along with secreting a poison if anyone gets too close!

Cool Card: Diamond and Pearl #104

Price Range: .10 - .20

#266 Silcoon

Type: Bug
Evolution: Evolves from Wurmple and into Beautifly
Description: Originally believed to not eat until its evolution, scientists have recently discovered that Silcoon actually drink rain water that collects on their skin.

Cool Card: Diamond and Pearl #63
Price Range: .20 - .50

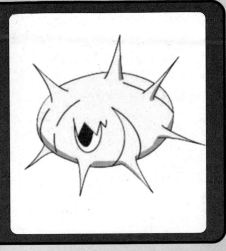

#267 Beautifly

Type: Bug/Flying
Evolution: Evolves from Silcoon
Description: Beautifly uses its long, needle-like mouth to collect pollen from flowers and its large, beautiful wings to flit along cool spring winds.

Cool Card: Diamond and Pearl #19
Price Range: .50 – 1.00

#268 Cascoon

Type: Bug
Evolution: Evolves from Wurmple and into Dustox
Description: This tough Pokémon cannot move, even if attacked by an enemy, otherwise its body upon evolution will be very weak. It wouldn't be wise though to take advantage of them; they never forgive any who hurt them.

Cool Card: Diamond and Pearl #44
Price Range: ,20 - .50

#269 Dustox

Type: Bug/Poison
Evolution: Evolves from Cascoon
Description: The fine dust that Dustox releases from its wings is extremely poisonous and will weaken even the strongest of enemies. It also uses its antennae to search for food.

Cool Card: Diamond and Pearl #25
Price Range: .50 – 1.00

#270 Lotad

Type: Water/Grass
Evolution: Evolves into Lombre
Description: Originally thought to have been a land-dweller, the leaf on the Lotad's head is so large now that it cannot do more than float on the surface of a lake or river.

Cool Card: EX Crystal Guardians #55
Price Range: .10 - .20

#271 Lombre

Type: Water/Grass
Evolution: Evolves from Lotad and into Ludicolo
Description: People who mistake this Pokémon for a child will be in for quite a shock when they try to touch it; a thin, slimy mucus covers its entire body.

Cool Card: EX Crystal Guardians #37
Price Range: .20 - .50

#272 Ludicolo

Type: Water/Grass
Evolution: Evolves from Lombre
Description: Play an upbeat and cheerful song and a Ludicolo will get up and dance around, even in battle!

Cool Card: EX Deoxys #19
Price Range: .50 – 1.00

#273 Seedot

Type: Grass
Evolution: Evolves into Nuzleaf
Description: This tiny Pokémon looks exactly like an acorn and uses leaves to polish its body at least once a day.

Cool Card: Diamond and Pearl #97
Price Range: .10 - .20

#274 Nuzleaf

Type: Grass/Dark

Evolution: Evolves from Seedot and into Shiftry

Description: Nuzleaf use the leaf atop their heads like a flute and play haunting, fearful melodies that strike terror in the hearts of anyone lost in the woods.

Cool Card: Diamond and Pearl #57

Price Range: .20 - .50

#275 Shiftry

Type: Grass/Dark

Evolution: Evolves from Nuzleaf

Description: Shiftry prefers to live in seclusion deep within forests, but if an enemy appears, it can use its fans to kick up powerful winds and blow them away!

Cool Card: EX Deoxys #25

Price Range: .50 – 1.00

#276 Taillow

Type: Normal/Flying
Evolution: Evolves into Swellow
Description: Having just left their nests, these young birds are often heard crying out at night from being lonely. They also love nibbling on Wurmples.

Cool Card: EX Ruby and Sapphire #72
Price Range: .10 - .20

#277 Swellow

Type: Normal/Flying
Evolution: Evolves from Taillow
Description: Extremely concerned with the glossy beauty of their wings, two Swellow will diligently take care of each other's wings.

Cool Card: EX Delta Species #32
Price Range: .50 – 1.00

#278 Wingull

Type: Water/Flying
Evolution: Evolves into Pelipper
Description: The Wingull's long, narrow wings allow them to glide easily upon high sea winds, and their beaks are perfect for catching fish.

Cool Card: EX Ruby and Sapphire #77
Price Range: .10 - .20

#279 Pelipper

Type: Water/Flying

Evolution: Evolves from Wingull

Description: Pelipper skim low over a surface of water, dipping their extremely large beaks into the water to catch both water and fish, and then swallow both in one huge gulp!

Cool Card: EX Crystal Guardians #26

Price Range: .50 – 1.00

#280 Ralts

Type: Psychic

Evolution: Evolves into Kirlia

Description: This empathetic Pokémon can sense the emotions of its trainer and reflects their mood; thus a happy trainer will raise a happy Ralts.

Cool Card: EX Dragon Frontiers #61

Price Range: .10 - .20

#281 Kirlia

Type: Psychic

Evolution: Evolves from Ralts and into Gardevoir or Gallade

Description: The horns on a Kirlia's head amplify its psychic powers, which distort the scenery and create illusions that don't really exist.

Cool Card: EX Ruby and Sapphire #34

Price Range: .20 - .50

#282 Gardevoir

Type: Psychic

Evolution: Evolves from Kirlia

Description: With psychic powers far more powerful than its earlier evolutions, the Gardevoir can actually open a small black hole to distort the dimensions. It's extremely protective of its trainer, and will die in order to protect them!

Cool Card: EX Dragon Frontiers #93

Price Range: 12.00 – 16.00

#283 Surskit

Type: Bug/Water

Evolution: Evolves into Masquerain

Description: If scared, the Surskit will secrete thick, sugary syrup from the tip of its head. The syrup is a favorite though of many Pokémon.

Cool Card: EX Holon Phantoms #82

Price Range: .10 - .20

#284 Masquerain

Type: Bug/Flying

Evolution: Evolves from Surskit

Description: The Masquerain's antennae look like giant, angry eyes in order to scare enemies away. It's said that if their antennae droop, a storm is coming.

Cool Card: EX Hidden Legends #20

Price Range: .50 – 1.00

#285 Shroomish

Type: Grass

Evolution: Evolves into Breloom

Description: If frightened, the Shroomish shakes violently and releases toxic spores that are so poisonous, they'll cause trees and grass around them wilt!

Cool Card: EX Ruby and Sapphire #69

Price Range: .10 - .20

#286 Breloom

Type: Grass/Fighting
Evolution: Evolves from Shroomish
Description: The bell-like seeds on Breloom's tail not only taste horrible, but will release a mild poison that'll give one a nasty tummy ache.

Cool Card: EX Deoxys #3
Price Range: 3.00 – 6.00

#287 Slakoth

Type: Normal
Evolution: Evolves into Vigoroth
Description: Slakoth is extremely sloth-like and would prefer loafing around to fighting. It's exceptionally rare to see them in motion.

Cool Card: EX Sandstorm #80
Price Range: .10 - .20

#288 Vigoroth

Type: Normal
Evolution: Evolves from Slakoth and into Slaking
Description: Completely the opposite from a Slakoth, the Vigoroth are so agitated that even when they try to sleep, their blood vibrates violently through their veins!

Cool Card: EX Ruby and Sapphire #47
Price Range: .20 - .50

#289 Slaking

Type: Normal

Evolution: Evolves from Vigoroth

Description: Returning to its sloth-like origins, Slaking leave small rings wherever they go since they simply eat all of the grass within reach.

Cool Card: EX Power Keepers #13

Price Range: 2.00 – 4.00

#290 Nincada

Type: Bug/Ground

Evolution: Evolves into Ninjask or Shedinja

Description: Nincada cannot stand sunlight, so they burrow and use their claws to cut into the roots of plants and trees before stealing all of their nutrients.

Cool Card: EX Dragon #68

Price Range: .10 - .20

#291 Ninjask

Type: Bug/Flying
Evolution: Evolves from Nincada
Description: If not trained properly, the Ninjask will start to cry loudly without stopping to give the poor trainer's ears a rest.

Cool Card: EX Dragon #18
Price Range: .50 – 1.00

#292 Shedinja

Type: Bug/Ghost
Evolution: Evolves from Nincada
Description: This unusual Pokémon simply appears without warning sometimes when a Nincada evolves. It doesn't move, nor does it even breathe!

Cool Card: EX Dragon #11
Price Range: 2.00 – 4.00

#293 Whismur

Type: Normal
Evolution: Evolves into Loudred
Description: The Whismur is a very fearful creature. If it starts to cry, the sound of its own sobs will scare it into crying even louder! Once it finally tires of crying, it lays down to sleep.

Cool Card: EX Crystal Guardians #69
Price Range: .10 - .20

#294 Loudred

Type: Normal

Evolution: Evolves from Whismur and into Exploud

Description: Loudred stomp their feet and scream very loudly at an enemy. Once they finish, they're actually temporarily deaf from the sound of their own voice.

Cool Card: EX Crystal Guardians #23

Price Range: .50 – 1.00

#295 Exploud

Type: Normal

Evolution: Evolves from Loudred

Description: Generally a quiet Pokémon unless in battle, Exploud use the tubes on their bodies to emit soft whistling sounds that allow them to express their feelings.

Cool Card: EX Crystal Guardians #92

Price Range: 12.00 – 15.00

#296 Makuhita

Type: Fighting
Evolution: Evolves into Hariyama
Description: Makuhita love to train heavily, eat heartily, and get plenty of sleep in order to forge themselves into perfectly balanced fighting machines.

Cool Card: EX Deoxys #65
Price Range: .10 - .20

#297 Hariyama

Type: Fighting
Evolution: Evolves from Makuhita
Description: Don't let Hariyama's appearance fool you; its body isn't covered in fat, but hardened muscle that, when tensed up, makes its body as hard as stone!

Cool Card: EX Deoxys #100
Price Range: 7.00 – 14.00

#298 Azurill

Type: Normal
Evolution: Evolves into Marill
Description: Azurill is a fun-loving Pokémon that uses the large, bouncy ball at the end of its tail to bounce around and play.

Cool Card: Diamond and Pearl #69
Price Range: .10 - .20

#299 Nosepass

Type: Rock

Evolution: Evolves into Probopass

Description: The Nosepass's nose always points north and it travels a mere 3/8ths of an inch every year!

Cool Card: EX Ruby and Sapphire #18

Price Range: .50 – 1.00

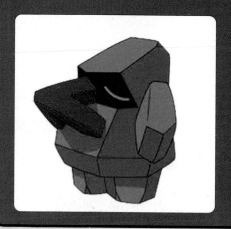

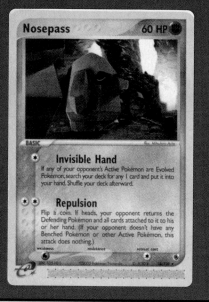

Nosepass — 60 HP

BASIC

Invisible Hand
If any of your opponent's Active Pokémon are Evolved Pokémon, search your deck for any 1 card and put it into your hand. Shuffle your deck afterward.

Repulsion
Flip a coin. If heads, your opponent returns the Defending Pokémon and all cards attached to it to his or her hand. (If your opponent doesn't have any Benched Pokémon or other Active Pokémon, this attack does nothing.)

weakness   resistance   retreat cost

#300 Skitty

Type: Normal

Evolution: Evolves into Delcatty

Description: Skitty love to chase their own tails around and are popular pets due to their adorable appearance.

Cool Card: EX Sandstorm #79

Price Range: .10 - .20

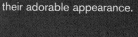

Skitty — 50 HP

BASIC

Energy Catch
Search your discard pile for a basic Energy card, show it to your opponent, and put it into your hand.

Double-edge   30
Skitty does 10 damage to itself.

weakness   resistance   retreat cost

#301 Delcatty

Type: Normal
Evolution: Evolves from Skitty
Description: Passive in nature, Delcatty will curl up anywhere they feel like and fall asleep there. If an enemy attacks them while asleep, they won't fight back; they'll simply move elsewhere.

Cool Card: EX Crystal Guardian #91
Price Range: 12.00 – 20.00

#302 Sableye

Type: Dark/Ghost
Evolution: None
Description: Sableye use their claws to dig up rocks full of wonderful minerals and eat them. The minerals crystallize and rise up into their skin, making them exceptionally dangerous Pokémon.

Cool Card: EX Deoxys #23
Price Range: .50 – 1.00

#303 Mawile

Type: Steel
Evolution: None
Description: Their cute face is extremely deceptive: Mawile use their horns, which have been transformed into a massive steel jaw, to chomp down on enemies!

Cool Card: EX Power Keepers #17
Price Range: .50 – 1.00

#304 Aron

Type: Steel/Rock

Evolution: Evolves into Lairon

Description: Though extremely small, the Aron packs a huge punch; it can tear through a dump truck, and then turn the twisted metal into a yummy meal!

Cool Card: EX Crystal Guardians #44
Price Range: .10 - .20

#305 Lairon

Type: Steel/Rock

Evolution: Evolves from Aron and into Aggron

Description: Lairon dine on iron found in both rocks and water. Generally found in rocky areas near iron caches, Lairon oftentimes clash with humans who try to mine the ore near them.

Cool Card: EX Crystal Guardians #36
Price Range: .20 - .50

#306 Aggron

Type: Steel/Rock
Evolution: Evolves from Lairon
Description: Extremely territorial, even if its countryside is ravaged by a landside or fire, the Aggron will haul rocks and trees from nearby to restore their home to its natural beauty.

Cool Card: EX Crystal Guardians #89
Price Range: 15.00 – 20.00

#307 Meditite

Type: Fighting/Psychic
Evolution: Evolves into Medicham
Description: Surviving on just one berry a day as part of its training, the Meditite meditates to focus its psychic abilities.

Cool Card: Diamond and Pearl #89
Price Range: .10 - .20

#308 Medicham

Type: Fighting/Psychic
Evolution: Evolves from Meditite
Description: Extensive meditation has opened the Medicham's third eye, giving it incredible psychic and telekinetic powers!

Cool Card: Diamond and Pearl #32
Price Range: .50 – 1.00

#309 Electrike

Type: Electric

Evolution: Evolves into Manectric

Description: Electrike run faster than the eye can see, converting the friction from running so fast into energy that's stored in their fur.

Cool Card: EX Crystal Guardians #52

Price Range: .10 - .20

#310 Manectric

Type: Electric

Evolution: Evolves from Electrike

Description: Strong electrical currents are stored in the Manectric's mane, which are collected from the atmosphere. It's not uncommon for thunderclouds to form over this Pokémon.

Cool Card: EX Ruby and Sapphire #9

Price Range: 2.00 – 4.00

#311 Plusle

Type: Electric
Evolution: None
Description: Electric sparks dance along the Plusle's body when cheering on its partner, though it'll cry loudly should they lose.

Cool Card: EX Deoxys #44
Price Range: .20 - .50

#312 Minun

Type: Electric
Evolution: None
Description: Like the Plusle, Minun love to cheer on their partners. If they see they're in trouble, they'll release a huge number of sparks in order to help them fight.

Cool Card: EX Emerald #37
Price Range: .20 - .50

#313 Volbeat

Type: Bug
Evolution: None
Description: Volbeat's tail glows like a light bulb and when around others, they love to draw designs in the night sky with them. They also love Illumise's sweet aroma.

Cool Card: EX Emerald #42
Price Range: .20 - .50

#314 Illumise

Type: Bug
Evolution: None
Description: Illumise lead groups of Volbeat as they light up designs in the night sky. The more complex the design, the greater renowned the Illumise will become among other Illumise.

Cool Card: EX Delta Species #45
Price Range: .20 - .50

#315 Roselia

Type: Grass/Poison
Evolution: Evolves from Budew and into Roserade
Description: Though generally quite beautiful and peaceful, a Roselia won't hold back in a battle: the thorns upon its head contain a deadly poison that'll stop anyone from stealing its beautiful flowers.

Cool Card: Diamond and Pearl #96
Price Range: .10 - .20

#316 Gulpin

Type: Poison
Evolution: Evolves into Swalot
Description: This gelatinous Pokémon has a tiny brain and heart; almost its entire body is filled with a massive stomach that can digest literally anything it consumes!

Cool Card: EX Crystal Guardians #33
Price Range: .20 - .50

#317 Swalot

Type: Poison
Evolution: Evolves from Gulpin
Description: Since the Swalot has no teeth, it swallows everything in one giant gulp. And boy, can it swallow; a tire could fit into its massive maw!

Cool Card: EX Emerald #40
Price Range: .20 - .50

#318 Carvanha

Type: Water/Dark
Evolution: Evolves into Sharpedo
Description: On its own, the Carvanha is quite timid and bashful. When in a large group, however, these little guys will tear apart anything that intrudes upon their territory with their sharp, jagged teeth!

Cool Card: EX Team Magma vs. Team Aqua #25
Price Range: .20 - .50

#319 Sharpedo

Type: Water/Dark
Evolution: Evolves from Carvanha
Description: This is one Pokémon that any would-be trainer had better be careful of. Capable of bursts of speeds up to 75 mph, Sharpedo's teeth can tear through iron in a single bite.

Cool Card: EX Holon Phantoms #53
Price Range: .20 - .50

#320 Wailmer

Type: Water
Evolution: Evolves into Wailord
Description: The water a Wailmer can store in its body not only acts as a fun prank when spraying an unsuspecting target, but it allows the Pokémon to bounce across short distances of land.

Cool Card: EX Sandstorm #83
Price Range: .10 - .20

#321 Wailord

Type: Water
Evolution: Evolves from Wailmer
Description: The Wailord is the largest Pokémon alive and they generally travel in pods. Alone they can catch krill simply by opening their mouths, but in a group they can take down larger prey.

Cool Card: EX Sandstorm #100
Price Range: 30.00 – 50.00

#322 Numel

Type: Fire/Ground
Evolution: Evolves into Camerupt
Description: Numel store super-heated lava within their bodies. If they get wet, that lava cools and the poor Pokémon becomes sluggish.

Cool Card: EX Ruby and Sapphire #61
Price Range: .10 - .20

#323 Camerupt

Type: Fire/Ground
Evolution: Evolves from Numel
Description: The strange humps on the back of Camerupt are known to erupt and spew lava whenever they get really mad!

Cool Card: EX Emerald #92
Price Range: 6.00 – 12.00

#324 Torkoal

Type: Fire
Evolution: None
Description: Torkoal actually burn coal within their bodies in order to fuel their bodies with steam and heat. If they don't burn enough coal, the fire within them dies down and then become extremely weak.

Cool Card: EX Team Magma vs. Team Aqua #12
Price Range: 2.00 - 4.00

#325 Spoink

Type: Psychic
Evolution: Evolves into Grumpig
Description: The beautiful pearl upon a Spoink's head amplifies its psychic powers. Because of this, they're constantly looking for bigger pearls to wear.

Cool Card: EX Dragon #73
Price Range: .10 - .20

#326 Grumpig

Type: Psychic
Evolution: Evolves from Spoink
Description: No longer relying upon a single giant pearl after evolving, Grumpig instead use numerous small black pearls to wield their fantastic psychic abilities.

Cool Card: EX Crystal Guardians #20
Price Range: .50 – 1.00

#327 Spinda

Type: Normal
Evolution: None
Description: No two Spinda are said to have the same pattern of spots, which just seems to emphasize their rather bizarre nature to wander around in a daze and confuse opponents with their strange movements.

Cool Card: EX Legend Maker #26
Price Range: .50 – 1.00

#328 Trapinch

Type: Ground
Evolution: Evolves into Vibrava
Description: Trapinch are patient hunters who dig elaborate traps and wait at the bottom of them with their mouths wide for an unsuspecting Pokémon to fall into their grasp.

Cool Card: EX Dragon #78
Price Range: .10 – .20

#329 Vibrava

Type: Ground/Dragon

Evolution: Evolves from Trapinch and into Flygon

Description: Still too underdeveloped for long-distance flying, the Vibrava instead rapidly vibrate their wings in order to generate ultrasonic waves.

Cool Card: EX Dragon Frontiers #24
Price Range: .50 – 1.00

#330 Flygon

Type: Ground/Dragon

Evolution: Evolves from Vibrava

Description: Flygon's wings are massive and strong, whipping up sandstorms with a single beat. Since they also make beautiful, song-like sounds, they're often thought of as desert spirits.

Cool Card: EX Dragon #4
Price Range: .10 - .20

#331 Cacnea

Type: Grass
Evolution: Evolves into Cacturne
Description: Cacnea thrive in harsh, unlivable conditions, which only increase how beautiful their flowers grow. In battle, they wield their massive, thorny arms like clubs.

Cool Card: EX Sandstorm #57
Price Range: .10 -.20

#332 Cacturne

Type: Grass/Dark
Evolution: Evolves from Cacnea
Description: During the day, Cacturne remain motionless to preserve their moisture. At night, they follow lost prey in packs until it tires, then attack and absorb all moisture from their prey.

Cool Card: EX Cryotal Guardians #15
Price Range: .50 – 1.00

#333 Swablu

Type: Normal/Flying
Evolution: Evolves into Altaria
Description: These puffy birds are extreme neat-freaks and will happily clean up any dirt they find with their soft, fluffy wings. They're also extremely friendly and like to perch on human's heads!

Cool Card: EX Dragon Frontiers #65
Price Range: .10 - .20

#334 Altaria

Type: Dragon/Flying

Evolution: Evolves from Swablu

Description: Altaria's soft plume lets them float upon the strongest and weakest breezes, and their beautiful voices can seduce anyone within earshot.

Cool Card: EX Dragon Frontier #90

Price Range: 12.00 – 16.00

#335 Zangoose

Type: Normal

Evolution: None

Description: When threatened, a Zangoose will stand up on their hind legs and swipe at enemies with their fast moves and sharp claws. Their hatred of Seviper is so deep and ancient, it's now instinctual.

Cool Card: EX Sandstorm #14

Price Range: .10 - .20

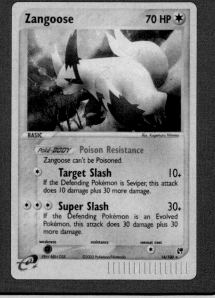

#336 Seviper

Type: Poison
Evolution: None
Description: Seviper's sword-like tail slices at enemies while poisoning them with nasty venom. Never get one near a Zangoose, otherwise they won't stop until one of them is dead!

Cool Card: EX Emerald #20
Price Range: .50 – 1.00

#337 Lunatone

Type: Rock/Psychic
Evolution: None
Description: Only active when there's a full moon out, a Lunatone will use its red eyes to paralyze any who look at it with fear.

Cool Card: EX Legend Maker #20
Price Range: .50 – 1.00

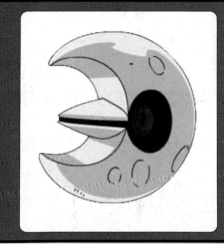

#338 Solrock

Type: Rock/Psychic
Evolution: None
Description: Solrock feed off of sunlight and will release intense heat from their bodies when rotating them. It's also theorized that these Pokémon can read the emotions of others.

Cool Card: EX Legend Maker #25
Price Range: .50 – 1.00

#339 Barboach

Type: Water/Ground

Evolution: Evolves into Whiscash

Description: The slimy film that covers a Barboach's body is its first and best means of defense, allowing it to slip through anything that might try to grab it. They become extremely weak if the film dries up though!

Cool Card: EX Dragon #51

Price Range: .10 - .20

#340 Whiscash

Type: Water/Ground

Evolution: Evolves from Barboach

Description: Not only can the Whiscash predict earthquakes but, should it become angry, it can also cause one that can be felt up to three miles away!

Cool Card: EX Dragon #48

Price Range: .10 - .20

#341 Corphish

Type: Water
Evolution: Evolves into Crawdaunt
Description: A Corphish will use its claws to catch food. It has no preferences, neither with what it eats nor what type of water it lives in (even the icky, murky stuff!).

Cool Card: EX Team Magma vs. Team Aqua #26
Price Range: .20 - .50

#342 Crawdaunt

Type: Water/Dark
Evolution: Evolves from Corphish
Description: Crawdaunt have vicious attitudes and seek out fights wherever they can find them. Due to this, they generally only live around other Crawdaunt since other Pokémon can't stand them.

Cool Card: EX Holon Phantoms #99
Price Range: 9.00 – 17.00

#343 Baltoy

Type: Ground/Psychic
Evolution: Evolves into Claydol
Description: Though most are unsure as to why, if a Baltoy meets another of its kind, they'll huddle together and cry noisily. Their psychic powers allow them to balance upon their single foot, which they even sleep on!

Cool Card: EX Team Magma vs. Team Aqua #32
Price Range: .20 - .50

#344 Claydol

Type: Ground/Psychic
Evolution: Evolves from Baltoy
Description: Claydol are even more mysterious than their predecessors, using their psychic powers to not only stay afloat even while asleep, but to keep their laser-shooting arms rotating slowly around their bodies.

Cool Card: EX Power Keepers #93
Price Range: 12.00 – 15.00

#345 Lileep

Type: Rock/Grass
Evolution: Evolves into Cradily
Description: An ancient Pokémon that was extinct until it was recently regenerated from a fossil, Lileep remain rooted upon a rock for their entire lives, scanning for prey with their two eyes.

Cool Card: EX Holon Phantoms #68
Price Range: .10 - .20

#346 Cradily

Type: Rock/Grass
Evolution: Evolves from Lileep
Description: Cradily are dangerous sea Pokémon that use their bodies to anchor themselves to the ground. When food gets too close, their petal-like tentacles capture and release a digestive fluid that "melts" their prey before eating them!

Cool Card: EX Team Magma vs. Team Aqua #90
Price Range: 7.00 – 15.00

#347 Anorith

Type: Rock/Bug
Evolution: Evolves into Armaldo
Description: Another ancient Pokémon, the Anorith use their eight "wings" to swim along through the water and their sharp claws to capture would-be food.

Cool Card: EX Legend Maker #29
Price Range: .20 - .50

#348 Armaldo

Type: Rock/Bug
Evolution: Evolves from Anorith
Description: The ancient, and once extinct, Armaldo relies on its massive hind legs to walk on land, where it seems to prefer to hunt and live.

Cool Card: EX Legend Maker #84
Price Range: .7.00 – 14.00

#349 Feebas

Type: Water
Evolution: Evolves into Milotic
Description: Rather slow and dimwitted, Feebas are easy to catch if you can find them. They love both salty and fresh water, though they're extremely weak fighters.

Cool Card: EX Hidden Legends #61
Price Range: .10 - .20

#350 Milotic

Type: Water
Evolution: Evolves from Feebas
Description: The beautiful Milotic live at the bottom of lakes and are often compared to mermaids. None can stay angry in their presence, and in cases of extreme anger, Milotic will turn red and release a pulse of calming energy!

Cool Card: EX Hidden Legends #12
Price Range: 5.00 – 10.00

#351 Castform

Type: Normal
Evolution: None
Description: Castform have the unique ability to absorb the powers of the sun, rain clouds, and snow clouds, giving it a huge variety of attacks and forms in battle!

Cool Card: EX Hidden Legends #23
Price Range: .50 – 1.00

#352 Kecleon

Type: Normal
Evolution: None
Description: Like a chameleon, a Kecleon's skin changes to match that of their surroundings. They wait quietly and strike out with their long tongue to ensnare food.

Cool Card: EX Legend Maker #07
Price Range: .20 - .50

#353 Shuppet

Type: Ghost
Evolution: Evolves into Banette
Description: The Shuppet is a rather nasty little Pokémon, floating around towns in search of dark and depressing emotions to feed on.

Cool Card: EX Crystal Guardians #40
Price Range: .20 - .50

#354 Banette

Type: Ghost
Evolution: Evolves from Shuppet
Description: Created when a Shuppet possesses a discarded stuffed toy, Banette can unleash devastating curses while they search for the child that abandoned them. If their mouths ever open, they'll lose all of their powers!

Cool Card: EX Crystal Guardians #1
Price Range: 3.00 – 6.00

#355 Duskull

Type: Ghost
Evolution: Evolves into Dusclops
Description: Duskull wander lost through the darkest places in the world. Mothers are prone to telling stories of how the Duskull will run off with children who are not quiet.

Cool Card: Diamond and Pearl #80
Price Range: .10 - .20

#356 Dusclops

Type: Ghost
Evolution: Evolves from Duskull and into Dusknoir
Description: Be wary of the Dusclops' single eye! If you become entranced by their hypnotic powers, you'll become their unwilling slave.

Cool Card: Diamond and Pearl #47
Price Range: .20 - .50

#357 Tropius

Type: Grass/Flying
Evolution: None
Description: Not only are Tropius very well-rounded fighters, but if you find yourself in the middle of nowhere without anything to eat, you can munch on the fruits that grow from their neck!

Cool Card: EX Dragon Frontiers #23
Price Range: .50 – 1.00

#358 Chimecho

Type: Psychic
Evolution: Evolves from Chingling
Description: Chimecho are beautiful Pokémon resembling chimes that stick to branches with the suction cup on their heads and eat berries with their long tails.

Cool Card: EX Emerald #12
Price Range: .50 – 1.00

#359 Absol

Type: Dark
Evolution: None
Description: The Absol's unique ability to foretell the future by observing subtle shifts in the world around it makes it a valuable, if exceedingly rare, Pokémon to possess.

Cool Card: EX Power Keepers #92
Price Range: 10.00 - 20.00

#360 Wynaut

Type: Psychic
Evolution: Evolves into Wobbuffet
Description: These adorable Pokémon love to gather and rub up against each other to practice their fighting techniques. Since they're always smiling, an observant trainer must look at a Wynaut's tail to tell its current mood.

Cool Card: Diamond and Pearl #42
Price Range: .50 – 1.00

#361 Snorunt

Type: Ice

Evolution: Evolves into Glalie or Froslass

Description: Living off of only ice and snow, Snorunt move around in small packs and hide when spring and summer roll around. It's said that when one visits a house, it'll bring good luck upon the house for generations!

Cool Card: EX Hidden Legends #73

Price Range: .10 - .20

#362 Glalie

Type: Ice

Evolution: Evolves from Snorunt

Description: This icy evolution is a master of freezing opponents and prey, thus giving it time to nibble on its new frozen treat.

Cool Card: EX Emerald #13

Price Range: .50 – 1.00

#363 Spheal

Type: Ice/Water

Evolution: Evolves into Sealeo

Description: The rotund Spheal moves about by rolling around on ice and other surfaces, having quite a "ball" as it does too!

Cool Card: EX Legend Maker #65

Price Range: .10 - .20

#364 Sealeo

Type: Ice/Water

Evolution: Evolves from Spheal and into Walrein

Description: Sealeo noses are extremely sensitive and accurate. They'll balance objects upon their noses in order to get an idea if it's something they'd like or not.

Cool Card: EX Team Magma vs. Team Aqua #31

Price Range: .20 - .50

#365 Walrein

Type: Ice/Water

Evolution: Evolves from Sealeo

Description: The Walrein's large layer of blubber and massive tusks allow for them to survive in the frigid, artic waters where they live.

Cool Card: EX Hidden Legends #15

Price Range: 4.00 – 7.00

#366 Clamperl

Type: Water
Evolution: Evolves into Huntail or Gorebyss
Description: The gentle pearl within every Clamperl grows slowly within its hardened shell. When the pearl becomes too large for its shell, it's a sure sign that it's about to evolve!

Cool Card: EX Legend Maker #51
Price Range: .10 - .20

#367 Huntail

Type: Water
Evolution: Evolves from Clamperl
Description: Having avoided detection until recently since it thrives in the darkest regions of the sea, the Huntail is a serpentine Pokémon capable of withstanding the challenges presented by its habitat.

Cool Card: EX Legend Maker #18
Price Range: .50 – 1.00

#368 Gorebyss

Type: Water
Evolution: Evolves from Clamperl
Description: Though thin and beautiful, the Gorebyss is extremely vicious. When it sees its prey, it sticks its thin nose into the creature and sucks it dry of all bodily fluids!

Cool Card: EX Legend Maker #17
Price Range: .50 – 1.00

#369 Relicanth

Type: Water/Rock

Evolution: None

Description: Another deep-sea Pokémon, its hard body can withstand heavy water pressure and it feeds on microscopic organisms that thrive in the sunless parts of the ocean.

Cool Card: EX Holon Phantoms #30

Price Range: .50 – 1.00

#370 Luvdisc

Type: Water

Evolution: None

Description: Not only its name, but its appearance is a symbol of the heart and love. It's said that a couple who finds a Luvdisc will be blessed with a happy life filled with love.

Cool Card: EX Crystal Guardians #7

Price Range: 3.00 – 6.00

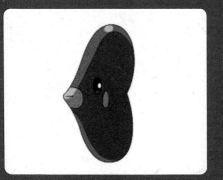

#371 Bagon

Type: Dragon
Evolution: Evolves into Shelgon
Description: The Bagon develop stone-hard heads from taking one too many jumps off of the edge of a cliff in the vain hope of being able to fly!

Cool Card: EX Dragon #23
Price Range: .20 - .50

#372 Shelgon

Type: Dragon
Evolution: Evolves from Bagon and into Salamence
Description: The bone-like shell surrounding Shelgon helps protect it as it prepares and fasts in order to evolve. Due to this, they tire very easily.

Cool Card: EX Dragon #42
Price Range: .20 - .50

#373 Salamence

Type: Dragon/Flying
Evolution: Evolves from Shelgon
Description: The seemingly futile dream of being able to fly is finally realized in this final evolution. Upon evolving, the Salamence are known to fly around happily while spewing fire everywhere!

Cool Card: EX Dragon Frontiers #98
Price Range: 15.00 – 25.00

#374 Beldum

Type: Steel/Psychic
Evolution: Evolves into Metang
Description: Beldum stay afloat by emitting a magnetic field around their bodies that repel against the earth's natural magnetism. When they sleep, they attach themselves to sturdy rocks.

Cool Card: EX Hidden Legends #28
Price Range: .20 - .50

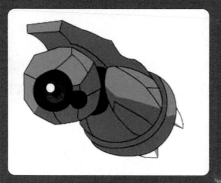

#375 Metang

Type: Steel/Psychic
Evolution: Evolves from Beldum and into Metagross
Description: When two Beldum join, they merge into a Metang. Arms with talons form where once there were only claws, and this new form allows for speedy travel.

Cool Card: EX Hidden Legends #44
Price Range: .20 - .50

#376 Metagross

Type: Steel/Psychic
Evolution: Evolves from Metang
Description: Metagross are formed when two Metang merge. These guys are pretty nasty though; once they've crushed their prey under their massive weight, they slowly eat them alive!

Cool Card: EX Hidden Legends #95
Price Range: 9.00 – 18.00

#377 Regirock

Type: Rock
Evolution: None
Description: Regirock's patchwork appearance is due to the fact that when a piece of its body chips off, it just picks up the nearest suitable rock and replaces the missing piece.

Cool Card: EX Emerald #99
Price Range: 4.00 – 9.00

#378 Regice

Type: Ice
Evolution: None
Description: Even getting near this Pokémon without freezing is a challenge, as it can be submerged in magma and not melt at all!

Cool Card: EX Emerald #98
Price Range: 5.00 – 10.00

#379 Registeel

Type: Steel

Evolution: None

Description: This Pokémon's body is made of an unidentifiable, and impossibly hard, metal. Registeel, along with Regice and Regirock, were imprisoned deep within the earth when an ancient race feared their powers.

Cool Card: EX Hidden Legends #99

Price Range: 10.00 – 20.00

#380 Latias

Type: Dragon/Psychic

Evolution: None

Description: Latias's uniquely reflective skin allows it to change its appearance by altering the way light reflects off of its skin. It can also understand human speech and is especially sensitive to emotions.

Cool Card: EX Dragon #93

Price Range: 7.00 – 15.00

#381 Latios

Type: Dragon/Psychic
Evolution: None
Description: Though very similar to Latias, Latios can fly as fast as a jet, communicate telepathically with humans, and can only be trained by a trainer with a pure heart!

Cool Card: EX Dragon Frontiers #96
Price Range: 12.00 – 22.00

#382 Kyogre

Type: Water
Evolution: None
Description: The legendary water Pokémon, it's said that Kyogre expanded the seas by covering the world in a torrential storm. It went to sleep after battling Groudon.

Cool Card: EX Crystal Guardians #95
Price Range: 10.00 – 15.00

#383 Groudon

Type: Ground
Evolution: None
Description: Groudon, another legendary Pokémon, can dismiss storm clouds and evaporate rain. It's hailed as a savior by many who were hurt by Kyogre's unending rainstorms.

Cool Card: EX Crystal Guardians #93
Price Range: 12.00 – 20.00

#384 Rayquaza

Type: Dragon/Flying

Evolution: None

Description: Living in the ozone for millions of years, the legendary Rayquaza wields incredible powers over all of the elements and can stop any battle that might arise between Kyogre and Groudon!

Cool Card: EX Deoxys #102

Price Range: 12.00 – 20.00

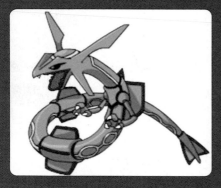

#385 Jirachi

Type: Steel/Psychic

Evolution: None

Description: This legendary Pokémon is rumored to awake and grant a single wish to anyone with a pure heart who sings to it! The line upon its stomach is actually a third eye.

Cool Card: EX Hidden Legends #8

Price Range: 4.00 – 8.00

#386 Deoxys

Type: Psychic
Evolution: None
Description: Originally born from a virus that came to earth within a meteor, Deoxys has incredible psychic attacks and the ability to change forms to better handle whatever situation it encounters.

Cool Card: EX Deoxys #98
Price Range: 7.00 – 14.00

#387 Turtwig

Type: Grass
Evolution: Evolves into Grotle
Description: Turtwig is the Grass starter in *Diamond* and *Pearl*. This marks the second time a turtle appears as a starter in *Pokémon*, with Squirtle being the first.

Cool Card: Diamond and Pearl #103
Price Range: .10 - .50

#388 Grotle

Type: Grass
Evolution: Evolves from Turtwig and into Torterra
Description: Grotle is patterned after the dinosaur Ankylosaurus. However it has shrubs instead of plates of armor on its back.

Cool Card: Diamond and Pearl #49
Price Range: .20 - .50

#389 Torterra

Type: Grass/Ground

Evolution: Evolves from Grotle

Description: Torterra is based off of the Native American Iroquois legend where the world actually rests on the back of a giant turtle. It is also the heaviest out of the four generations of starter Pokémon.

Cool Card: Diamond and Pearl #122

Price Range: 18.00 – 33.00

#390 Chimchar

Type: Fire

Evolution: Evolves into Monferno

Description: Chimchar is the Fire starter in *Diamond & Pearl*. He is a monkey with a flaming tail, similar to the original Fire starter, Charmander.

Cool Card: Diamond and Pearl #76

Price Range: .10 - .50

#391 Monferno

Type: Fire
Evolution: Evolves from Chimchar and into Infernape
Description: Monferno is the evolution of Chimchar. Its tail goes from a little nub to a long prehensile tail. Monferno's face is also patterned after the 1980/90's pro wrestler: The Ultimate Warrior.

Cool Card: Diamond and Pearl #56
Price Range: .20 - .50

#392 Infernape

Type: Fire/Fighting
Evolution: Evolves from Infernape
Description: Infernape is the final evolution of Chimchar. With Infernape, the fire that was on his tail in the first two evolutions has now moved to his head. He is also a Fire/Fighting Pokémon, which makes this the second straight game where this combo is the final form of the Fire starter.

Cool Card: Diamond and Pearl #121
Price Range: 20.00 – 35.00

#393 Piplup

Type: Water
Evolution: Evolves into Prinplup
Description: Piplup is the Water starter for *Diamond & Pearl*. All of its evolutionary forms are patterned after Penguins. Piplup is the first Pokémon owned by Dawn in the current season of the anime.

Cool Card: Diamond and Pearl #93
Price Range: .10 - .50

#394 Prinplup

Type: Water

Evolution: Evolves from Piplup and into Empoleon

Description: Prinplup is the next evolution in the Piplup line. Although it is a bird, Prinplup cannot fly, but it does learn several Flying type moves.

Cool Card: Diamond and Pearl #58

Price Range: .20 - .50

#395 Empoleon

Type: Water/Steel

Evolution: Evolves from Prinplup

Description: Although being a Penguin, Empoleon's final type is not Water/Ice. Instead, it's Water/Steel. Because of how strong Steel is against most other types, Empoleon is currently the most chosen of the three Sinnoh starters.

Cool Card: Diamond and Pearl #120

Price Range: 20.00 – 35.00

#396 Starly

Type: Normal/Flying
Evolution: Evolves into Staravia
Description: Starly is this generation's version of Pidgey. They both have three forms, and are Normal/Flying type Pokémon. The tuft of feathers on its head becomes a crest as it evolves.

Cool Card: Diamond and Pearl #101
Price Range: .10 - .20

#397 Staravia

Type: Normal/Flying
Evolution: Evolves from Starly and into Staraptor
Description: Like all forms of Starly, Staravia is patterned after a Starling. Its tuft has now become a curled crest. Ash's Starly evolves into a Staravia in the episode "Good Luck Starly!"

Cool Card: Diamond and Pearl #64
Price Range: .20 - .50

#398 Staraptor

Type: Normal/Flying
Evolution: Evolves from Staravia
Description: Staraptor is one of the fastest and strongest Pokémon in the game. Although most competitive gamers in the past have eschewed both Normal and Flying type Pokémon, Staraptor is one of the best new Pokémon in the game and has made a lot of people think twice about the type combination.

Cool Card: Diamond and Pearl #16
Price Range: 5.00 – 10.00

#399 Bidoof

Type: Normal
Evolution: Evolves into Bibarel
Description: Bidoof is a Pokémon based on many different real life animals, ranging from guinea pigs to woodchucks. In the game, it's really only used as a "Swiss Army Knife," meaning that trainers use Bidoof and its evolution for HM moves and never actually battle with it due to its poor stats and moves.

Cool Card: Diamond and Pearl #70
Price Range: .10 - .20

#400 Bibarel

Type: Normal/Water
Evolution: Evolves from Bidoof
Description: Bibarel resembles a beaver. Bibarel can learn every HM except Fly. It can learn strong moves, but has poor stats, so it's only useful as an HM Pokémon.

Cool Card: Diamond and Pearl #20
Price Range: .50 – 1.00

#401 Kricketot

Type: Bug
Evolution: Evolves into Kricketune
Description: Kricketot is the first Bug type Pokémon you can get in *D&P*. It only learns two moves: Bide and Growl. It also evolves faster than any of the new Pokémon.

Cool Card: Mysterious Treasures #86
Price Range: .10 - .20

#402 Kricketune

Type: Bug
Evolution: Evolves from Kricketot
Description: Kricketune is the evolution of Kricketot. Its body is shaped like a violin. Kricketune learns great Bug type moves like X-Scissor and Fury Cuttor, but its stats are very low.

Cool Card: Mysterious Treasures #27
Price Range: .50 - 1.00

#403 Shinx

Type: Electric
Evolution: Evolves into Luxio
Description: Shinx is the first Electric Pokémon a Trainer can find in *D&P*. Like the rest of its evolutionary forms, this "Thunder Cat" pays homage to a popular 1980's cartoon.

Cool Card: Diamond and Pearl #98
Price Range: .10 - .20

#404 Luxio

Type: Electric

Evolution: Evolves from Shinx and into Luxray

Description: Luxio is the first of two evolutions that Shinx gets. It learns mainly Electric, Normal, and Dark attacks. Lux is the International System of Units measurement for luminance.

Cool Card: Diamond and Pearl #52

Price Range: .20 - .50

#405 Luxray

Type: Electric

Evolution: Evolves from Luxio

Description: The Luxray family is one of only four Electric types that have three evolutions. The others are the Mareep, Pikachu, and Electabuzz families. It gains a yellow ring on its front legs for each stage of its evolution.

Cool Card: Diamond and Pearl #7

Price Range: 2.00 – 6.00

#406 Budew

Type: Grass
Evolution: Evolves into Roselia
Description: Although Roselia had no evolutions in *Ruby/Sapphire/Emerald*, in *D/P* it gains two! Budew is the first stage and Roserade is the final.

Cool Card: Diamond and Pearl #43
Price Range: .10 - .20

#407 Roserade

Type: Grass/Poison
Evolution: Evolves from Roselia
Description: Roserade is the final evolution for Budew. To get it, you must use a Shiny Stone on Roselia. It has excellent stats, and is the only Pokémon who can learn Weather Ball other than Castform.

Cool Card: Diamond and Pearl #13
Price Range: 2.00 – 4.00

#408 Cranidos

Type: Rock
Evolution: Evolves into Rampardos
Description: Cranidos is a fossil Pokémon. In order to catch one, you need to be playing *Pokémon Diamond* and find a Skull fossil in the Underground. It has a higher attack than most fully evolved Pokémon.

Cool Card: Mysterious Treasures #43
Price Range: .20 – .50

#409 Rampardos

Type: Rock

Evolution: Evolves from Cranidos

Description: Rampardos is based off the dinosaur Pachycephalosaur. It is a Rock type Pokémon and has the highest attack out of any Pokémon other than Deoxys. Along with Staraptor, it is one of the most popular Pokémon in *Diamond & Pearl*.

Cool Card: Mysterious Treasures #33

Price Range: .50 – 1.00

#410 Shieldon

Type: Rock/Steel

Evolution: Evolves from Bastiodon

Description: Like Cranidos, Shieldon can only be obtained if you find its fossil in the Underground. However, Shieldon can only be found in *Pokémon Pearl*.

Cool Card: Mysterious Treasures #63

Price Range: .20 – .50

#411 Bastiodon

Type: Rock/Steel
Evolution: Evolves from Shieldon
Description: Bastiodon is one of the best defensive Pokémon in the game. It is a Rock/Steel type Pokémon and has amazingly high Defense and Special Defense stats. Its head is shaped like a tower shield.

Cool Card: Mysterious Treasures #21
Price Range: .50 – 1.00

#412 Burmy

Type: Bug
Evolution: Evolves into Wormadam or Mothim
Description: Burmy changes its form depending on the area you last battled in. If you were in a cave, it has a yellow coat. If you battled in grass or a forest, it puts on a green coat. If you last battled inside a building, it will have a pink coat.

Cool Card: N/A

#413 Wormadam

Type: Bug/??
Evolution: Evolves from Burmy
Description: Wormadam is one of the two Pokémon Burmy will evolve into. Only female Burmy become a Wormadam. Wormadam will either be Bug/Grass, Bug/Steel, or Bug/Ground, depending on what coat the Burmy had on when it evolved.

Cool Card: N/A

#414 Mothim

Cool Card: N/A

Type: Bug/Flying
Evolution: Evolves from Burmy
Description: Mothim is the Pokémon that all male Burmy evolve into. Although Mothim has strong Attack and Special Attack scores, its defensive stats and Speed are very low. Being Bug/Flying also leaves it weak to a lot of different attacks.

#415 Combee

Cool Card: Diamond and Pearl #79
Price Range: .10 - .20

Type: Bug/Flying
Evolution: Evolves into Vespiquen
Description: Combee has the ability Honey Gather. Honey Gather allows Combee to pick up honey as you walk around with it if it doesn't hold any items. Only female Combee evolve.

#416 Vespiquen

Type: Bug/Flying

Evolution: Evolves from Combee

Description: Only female Combees evolve into Vespiquen and they are very rare in both *Diamond & Pearl* because 75% of all Combee are male. She has excellent moves and stats, making her a much sought after Pokémon.

Cool Card: Diamond and Pearl #39

Price Range: .50 – 1.00

#417 Pachirisu

Type: Electric

Evolution: None

Description: Pachirisu is an Electric squirrel Pokémon. It does not evolve and its electricity is colored blue where all other Electric Pokémon have a yellow tint to their Electric attacks. It is meant to be this generation's Pikachu and Dawn eventually gets one in the anime.

Cool Card: Diamond and Pearl #35

Price Range: .50 – 1.00

#418 Buizel

Type: Water

Evolution: Evolves into Floatzel

Description: Buizel is a Water Pokémon who actually pays homage to a character from the Sega video game franchise, Sonic the Hedgehog. Both Buizel and Miles "Tails" Prower have multiple tails that spin like a propeller when they move quickly.

Cool Card: Diamond and Pearl #72

Price Range: .10 - .20

#419 Floatzel

Type: Water
Evolution: Evolves from Buizel
Description: Floatzel is an exceptionally fast Pokémon and its ability of Swift Swim doubles its speed if it is raining. Under rainy weather, Floatzel is the fastest Pokémon out of all 493 Pokémon.

Cool Card: Diamond and Pearl #26
Price Range: .50 – 1.00

#420 Cherubi

Type: Grass
Evolution: Evolves into Cherrim
Description: Cherubi can only be found by slathering honey on special trees. It is the only Pokémon based on a fruit. It is similar is appearance to Weezing in that its main body is connected to a smaller version of it.

Cool Card: Diamond and Pearl #75
Price Range: .10 - .20

#421 Cherrim

Type: Grass
Evolution: Evolves from Cherubi
Description: Cherrim is the evolution of Cherubi. Its appearance changes depending on if it is a Sunny Day out or not. It evolves from Cherubi at level 25. It also knows an attack called Lucky Chant that prevents critical hits.

Cool Card: Diamond and Pearl #45
Price Range: .20 - .50

#422 Shellos

Type: Water
Evolution: Evolves into Gastrodon
Description: Shellos is a Pokémon whose color scheme varies depending on where you caught it. On the East side of Sinnoh, Shellos are blue, but on the West side, they are pink. It also has two Shiny forms because of this.

Cool Card: N/A

#423 Gastrodon

Type: Water/Ground
Evolution: Evolves from Shellos
Gastrodon is the evolved form of Shellos. It also follows the special color scheme of Shellos. Its form is based off of the sea slug. Gastrodon is one of the Pokémon used by Sinnoh's Champion, Cynthia.

Cool Card: N/A

#424 Ambipom

Type: Normal
Evolution: Evolves from Aipom
Description: Ambipom gains a second tail when Aipom evolves and it is a very fast Pokémon. Before *D/P*, Aipom had no evolutionary forms. Ambipom's name in Japanese is Eteboth, which means "Both Hands;" this refers to the fact that its tails resemble hands.

Cool Card: Mysterious Treasures #3
Price Range: 3.00 – 6.00

#425 Drifloon

Type: Ghost/Flying
Evolution: Evolves into Drifblim
Description: Drifloon can only be caught on Fridays outside the Valley Windworks. It has very low stats, and is also one of the more sinister Pokémon, seeking to take small children to the Underworld. It is shaped like a helium balloon.

Cool Card: Diamond and Pearl #46
Price Range: .20 - .50

#426 Drifblim

Type: Ghost/Flying

Evolution: Evolves from Drifloon

Description: Drifblim resembles a hot air balloon. Drifblim has Chansey level hit points, but very weak stats, so it is easy to knock out. Drifblim is immune to three different attack types: Ground, Fighting & Normal.

Cool Card: Diamond and Pearl #24

Price Range: .50 – 1.00

#427 Buneary

Type: Normal

Evolution: Evolves into Lopunny

Description: Buneary can have one of the few negative Pokémon Abilities in Klutz that prevents a Buneary with this Ability from using held items. In the anime, Dawn has a Buneary who is in love with Ash's Pikachu.

Cool Card: Diamond and Pearl #73

Price Range: .10 - .20

#428 Lopunny

Type: Normal

Evolution: Evolves from Buneary

Description: Even the male Lopunny's resemble a shapely human female. This is actually a reference to the "Playboy Bunnies" from the 1960's. It has good all-around stats and learns many different types of moves.

Cool Card: Diamond and Pearl #30

Price Range: .50 – 1.00

#429 Mismagius

Type: Ghost

Evolution: Evolves from Misdreavus

Description: Misdreavus is a Pokémon that first appeared in *Gold & Silver*. Misdreavus evolves into Mismagius with help from a Dusk Stone. Mismagius has very high Special Attack, Special Defense, and Speed stats. Its head is shaped like a witch's hat.

Cool Card: Diamond and Pearl #10

Price Range: 2.00 – 5.00

#430 Honchkrow

Type: Dark/Flying

Evolution: Evolves from Murkrow

Description: Murkrow, Honchkrow's base form, debuted in *Gold & Silver*. You will need a Dusk Stone to evolve it into Honchkrow. Honchkrow's special ability is Super Luck, which raises its chance of scoring a critical hit.

Cool Card: Mysterious Treasures #10

Price Range: 3.00 – 6.00

#431 Glameow

Type: Normal
Evolution: Evolves into Purugly
Description: Glameow learns a lot of
Dark type attacks. 75% of all Glameow
found in *Diamond* and *Pearl* are female. In
the anime, Dawn's mother owns a
Glameow. It is the most common
Pokémon owned by Team Galactic.

Cool Card: Diamond and Pearl #83
Price Range: .10 – .20

#432 Purugly

Type: Normal
Evolution: Evolves from Glameow
Description: Purugly is the evolved form of
Glameow. It has a high Speed and can only
be caught in *Pokémon Pearl*. When
Glameow evolves into Purugly, its body
weight multiplies by 12! That's one hefty kitty.

Cool Card: Diamond and Pearl #36
Price Range: .50 – 1.00

#433 Chingling

Type: Psychic
Evolution: Evolves into Chimecho
Description: Chingling is patterned after
the bells one finds at a Chinese temple. It
is the pre-evolutionary form for Chimecho.
Chingling will only evolve into Chimecho at
night and only if it really likes its Trainer.

Cool Card: Mysterious Treasures #42
Price Range: .20 – .50

#434 Stunky

Type: Dark/Poison

Evolution: Evolves into Skuntank

Description: If you listen to the Stunky's cry in your Pokédex, it sounds like flatulence. Its face is designed to look like a human butt. In Sinnoh, it is used by Officer Joy instead of a Growlithe.

Cool Card: Diamond and Pearl #102
Price Range: .10 - .20

#435 Skuntank

Type: Dark/Poison

Evolution: Evolves from Stunky

Description: Skuntank is a popular Pokémon in the game right now because it is very powerful and learns many different types of moves. It is exclusive to *Pokémon Diamond*. Its tail is the size of the rest of its body.

Cool Card: Diamond and Pearl #15
Price Range: 2.00 – 4.00

#436 Bronzor

Type: Steel/Psychic

Evolution: Evolves into Bronzong

Description: Bronzor is a defensive Pokémon and has below average Attack statistics. It can either have Levitate, making it immune to Ground attacks, which Steel types are usually weak against, or it will know Heatproof, which cuts Fire damage in half.

Cool Card: Mysterious Treasures #74

Price Range: .10 – .20

#437 Bronzong

Type: Steel/Psychic

Evolution: Evolves from Bronzor

Description: Bronzong resembles a giant bell. It can learn both Sunny Day and Rain Dance and is best used as a defensive Pokémon in tag matches. It was once worshiped by humans as a Harvest God.

Cool Card: Mysterious Treasures #6

Price Range: 3.00 – 6.00

#438 Bonsly

Type: Rock

Evolution: Evolves into Sudowoodo

Description: Bonsly is the pre-evolution of Sudowoodo. Although Bonsly is listed as being new to *D&P*, it actually first appeared in *Pokémon XD: Gale of Darkness* for the Nintendo GameCube. It looks like a tree but it's a Rock type Pokémon.

Cool Card: Diamond and Pearl #71

Price Range: .10 - .20

#439 Mime Jr.

Type: Psychic

Evolution: Evolves into Mr. Mime

Description: Mime Jr. is the pre-evolutionary form of Mr. Mime. Mime Jr. will evolve into Mr. Mime after it learns the move Mimic. It first appeared in *Pokémon Mystery Dungeon*. It can only be caught in *Pokémon Diamond*.

Cool Card: Diamond and Pearl #90

Price Range: .10 - .20

#440 Happiny

Type: Normal

Evolution: Evolves into Chansey

Description: Happiny is the pre-evolutionary form of Chansey and Blissey. It only evolves into a Chansey with an Oval Stone. Brock will eventually get a Happiny who hatches from an egg he finds.

Cool Card: Mysterious Treasures #52

Price Range: .20 - .50

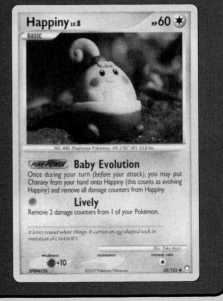

#441 Chatot

Type: Normal/Flying
Evolution: None
Description: Once Chatot gains the move Chatter, use it and say something into the DS Microphone. Now Chatot will mimic whatever was said when it uses this move or enters a battle. Its head is shaped like an eighth note.

Cool Card: Diamond and Pearl #74
Price Range: .10 - .20

#442 Spiritomb

Type: Dark/Ghost
Evolution: None
Description: The combination of Dark and Ghost types leaves Spiritomb with absolutely NO WEAKNESSES. For this reason, it is quite popular with trainers. It is amazingly hard to find however. The Pokémon also has a special connection to the number 108.

Cool Card: N/A

#443 Gible

Type: Ground/Dragon
Evolution: Evolves into Gabite
Description: Gible's head resembles a shark fin, earning it the nickname "Land shark." Gible can only be found in the bottom level of the Wayward Cave in a secret entrance hidden under Cycling Road. Its Japanese name is Fukamaru.

Cool Card: Mysterious Treasures #85
Price Range: .10 - .20

#444 Gabite

Type: Ground/Dragon

Evolution: Evolves from Gible and into Garchomp

Description: Gabite's back and tail continues to resemble a shark. It also resembles a blue Sceptile. All forms of Gible pay homage to an old Saturday Night Live skit. The Gabite family takes four times the normal damage from Ice attacks.

Cool Card: Mysterious Treasures #48

Price Range: .20 – .50

#445 Garchomp

Type: Ground/Dragon

Evolution: Evolves from Gabite

Description: Garchomp is the final form for a Gabite. Its head resembles a Hammerhead Shark. The Gible family are the only Dragon type Pokémon you can find in *D/P* before you beat the Elite Four. It has two fins on its arms, continuing the "Land Shark" theme.

Cool Card: Mysterious Treasures #9

Price Range: 8.00 – 16.00

#446 Munchlax

Type: Normal
Evolution: Evolves into Snorlax
Description: Munchlax is the pre-evolutionary form for Snorlax. Munchlax can only be found by slathering honey on specific trees in Sinnoh. Even so, it is a very rare Pokémon. Munchlax first appeared in *Pokémon Dash*. While Snorlax is always sleepy, Munchlax is always ravenously hungry.

Cool Card: Diamond and Pearl #33
Price Range: .50 – 1.00

#447 Riolu

Type: Steel/Fighting
Evolution: Evolves into Lucario
Description: The only way to receive a Riolu is to be given the egg by a trainer named Riley. This is one of the few Pokémon that is not based on a real life creature or legend of some sort. It can only evolve during the day and only then when its happiness is maxed out.

Cool Card: Diamond and Pearl #61
Price Range: .20 - .50

#448 Lucario

Type: Steel/Fighting
Evolution: Evolves from Riolu
Description: Lucario is meant to resemble Anubis, the Egyptian Jackal-headed God of the Dead. Lucario is also the star of the seventh Pokémon film. If you reach 15,000 points in *Pokémon Mysterious Dungeon*, you will receive a Lucario statue.

Cool Card: Diamond and Pearl #6
Price Range: 10.00 - 20.00

#449 Hippopotas

Type: Ground

Evolution: Evolves into Hippowdon

Description: Hippopotas is a Ground Pokémon that can only be found in the Ruin Maniac cave in *Diamond & Pearl*. Whenever it enters a battle, it causes a Sandstorm to erupt. It can learn the most powerful Ground and Dark attacks.

Cool Card: Diamond and Pearl #51

Price Range: .20 - .50

#450 Hippowdon

Type: Ground

Evolution: Evolves from Hippopotas

Description: Hippowdon somewhat resembles the fire Pokémon Torkoal in that they both have black armor. Sand is constantly streaming from the holes in Hippowdon's back. It is one of the Pokémon used by Bertha of the Elite Four.

Cool Card: Diamond and Pearl #29

Price Range: .50 - 1.00

#451 Skorupi

Type: Poison/Bug
Evolution: Evolves into Drapion
Description: Skorupi can only be found in the Great Marsh of Pastoria City. Skorupi only learns a single Bug type attack though: Pin Missile. Skorupi is based off a scorpion and is one of the rarest non-Legends to find.

Cool Card: Diamond and Pearl #99
Price Range: .10 - .20

#452 Drapion

Type: Poison/Dark
Evolution: Evolves from Skorupi
Description: Drapion is a Poison/Dark Pokémon rather than Skorupi's Poison/Bug types. The only type of attacks Drapion is weak against is Ground. In the anime, Drapion is owned by a trainer who pays homage to Vampire Hunter D.

Cool Card: Diamond and Pearl #23
Price Range: .50 – 1.00

#453 Croagunk

Type: Poison/Fighting
Evolution: Evolves into Toxicroak
Description: Croagunk can only be found in the Great Marsh of Pastoria City. Croagunk and its evolution are the only Poison/Fighting type combination out of all 493 Pokémon. It is based off of poison toads and Muay Thai kick boxers.

Cool Card: Mysterious Treasures #78
Price Range: .10 – .20

#454 Toxicroak

Type: Poison/Fighting
Evolution: Evolves from Croagunk
Description: Although a very powerful Pokémon, Toxicroak takes four times the normal damage from Psychic attacks, meaning even a single low power Psychic move can knock it out in one hit. It has bright red spikes on its fist filled with powerful poison.

Cool Card: Mysterious Treasures #36
Price Range: .50 - 1.00

#455 Carnivine

Type: Grass
Evolution: None
Description: Carnivine can only be found in the great Marsh of Pastoria City. Although it is based on a Venus Flytrap, a type of plant that actually eats bugs, Grass type Pokémon are weak against Bug types. Its ability is Levitate, making it immune to Ground attacks.

Cool Card: Diamond and Pearl #21
Price Range: .50 – 1.00

#456 Finneon

Type: Water

Evolution: Evolves into Lumineon

Description: Finneon appears in various bodies of water in *Diamond & Pearl*. You will need the Super Rod to catch it. Its Japanese name is Keikouo and it means "fluorescence fish." Finneon is based on the Tetra fish.

Cool Card: Mysterious Treasures #83

Price Range: .10 - .20

#457 Lumineon

Type: Water

Evolution: Evolves from Finneon

Description: Lumineon is a very fast Pokémon and tends to surprise trainers with its ability to use Silver Wind, which is a strong Bug type attack. Lumineon is based off of the butterfly fish. Lumineon is primarily a defensive Pokémon with its Special Defense being its best stat.

Cool Card: Mysterious Treasures #11

Price Range: 2.00 - 4.00

#458 Mantyke

Type: Water/Flying

Evolution: Evolves into Mantine

Description: Mantyke is the pre-evolutionary form of Mantine. Mantyke will only evolve into a Mantine if you have both it and a Remoraid in your party. Mantine will only give birth to a Mantyke if it is holding some Wave Incense.

Cool Card: Diamond and Pearl #55

Price Range: .20 - .50

#459 Snover

Type: Grass/Ice
Evolution: Evolves into Abomasnow
Description: Snover and its evolution are the only Grass/Ice type Pokémon. Snover resembles a Daikon, also known as the "Chinese Radish." Whenever a Snover enters a battle, it begins to Hail. Fire type attacks do four times their normal damage against the Snover family.

Cool Card: Mysterious Treasures #101
Price Range: .10 – .20

#460 Abomasnow

Type: Grass/Ice
Evolution: Evolves from Snover
Description: Abomasnow resembles both a pine tree and the legendary Abominable Snowman (also called a yeti). Its Japanese name is Yukinooh, which means "King of Snow." It can only be caught on the top of Mt. Coronet.

Cool Card: Mysterious Treasures #19
Price Range: .50 – 1.00

#461 Weavile

Type: Dark/Ice
Evolution: Evolves from Sneasel
Description: Sneasel is a Pokémon introduced back in *Silver/Gold*. Sneasel only evolves into a Weavile if it levels up at night while really liking its Trainer. Weavile is the main Pokémon used by the head of Team Galactic, Cyrus.

Cool Card: Diamond and Pearl #40
Price Range: .50 – 1.00

#462 Magnezone

Type: Electric/Steel
Evolution: Evolves from Magneton
Description: Magnezone is the brand new final evolution for Magnemite. When a Magneton evolves into a Magnezone, only its Special Attack is raised. The rest of its stats stay the same. A Magneton only evolves into a Magnezone if it levels up on Mt. Coronet.

Cool Card: Diamond and Pearl #8
Price Range: 4.00 – 8.00

#463 Lickilicky

Type: Normal
Evolution: Evolves from Lickitung
Description: Lickilicky is the first ever evolution for Lickitung, a Pokémon that has been around since the very beginning. In order to evolve your Lickitung, it must learn the move Rollout. Then the next time it levels up, it will evolve.

Cool Card: N/A

#464 Rhyperior

Type: Rock/Ground
Evolution: Evolves from Rhydon
Description: In order to evolve a Rhydon into a Rhyperior, a Rhydon must be given the Protector item and then traded, much like how a Haunter evolves into a Gengar. Rhyperior gains no real stat changes from Rhydon. It can learn Surf though, making it one of the few Rock or Ground Pokémon that's able to use Water attacks.

Cool Card: Diamond and Pearl #12
Price Range: 6.00 – 12.00

Rhyperior LV.61 HP140
STAGE 2 Evolves from Rhydon

NO. 464 Drill Pokémon. HT. 7'10" WT. 623.5 lbs.

Pokémon Power **Earth Fissure**
Once during your turn, when you play Rhyperior from your hand to evolve 1 of your Pokémon, you may discard the top 3 cards from your opponent's deck.

Rock Wrecker 80
This attack's damage isn't affected by Weakness or Resistance. Rhyperior can't attack during your next turn.

It puts rocks in holes in its palms and uses its muscles to shoot them. GEODUDE are shot at rare times.

Illus. Nakaoka

weakness +30 resistance -20 retreat cost

#465 Tangrowth

Type: Grass
Evolution: Evolves from Tangela
Description: Tangrowth is the very first evolution for Tangela, a Pokémon that's remained untouched since *Red, Green,* and *Blue*. It will only level up once it learns the move Ancient Power. It has excellent stats all around except for its Special Defense and Speed, which are quite low.

Cool Card: N/A

#466 Electivire

Type: Electric
Evolution: Evolves from Electabuzz
Description: An Electabuzz will only evolve into Electivire when it holds an Electirizer item. Electivire can also learn Ground and Fire's best attacks in addition to its powerful Giga Impact. Electivire is arguably the best Electric Pokémon in the game.

Cool Card: Diamond and Pearl #3
Price Range: 5.00 – 11.00

#467 Magmortar

Type: Fire
Evolution: Evolves from Magmar
Description: Magmar will only evolve into Magmortar if it is holding the Magmarizer and is then traded. Magmortar can learn Grass, Electric, Ground, Dark and even Ghost moves, making it exceptionally versatile. Sadly, the Magmarizer can only be found on 5% of all Magby and then only when you have Pokémon Emerald in your DS.

Cool Card: Mysterious Treasures #12
Price Range: 4.00 – 8.00

#468 Togekiss

Type: Normal/Flying
Evolution: Evolves from Togetic
Description: Togekiss evolves through the use of a Shiny Stone. Togekiss has great Special and Speed stats and can learn a wide variety of TM's. Togekiss' shape resembles a stealth bomber. Togekiss's previous forms can only be imported from a previous Pokémon game as they do not appear in *Diamond* or *Pearl*.

Cool Card: N/A

#469 Yanmega

Type: Bug/Flying
Evolution: Evolves from Yanma
Description: Yanmega is based on the prehistoric dragonfly Meganeura, which had a two foot long wingspan. Its wings move so fast, the ultrasonic vibrations emanating from them can turn its opponent's internal organs into pulp.

#470 Leafeon

Type: Grass
Evolution: Evolves from Eevee
Description: Leafeon is one of two new Eevee evolutions in *D/P*. An Eevee becomes a Leafeon if you level it up in front of Moss Rock in Eterna Forest. It is the only Pokémon other than the Treecko family to learn Leaf Blade.

#471 Glaceon

Type: Ice
Evolution: Evolves from Eevee
Description: In order to obtain a Glaceon, you must level up an Eevee in front of the Ice Rock on Route 217. Glaceon has the highest Special Attack of any Ice Pokémon, including Articuno. Its ability Snow Cloak makes it especially hard to hit when it is hailing out.

Cool Card: N/A

#472 Gliscor

Type: Ground/Flying
Evolution: Evolves from Gligar
Description: Gliscor is the first evolution for Gligar. A Gliscor is meant to be a combination of a scorpion and a vampire in appearance. In the past two generations, Gligar was practically unplayable due to bad stats and moves. With a better moveset and superior stats, Gliscor might see some use in player vs. player battles.

Cool Card: N/A

#473 Mamoswine

Type: Ice/Ground
Evolution: Evolves from Piloswine
Description: Mamoswine is the newest member of the Swinub family. Mamoswine has a high Attack and a lot of Hit Points, but is average to below average in all other stats. A Piloswine becomes a Mamoswine by leveling up while knowing the move Ancient Power. It looks like a mammoth but it has a pig's snout.

Cool Card: N/A

#474 Porygon-Z

Cool Card: N/A

Type: Normal
Evolution: Evolves from Porygon2
Description: Porygon-Z has the highest
Special Attack for any Normal type Pokémon and
is equal in power to an Alakazam or a Darkrai in
this category. It is the only Pokémon that needs to
be traded twice in order to get both evolutions.

#475 Gallade

Cool Card: N/A

Type: Ice
Evolution: Evolves from Kirlia
Description: Gallade is the fourth form for
the Ralts family. Only male Kirlia can become
a Gallade, and then only with the help of a
Dawn Stone. Gallade are Psychic/Fighting
type Pokémon.

#476 Probopass

Type: Rock/Steel
Evolution: Evolves from Nosepass
Description: Nosepass was a little used Pokémon from *Ruby* and *Sapphire*. Probopass gains the Steel type in addition to the Rock type from its previous evolution. It can also learn Electric attacks, which is quite unusual for its types. It is primarily a defensive Pokémon.

Cool Card: N/A

#477 Dusknoir

Type: Ghost
Evolution: Evolves from Dusclops
Description: A Dusknoir can only be obtained when you trade a Dusclops while it is holding a Reaper Cloth. The Dusknoir family is the only three-stage evolution Pokémon that are a pure Ghost type. It is believed that Dusknoir is related somehow to the Grim Reaper itself.

Cool Card: Diamond and Pearl #2
Price Range: 2.00 – 5.00

#478 Froslass

Type: Ghost/Ice
Evolution: Evolves from Snorunt
Description: A Froslass can only be obtained by evolving a female Snorunt with a Dawn Stone. Otherwise it will evolve, regardless of gender, into a Glalie. It is the only Ghost/Ice type Pokémon in the game. It has poor stats, so many Trainers get it simply to complete their Pokédex. It is the only Pokémon besides Cubone and Marowak that wear helmets to conceal their true faces.

Cool Card: N/A

#479 Rotom

Cool Card: N/A

Type: Ghost/Electric

Evolution: None

Description: Rotom can only be found by peering into the television inside the Old Chateau very late at night. There is only one Rotom in the entire game. Although it can be bred with a Ditto, it has the special Legendary music when you encounter it. Rotom is immune to Normal, Ghost, and Ground type attacks.

#480 Uxie

Cool Card: Mysterious Treasures #18

Price Range: 2.00 – 5.00

Type: Psychic

Evolution: None

Description: Uxie is one of the three Psychic Pokémon used by Team Galactic to bring either Dialga or Palkia back to life. It has poor moves, and is primarily a defensive Pokémon. It is referred to as the "Being of Knowledge." Uxie's eyes are never open because if it looks at someone directly, it will erase their mind.

#481 Mesprit

Type: Psychic
Evolution: None
Description: Mesprit is the second of the three Psychic brothers in *Diamond & Pearl*. Unlike Uxie and Azelf, Mesprit runs all over Sinnoh, making you chase it akin to Latios and Latias. Mesprit is the best overall stats wise of the three legends. It is known as the "Being of Emotion."

Cool Card: Mysterious Treasures #14
Price Range: 3.00 – 6.00

#482 Azelf

Type: Psychic
Evolution: None
Description: Azelf is the final of the three Psychic brothers. Azelf has a high Special Attack, and thanks to its move, Nasty Plot, which raises its Special Attack by two stages, it is the hardest of the three Psychic brothers to catch. It is known as the "Being of Willpower" and its eyes do not blink.

Cool Card: Mysterious Treasures #4
Price Range: 5.00 – 8.00

#483 Dialga

Type: Steel/Dragon
Evolution: None
Description: Dialga is the Legendary Pokémon summoned by Team Galactic if you are playing *Pokémon Diamond*. Dialga and Celebi both have mastery over time. It is a Steel/Dragon type Pokémon and is only weak against Fighting and Ground attacks.

Cool Card: Diamond and Pearl #1
Price Range: 10.00 - 15.00

#484 Palkia

Type: Water/Dragon

Evolution: None

Description: Palkia is the Legendary Pokémon brought back to life by Team Galactic if you are playing *Pokémon Pearl*. Palkia is the master of space. It is weak only to Dragon type moves, and as it can learn very powerful Ice type attacks, Palkia has little to fear from Dragon type Pokémon.

Cool Card: Diamond and Pearl #11
Price Range: 10.00 – 20.00

#485 Heatran

Type: Fire/Steel

Evolution: None

Description: Heatran is one of the few Legendary Pokémon with a gender. It has an equal chance of being found as a male or female Pokémon on Stark Mountain. However, like most other Legends, it cannot breed. As it is a Fire/Steel type, it takes four times the usual damage from Ground type attacks.

Cool Card: N/A

#486 Regigigas

Type: Normal
Evolution: None
Description: Regigigas is the first Normal type Legend. It can only be found in the Snowpoint temple, but can only be battled and thus caught if you bring the three Regis from *Ruby/Sapphire/Emerald* to it. Its Pokémon Ability "Slow Start" makes Regigigas worthless in actual battles as it severely hampers it for the first five rounds, allowing your opponent to take it out quickly.

Cool Card: N/A

#487 Giratina

Type: Ghost/Dark
Evolution: None
Description: Giratina is a Ghost/Dragon Pokémon that can be found in Turnback Cave. It is level 70 when you encounter it, making it very dangerous. In the eventual upgrade version of *D/P* (ala *Yellow*, *Crystal*, and *Emerald*), it is believed that Giratina will be the focus. It is the only double type Pokémon in the game that is weak to both its types.

Cool Card: N/A

#488 Cresselia

Type: Psychic
Evolution: None
Description: Cresselia is a female Legend that can only be found on Fullmoon Island. Once encountered, it will flee from your Trainer and roam Sinnoh like Mesprit. It is a pure Psychic Pokémon and will always run the first chance it gets.

Cool Card: N/A

#489 Phione

Cool Card: N/A

Type: Water

Evolution: None

Description: Phione is the only Legend that is obtained by breeding. It is the off-spring of Manaphy. It is weaker than Manaphy in all respects yet it is larger and heavier than its parent. Phione do not evolve into Manaphy either.

#490 Manaphy

Cool Card: Diamond and Pearl #9

Price Range: 2.00 - 6.00

Type: Water

Evolution: None

Description: Manaphy is a Legendary Water Pokémon that can only be obtained if you have beaten *Pokémon Ranger* and then performed a special bonus quest. Manaphy is a powerful Pokémon with roughly the same stats as Jirachi or Mew. Manaphy is the star of the ninth Pokémon film, *Pokémon Ranger and the Temple of the Sea.*

#491 Darkrai

Type: Dark
Evolution: None
Description: Darkrai is a pure Dark Pokémon. It can be obtained in one of two ways. The first involves seeing the 10th Pokémon film in theatres in Japan. There you will be given an extra powerful Darkrai. The other involves gaining a Member's Card and traveling to Newmoon Island. However, due to a bug in *D/P* in Japan, this optional quest has been scrapped for both US and Japanese audiences. It is unknown how Americans will receive Darkrai at this time.

Cool Card: N/A

#492 Shaymin

Type: Grass
Evolution: None
Description: Shaymin resembles a hedgehog but has grass instead of quills on its body. It can only be obtained by receiving Oak's Letter via a special Nintendo Event. Oak's Letter will allow you to travel to the Flower Paradise and encounter a Level 30 Shaymin.

Cool Card: N/A

#493 Arceus

Type: Normal
Evolution: None
Description: Arceus is the "Original One" as mentioned in various texts throughout *Diamond & Pearl*. Arceus can only be obtained through a Nintendo Event where you are given the Azure Flute. You must play the flute in the same spot where you fought Dialga or Palkia and a gateway to the Hall of Origin will open. There you will encounter a Level 80 Arceus. It has the highest combined stats of all Pokémon. It can also change its type depending on what Plate you attach to it.

Cool Card: N/A

HOW TO USE

What's Listed
Products listed in the Price Guide typically: 1) are produced by licensed manufacturers, 2) are widely available and 3) have market activity on single items.

What the Columns Mean
The LO and HI columns reflect current retail selling ranges. The HI column on the right generally represents the full retail selling price. The LO column on the left generally represents the lowest price one would expect to find with extensive shopping.

What the Arrows Mean
Up arrows denote prices that went up since the last issue. Down arrows denote prices that went down since the last issue. Arrows don't mean a card or set is "going up" or "going down."

Grading
All cards in the Price Guide are based on NrMint to Mint condition. Damaged cards are generally sold for 25 to 75 percent of Mint value.

Currency
This Price Guide is intended to reflect the entire North American market. All listed prices are in U.S. dollars.

Legend

(C) - Common card.

(P) - Promo card.

(R) - Rare card.

(HR) - Hidden rare card.

(F) - Fixed card.

(SCR) - Secret rare card.

(U) - Uncommon card.

(UER) - Uncorrected error.

(UR) - Ultra rare card.

NNO - No number.

HOLO - Holographic card.

Please Note: Beckett does not sell individual Pokémon cards.

GAMING CARDS

Price Range

Base 1st Edition Wizards of the Coast

		LO	HI
	Complete Set (102)	150.00	275.00
	Booster Box (36 ct)	200.00	300.00
	Booster Pack (11 cards)	7.00	12.00
	Common Card (not listed) (C)	.30	.75
	Uncommon Card (not listed) (U)	.50	1.00
	Rare Card (not listed) (R)	1.00	2.00
❏ 1	Alakazam (holo) (R)	15.00	27.00
❏ 2	Blastoise (holo) (R)	20.00	40.00
❏ 3	Chansey (holo) (R)	10.00	20.00
❏ 4	Charizard (holo) (R)	50.00	100.00
❏ 5	Clefairy (holo) (R)	10.00	20.00
❏ 6	Gyarados (holo) (R)	8.00	16.00
❏ 7	Hitmonchan (holo) (R)	8.00	18.00
❏ 8	Machamp (holo) (R)	3.00	5.00
❏ 9	Magneton (holo) (R)	7.00	18.00
❏ 10	Mewtwo (holo) (R)	10.00	20.00
❏ 11	Nidoking (holo) (R)	8.00	20.00
❏ 12	Ninetales (holo) (R)	12.00	20.00
❏ 13	Poliwrath (holo) (R)	8.00	20.00
❏ 14	Raichu (holo) (R)	8.00	16.00
❏ 15	Venusaur (holo) (R)	10.00	20.00
❏ 16	Zapdos (holo) (R)	15.00	25.00
❏ 17	Beedrill (R)	1.00	2.00

Arcanine 100 HP

STAGE 1 *Evolves from Growlithe* Put Arcanine on the Basic Pokémon

Legendary Pokémon. Length: 6' 3", Weight: 342 lbs.

Flamethrower Discard 1 Energy card attached to Arcanine in order to use this attack. 50

Take Down Arcanine does 30 damage to itself. 80

weakness · resistance · retreat cost

A Pokémon that has been long admired for its beauty. It runs gracefully, as if on wings. LV. 45 #59

23/102

Pidgeotto 60 HP

STAGE 1 *Evolves from Pidgey* Put Pidgeotto on the Basic Pokémon

Bird Pokémon. Length: 3' 7", Weight: 66 lbs.

Whirlwind If your opponent has any Benched Pokémon, he or she chooses 1 of them and switches it with the Defending Pokémon. (Do the damage before switching the Pokémon.) 20

Mirror Move If Pidgeotto was attacked last turn, do the final result of that attack on Pidgeotto to the Defending Pokémon.

weakness · resistance · retreat cost

-30

Very protective of its sprawling territory, this Pokémon will fiercely peck at any intruder. LV. 36 #17

22/102

		LO	HI
❏ 18	Dragonair (R)	1.00	2.00
❏ 19	Dugtrio (R)	1.00	2.00
❏ 20	Electabuzz (R)	1.00	2.00
❏ 21	Electrode (R)	1.00	2.00
❏ 22	Pidgeotto (R)	1.00	2.00
❏ 23	Arcanine (U)	.50	1.00
❏ 24	Charmeleon (U)	.50	1.00
❏ 25	Dewgong (U)	.50	1.00
❏ 26	Dratini (U)	.50	1.00
❏ 27	Farfetch'd (U)	.50	1.00
❏ 28	Growlithe (U)	.50	1.00
❏ 29	Haunter (U)	.50	1.00
❏ 30	Ivysaur (U)	.50	1.00
❏ 31	Jynx (U)	.50	1.00
❏ 32	Kadabra (U)	.50	1.00
❏ 33	Kakuna (UER) (U)	1.00	3.50
❏ 34	Machoke (U)	.50	1.00
❏ 35	Magikarp (U)	.50	1.00
❏ 36	Magmar (U)	.50	1.00
❏ 37	Nidorino (U)	.50	1.00
❏ 38	Poliwhirl (U)	.50	1.00
❏ 39	Porygon (U)	.50	1.00
❏ 40	Raticate (U)	.50	1.00
❏ 41	Seel (U)	.50	1.00
❏ 42	Wartortle (U)	.50	1.00
❏ 43	Abra (C)	.30	.75
❏ 44	Bulbasaur (UER) (C)	2.00	4.00
❏ 45	Caterpie (UER) (C)	1.00	3.00

		LO	HI
❏ 46	Charmander (C)	.30	.75
❏ 47	Diglett (C)	.30	.75
❏ 48	Doduo (C)	.30	.75
❏ 49	Drowzee (C)	.30	.75
❏ 50	Gastly (C)	.30	.75
❏ 51	Koffing (C)	.30	.75
❏ 52	Machop (C)	.30	.75
❏ 53	Magnemite (C)	.30	.75
❏ 54	Metapod (UER) (C)	1.00	3.00
❏ 55	Nidoran-M (C)	.30	.75
❏ 56	Onix (C)	.30	.75
❏ 57	Pidgey (C)	.30	.75
❏ 58	Pikachu (Red cheeks Error) (C)	5.00	12.00
❏ 58	Pikachu (Yellow cheeks Corr.) (C)	2.00	4.00
❏ 59	Poliwag (C)	.30	.75
❏ 60	Ponyta (C)	.30	.75
❏ 61	Rattata (C)	.30	.75
❏ 62	Sandshrew (C)	.30	.75
❏ 63	Squirtle (C)	.30	.75
❏ 64	Starmie (C)	.30	.75
❏ 65	Staryu (C)	.30	.75
❏ 66	Tangela (C)	.30	.75

TRAINER

Full Heal

Your Active Pokémon is no longer Asleep, Confused, Paralyzed, or Poisoned.

82/102

		LO	HI
❏ 67	Voltorb (UER) (C)	1.00	3.00
❏ 68	Vulpix (UER) (C)	1.00	2.50
❏ 69	Weedle (C)	.30	.75
❏ 70	Clefairy Doll (R)	1.00	2.00

❑ 71	Computer Search (R)	1.00	2.00
❑ 72	Devolution Spray (R)	1.00	2.00
❑ 73	Impostor Professor Oak (R)	1.00	2.00
❑ 74	Item Finder (R)	1.00	2.00
❑ 75	Lass (R)	1.00	2.00
❑ 76	Pokemon Breeder (R)	1.00	2.00
❑ 77	Pokemon Trader (R)	1.00	2.00
❑ 78	Scoop Up (R)	1.00	2.00
❑ 79	Super Energy Removal (R)	1.00	2.00
❑ 80	Defender (U)	.50	1.00
❑ 81	Energy Retrieval (U)	.50	1.00
❑ 82	Full Heal (U)	.50	1.00
❑ 83	Maintenance (U)	.50	1.00
❑ 84	Plus Power (U)	.50	1.00
❑ 85	Pokemon Center (U)	.50	1.00
❑ 86	Pokemon Flute (U)	.50	1.00
❑ 87	Pokedex (U)	.50	1.00
❑ 88	Professor Oak (U)	.50	1.00
❑ 89	Revive (U)	.50	1.00
❑ 90	Super Potion (U)	.50	1.00
❑ 91	Bill (C)	.30	.75
❑ 92	Energy Removal (C)	.30	.75
❑ 93	Gust of Wind (C)	.30	.75
❑ 94	Potion (C)	.30	.75
❑ 95	Switch (C)	.30	.75
❑ 96	Double Colorless Energy (C)	.50	1.00
❑ 97	Fighting Energy	.30	.75
❑ 98	Fire Energy	.30	.75
❑ 99	Grass Energy	.30	.75
❑ 100	Lightning Energy	.30	.75
❑ 101	Psychic Energy	.30	.75
❑ 102	Water Energy	.30	.75

Base Unlimited Wizards of the Coast

Complete Set (101)		50.00	80.00
Complete Set (w/Machamp) (102)		60.00	85.00
Booster Box (36 ct)		45.00	75.00
Booster Pack (11 cards)		1.75	3.00
Common Card (not listed) (C)		.10	.25
Uncommon Card (not listed) (U)		.25	.75
Rare Card (not listed)		.50	1.00
Starter Set (60 cards)		8.00	11.00
Blackout Deck (60 cards)		6.00	10.00
Brushfire Deck (60 cards)		6.00	10.00
OverGrowth Deck (60 cards)		6.00	10.00
Zap Deck (60 cards)		6.00	10.00

Shadowless Cards 2 X hi column
Card 8 Machamp is only in Starter Decks

❑ 1	Alakazam (holo) (R)	3.00	6.00
❑ 2	Blastoise (holo) (R)	5.00	10.00
❑ 3	Chansey (holo) (R)	3.00	6.00
❑ 4	Charizard (holo) (R)	12.50	25.00
❑ 5	Clefairy (holo) (R)	3.00	6.00

❑ 6	Gyarados (holo) (R)	3.00	6.00
❑ 7	Hitmonchan (holo) (R)	3.00	6.00
❑ 8	Machamp (holo) (R) 1st Ed. Only	3.00	5.00
❑ 9	Magneton (holo) (R)	3.00	6.00
❑ 10	Mewtwo (holo) (R)	4.00	8.00
❑ 11	Nidoking (holo) (R)	3.00	6.00
❑ 12	Ninetales (holo) (R)	3.00	6.00

❑ 13	Poliwrath (holo) (R)	3.00	6.00
❑ 14	Raichu (holo) (R)	3.00	7.00
❑ 15	Venusaur (holo) (R)	3.00	6.00
❑ 16	Zapdos (holo) (R)	3.00	6.00
❑ 17	Beedrill (R)	.50	1.00
❑ 18	Dragonair (R)	.50	1.00
❑ 19	Dugtrio (R)	.50	1.00
❑ 20	Electabuzz (R)	.50	1.00
❑ 21	Electrode (R)	.50	1.00
❑ 22	Pidgeotto (R)	.50	1.00
❑ 23	Arcanine (U)	.25	.75
❑ 24	Charmeleon (U)	.25	.75
❑ 25	Dewgong (U)	.25	.75
❑ 26	Dratini (U)	.25	.75
❑ 27	Farfetch'd (U)	.25	.75
❑ 28	Growlithe (U)	.25	.75
❑ 29	Haunter (U)	.25	.75
❑ 30	Ivysaur (U)	.25	.75
❑ 31	Jynx (U)	.25	.75
❑ 32	Kadabra (U)	.25	.75
❑ 33	Kakuna (Length/Length Error) (U)	1.00	2.00
❑ 33	Kakuna (Length/Weight Corr.) (U)	.50	1.00
❑ 34	Machoke (U)	.25	.75
❑ 35	Magikarp (U)	.25	.75
❑ 36	Magmar (U)	.25	.75
❑ 37	Nidorino (U)	.25	.75
❑ 38	Poliwhirl (U)	.25	.75
❑ 39	Porygon (U)	.25	.75
❑ 40	Raticate (U)	.25	.75
❑ 41	Seel (U)	.25	.75
❑ 42	Wartortle (U)	.25	.75
❑ 43	Abra (C)	.10	.25
❑ 44	Bulbasaur (Length/Length Error) (C)	1.00	2.00
❑ 44	Bulbasaur (Length/Weight Corr.) (C)	.25	.50
❑ 45	Caterpie (HP 40 Error) (C)	1.00	2.00
❑ 45	Caterpie (40 HP Corr.) (C)	.25	.50
❑ 46	Charmander (C)	.10	.25
❑ 47	Diglett (C)	.10	.25
❑ 48	Doduo (C)	.10	.25
❑ 49	Drowzee (C)	.10	.25
❑ 50	Gastly (C)	.10	.25
❑ 51	Koffing (C)	.10	.25
❑ 52	Machop (C)	.10	.25
❑ 53	Magnemite (C)	.10	.25
❑ 54	Metapod (HP 70 Error) (C)	1.00	2.00

❑ 54	Metapod (70 HP Corr.) (C)	.25	.50
❑ 55	Nidoran (C)	.10	.25
❑ 56	Onix (C)	.10	.25
❑ 57	Pidgey (C)	.10	.25
❑ 58	Pikachu (Red cheeks Error) (C)	3.00	7.00
❑ 58	Pikachu (Yellow cheeks Corr.)(C)	.50	1.00
❑ 59	Poliwag (C)	.10	.25
❑ 60	Ponyta (C)	.10	.25
❑ 61	Rattata (C)	.10	.25
❑ 62	Sandshrew (C)	.10	.25
❑ 63	Squirtle (C)	.10	.25
❑ 64	Starmie (C)	.10	.25
❑ 65	Staryu (C)	.10	.25
❑ 66	Tangela (C)	.10	.25
❑ 67	Voltorb (Monster Ball Error) (C)	1.00	2.00
❑ 67	Voltorb (Poke Ball Corr.) (C)	.25	.50
❑ 68	Vulpix (UER) (C)	.50	1.00
❑ 69	Weedle (C)	.10	.25
❑ 70	Clefairy Doll (R)	.50	1.00
❑ 71	Computer Search (R)	.50	1.00
❑ 72	Devolution Spray (R)	.50	1.00
❑ 73	Impostor Professor Oak (R)	.60	1.00
❑ 74	Item Finder (R)	.50	1.00
❑ 75	Lass (R)	.50	1.00
❑ 76	Pokemon Breeder (R)	.50	1.00
❑ 77	Pokemon Trader (R)	.50	1.00
❑ 78	Scoop Up (R)	.50	1.00
❑ 79	Super Energy Removal (R)	.50	1.00
❑ 80	Defender (U)	.25	.75
❑ 81	Energy Retrieval (U)	.25	.75
❑ 82	Full Heal (U)	.25	.75
❑ 83	Maintenance (U)	.25	.75

84	Plus Power (U)	.25	.75
85	Pokemon Center (U)	.25	.75
86	Pokemon Flute (U)	.25	.75
87	Pokedex (U)	.25	.75
88	Professor Oak (U)	.25	.75
89	Revive (U)	.25	.75
90	Super Potion (U)	.25	.75
91	Bill (C)	.10	.25
92	Energy Removal (C)	.10	.25
93	Gust of Wind (C)	.10	.25
94	Potion (C)	.10	.25
95	Switch (C)	.10	.25
96	Double Colorless Energy (U)	.25	.75
97	Fighting Energy (C)	.10	.25
98	Fire Energy (C)	.10	.25
99	Grass Energy (C)	.10	.25
100	Lightning Energy (C)	.10	.25
101	Psychic Energy (C)	.10	.25
102	Water Energy (C)	.10	.25

Jungle 1st Edition Wizards of the Coast

Complete Set (64)		60.00	85.00
Booster Box (36 ct)		55.00	75.00
Booster Pack (11 cards)		2.00	4.00
Common Card (not listed) (C)		.25	.50
Uncommon Card (not listed) (U)		.30	.75
Rare Card (not listed) (R)		1.00	2.00
1	Clefable (holo) (R)	3.00	6.00
2	Electrode (holo) (R)	3.00	6.00

3	Flareon (holo) (R)	4.00	7.00
4	Jolteon (holo) (R)	3.00	6.00
5	Kangaskhan (holo) (R)	3.00	6.00
6	Mr. Mime (holo) (R)	3.00	6.00
7	Nidoqueen (holo) (R)	3.00	6.00
8	Pidgeot (holo) (R)	3.00	6.00
9	Pinsir (holo) (R)	3.00	6.00
10	Scyther (holo) (R)	3.00	6.00
11	Snorlax (holo) (R)	3.00	6.00
12	Vaporeon (holo) (R)	3.00	6.00
13	Venomoth (holo) (R)	3.00	6.00
14	Victreebel (holo) (R)	3.00	6.00
15	Vileplume (holo) (R)	3.00	6.00
16	Wigglytuff (holo) (R)	3.00	6.00
17	Clefable (R)	2.00	4.00
18	Electrode (UER) (R)	2.00	4.00
19	Flareon (R)	2.00	4.00
20	Jolteon (R)	2.00	4.00
21	Kangaskhan (R)	2.00	4.00
22	Mr. Mime (R)	1.00	3.00
23	Nidoqueen (R)	2.00	4.00
24	Pidgeot (R)	2.00	4.00
25	Pinsir (R)	2.00	4.00

26	Scyther (R)	2.00	4.00
27	Snorlax (R)	2.00	4.00
28	Vaporeon (R)	2.00	4.00
29	Venomoth (R)	2.00	4.00
30	Victreebel (R)	2.00	4.00
31	Vileplume (R)	2.00	4.00
32	Wigglytuff (R)	2.00	4.00
33	Butterfree ("d" Edition Error) (U)	2.00	5.00
33	Butterfree (1 Edition Corr.) (U)	2.00	5.00
34	Dodrio (U)	.30	.75
35	Exeggutor (U)	.30	.75
36	Fearow (U)	.30	.75
37	Gloom (U)	.30	.75
38	Lickitung (U)	.30	.75
39	Marowak (U)	.30	.75
40	Nidorina (U)	.30	.75
41	Parasect (U)	.30	.75
42	Persian (U)	.30	.75
43	Primeape (U)	.30	.75
44	Rapidash (U)	.30	.75
45	Rhydon (U)	.30	.75
46	Seaking (U)	.30	.75
47	Tauros (U)	.30	.75
48	Weepingbell (U)	.30	.75
49	Bellsprout (C)	.25	.50
50	Cubone (C)	.25	.50
51	Eevee (C)	.25	.50
52	Exeggcute (C)	.25	.50
53	Goldeen (C)	.25	.50
54	Jigglypuff (C)	.25	.50
55	Mankey (C)	.25	.50
56	Meowth (C)	.25	.50
57	Nidoran-F (C)	.25	.50
58	Oddish (C)	.25	.50
59	Paras (C)	.25	.50
60	Pikachu (C)	1.00	2.00
61	Rhyhorn (C)	.25	.50
62	Spearow (C)	.25	.50
63	Venonat (C)	.25	.50
64	Trainer: Poke Ball (C)	.25	.50

Jungle Unlimited Wizards of the Coast

Complete Set (64)		35.00	50.00
Booster Box (36 ct)		35.00	50.00
Booster Pack (11 cards)		1.25	2.00
Common Card (not listed) (C)		.10	.25
Uncommon Card (not listed) (U)		.20	.50
Rare Card (not listed)		.50	1.00
Power Reserve Deck (60 cards)		8.00	13.00
Water Blast Deck (60 cards)		8.00	13.00
Holo Errors are missing Jungle Logo			
1	Clefable (holo) (R)	2.00	4.00
1	Clefable (holo) (R) (Error)	3.00	6.00
2	Electrode (holo) (R)	2.00	4.00
2	Electrode (holo) (R) (Error)	3.00	6.00
3	Flareon (holo) (R)	2.00	4.00
3	Flareon (holo) (R) (Error)	3.00	6.00
4	Jolteon (holo) (R)	2.00	4.00
4	Jolteon (holo) (R) (Error)	3.00	6.00
5	Kangaskhan (holo) (R)	2.00	4.00
5	Kangaskhan (holo) (R) (Error)	3.00	6.00
6	Mr. Mime (holo) (R)	2.00	4.00
6	Mr Mime (holo) (R) (Error)	3.00	6.00
7	Nidoqueen (holo) (R)	2.00	4.00
7	Nidoqueen (holo) (R) (Error)	3.00	6.00
8	Pidgeot (holo) (R)	2.00	4.00
8	Pidgeot (holo) (R) (Error)	3.00	6.00
9	Pinsir (holo) (R)	2.00	4.00
9	Pinsir (holo) (R) (Error)	3.00	6.00
10	Scyther (holo) (R)	2.00	4.00
10	Scyther (holo) (R) (Error)	3.00	6.00
11	Snorlax (holo) (R)	2.00	4.00
11	Snorlax (holo) (R) (Error)	3.00	6.00
12	Vaporeon (holo) (R)	2.00	4.00
12	Vaporeon (holo) (R) (Error)	3.00	6.00

Basic Pokémon
Kangaskhan 90 HP

Parent Pokémon. Length: 7' 3", Weight: 176 lbs.

Fetch Draw a card.

Comet Punch Flip 4 coins.
This attack does 20 damage times
the number of heads. 20x

weakness ✦ -30 resistance retreat cost ✦✦✦

The infant rarely ventures out of its mother's protective
pouch until it is three years old. LV. 40 #115
Illus. Mitsuhiro Arita ©1995, 96, 98 Nintendo, Creatures, GAMEFREAK. ©1999 Wizards. 5/64 ★

13	Venomoth (holo) (R)	2.00	4.00
13	Venomoth (holo) (R) (Error)	3.00	6.00
14	Victreebel (holo) (R)	2.00	4.00
14	Victreebel (holo) (R) (Error)	3.00	6.00
15	Vileplume (holo) (R)	2.00	4.00
15	Vileplume (holo) (R) (Error)	3.00	6.00
16	Wigglytuff (holo) (R)	2.00	4.00
16	Wigglytuff (holo) (R) (Error)	3.00	6.00
17	Clefable (R)	.50	1.00
18	Electrode (R)	.50	1.00
19	Flareon (R)	.50	1.00
20	Jolteon (R)	.50	1.00
21	Kangaskhan (R)	.50	1.00
22	Mr. Mime (R)	.50	1.00
23	Nidoqueen (R)	.50	1.00
24	Pidgeot (R)	.50	1.00
25	Pinsir (R)	.50	1.00
26	Scyther (R)	.50	1.00
27	Snorlax (R)	.50	1.00
28	Vaporeon (R)	.50	1.00
29	Venomoth (R)	.50	1.00
30	Victreebel (R)	.50	1.00
31	Vileplume (R)	.50	1.00
32	Wigglytuff (R)	.50	1.00
33	Butterfree (U)	.20	.50
34	Dodrio (U)	.20	.50
35	Exeggutor (U)	.20	.50
36	Fearow (U)	.20	.50
37	Gloom (U)	.20	.50
38	Lickitung (U)	.20	.50
39	Marowak (U)	.20	.50
40	Nidorina (U)	.20	.50

Evolves from Clefairy Put Clefable on the Basic Pokémon
STAGE 2
Clefable 70 HP

Fairy Pokémon. Length: 4' 3", Weight: 88 lbs.

Metronome Choose 1 of the Defending
Pokémon's attacks. Metronome copies that attack
except for its Energy costs and anything else
required in order to use that attack, such as
discarding Energy cards. (No matter what type the
Defending Pokémon is, Clefable's type is still Colorless.)

Minimize All damage done by attacks to Clefable
during your opponent's next turn is reduced by 20
(after applying Weakness and Resistance).

weakness ✦ -30 resistance retreat cost ✦

A timid Fairy Pokémon that is rarely seen. It will run and hide
the moment it senses people. LV. 34 #36
Illus. Mitsuhiro Arita ©1995, 96, 98 Nintendo, Creatures, GAMEFREAK. ©1999 Wizards. 17/64 ★

❑ 1	Aerodactyl (holo) (R)	4.00 7.00
❑ 2	Articuno (holo) (R)	4.00 8.00
❑ 3	Ditto (holo) (R)	3.00 7.00
❑ 4	Dragonite (holo) (R)	4.00 8.00
❑ 5	Gengar (holo) (R)	3.00 6.00
❑ 6	Haunter (holo) (R)	3.00 6.00
❑ 7	Hitmonlee (holo) (R)	3.00 7.00

❑ 53	Psyduck (C)	.25 .50
❑ 54	Shellder (C)	.25 .50
❑ 55	Slowpoke (C)	.25 .50
❑ 56	Tentacool (C)	.25 .50
❑ 57	Zubat (C)	.25 .50
❑ 58	Old Man Fuji (U)	.30 .75
❑ 59	Energy Search (C)	.25 .50
❑ 60	Gambler (C)	.25 .50
❑ 61	Recycle (C)	.25 .50
❑ 62	Mysterious Fossil (C)	.25 .50

Fossil Unlimited Wizards of the Coast

Complete Set (62)		35.00 40.00
Booster Box (36 ct)		35.00 50.00
Booster Pack (11 cards)		1.25 2.00
Common Card (not listed) (C)		.10 .25
Uncommon Card (not listed) (U)		.20 .50
Rare Card (not listed) (R)		.50 1.00
Bodyguard Deck (60)		4.00 10.00
Lock Down Deck (60)		4.00 10.00
❑ 1	Aerodactyl (holo) (R)	2.00 5.00
❑ 2	Articuno (holo) (R)	2.00 5.00
❑ 3	Ditto (holo) (R)	2.00 4.00
❑ 4	Dragonite (holo) (R)	2.00 4.00
❑ 5	Gengar (holo) (R)	2.00 4.00

❑ 41	Parasect (U)	.20 .50
❑ 42	Persian (U)	.20 .50
❑ 43	Primeape (U)	.20 .50
❑ 44	Rapidash (U)	.20 .50
❑ 45	Rhydon (U)	.20 .50
❑ 46	Seaking (U)	.20 .50
❑ 47	Tauros (U)	.20 .50
❑ 48	Weepingbell (U)	.20 .50
❑ 49	Bellsprout (C)	.10 .25
❑ 50	Cubone (C)	.10 .25
❑ 51	Eevee (C)	.10 .25
❑ 52	Exeggcute (C)	.10 .25
❑ 53	Goldeen (C)	.10 .25
❑ 54	Jigglypuff (C)	.10 .25
❑ 55	Mankey (C)	.10 .25
❑ 56	Meowth (C)	.10 .25
❑ 57	Nidoran-F (C)	.10 .25
❑ 58	Oddish (C)	.10 .25
❑ 59	Paras (C)	.10 .25
❑ 60	Pikachu (C)	.50 1.00
❑ 61	Rhyhorn (C)	.10 .25
❑ 62	Spearow (C)	.10 .25
❑ 63	Venonat (C)	.10 .25
❑ 64	Trainer Poke Ball (C)	.10 .25

Fossil 1st Edition Wizards of the Coast

Complete Set (62)		45.00 60.00
Booster Box (36 ct)		50.00 75.00
Booster Pack (11cards)		2.00 4.00
Common Card (not listed) (C)		.25 .50
Uncommon Card (not listed) (U)		.30 .75
Rare Card (not listed) (R)		.50 1.00

❑ 8	Hypno (holo) (R)	3.00 6.00
❑ 9	Kabutops (holo) (R)	3.00 6.00
❑ 10	Lapras (holo) (R)	3.00 6.00
❑ 11	Magneton (holo) (R)	3.00 6.00
❑ 12	Moltres (holo) (R)	3.00 7.00
❑ 13	Muk (holo) (R)	3.00 6.00
❑ 14	Raichu (holo) (R)	3.00 7.00
❑ 15	Zapdos (holo) (R)	2.00 4.00
❑ 16	Aerodactyl (R)	2.00 4.00
❑ 17	Articuno (R)	.50 1.00
❑ 18	Ditto (R)	.50 1.00
❑ 19	Dragonite (R)	.50 1.00
❑ 20	Gengar (R)	.50 1.00
❑ 21	Haunter (R)	.50 1.00
❑ 22	Hitmonlee (R)	.50 1.00
❑ 23	Hypno (R)	.50 1.00
❑ 24	Kabutops (R)	.50 1.00
❑ 25	Lapras (R)	.50 1.00
❑ 26	Magneton (R)	.50 1.00
❑ 27	Moltres (R)	.50 1.00
❑ 28	Muk (R)	.50 1.00
❑ 29	Raichu (R)	.50 1.00
❑ 30	Zapdos (R)	.50 1.00
❑ 31	Arbok (U)	.30 .75
❑ 32	Cloyster (U)	.30 .75
❑ 33	Gastly (U)	.30 .75
❑ 34	Golbat (U)	.30 .75
❑ 35	Golduck (U)	.30 .75
❑ 36	Golem (U)	.30 .75
❑ 37	Graveler (U)	.30 .75
❑ 38	Kingler (U)	.30 .75
❑ 39	Magmar (U)	.30 .75
❑ 40	Omastar (U)	.30 .75
❑ 41	Sandslash (U)	.30 .75
❑ 42	Seadra (U)	.30 .75
❑ 43	Slowbro (U)	.30 .75
❑ 44	Tentacruel (U)	.30 .75
❑ 45	Weezing (U)	.30 .75
❑ 46	Ekans (C)	.25 .50
❑ 47	Geodude (C)	.25 .50
❑ 48	Grimer (C)	.25 .50
❑ 49	Horsea (C)	.25 .50
❑ 50	Kabuto (C)	.25 .50
❑ 51	Krabby (C)	.25 .50
❑ 52	Omanyte (C)	.25 .50

❑ 6	Haunter (holo) (R)	2.00 4.00
❑ 7	Hitmonlee (holo) (R)	2.00 4.00
❑ 8	Hypno (holo) (R)	2.00 4.00
❑ 9	Kabutops (holo) (R)	2.00 4.00
❑ 10	Lapras (holo) (R)	2.00 4.00
❑ 11	Magneton (holo) (R)	2.00 4.00
❑ 12	Moltres (holo) (R)	2.00 4.00
❑ 13	Muk (holo) (R)	2.00 4.00
❑ 14	Raichu (holo) (R)	2.00 4.00
❑ 15	Zapdos (holo) (R)	2.00 4.00
❑ 16	Aerodactyl (R)	1.00 2.00
❑ 17	Articuno (R)	.50 1.00
❑ 18	Ditto (R)	.50 1.00
❑ 19	Dragonite (R)	.50 1.00
❑ 20	Gengar (R)	.50 1.00
❑ 21	Haunter (R)	.50 1.00
❑ 22	Hitmonlee (R)	.50 1.00
❑ 23	Hypno (R)	.50 1.00
❑ 24	Kabutops (R)	.50 1.00
❑ 25	Lapras (R)	.50 1.00
❑ 26	Magneton (R)	.50 1.00
❑ 27	Moltres (R)	.50 1.00
❑ 28	Muk (R)	.50 1.00
❑ 29	Raichu (R)	.50 1.00
❑ 30	Zapdos (R)	.50 1.00
❑ 31	Arbok (U)	.20 .50

#	Card		
32	Cloyster (U)	.20	.50
33	Gastly (U)	.20	.50
34	Golbat (U)	.20	.50
35	Golduck (U)	.20	.50
36	Golem (U)	.20	.50
37	Graveler (U)	.20	.50
38	Kingler (U)	.20	.50
39	Magmar (U)	.20	.50
40	Omastar (U)	.20	.50
41	Sandslash (U)	.20	.50
42	Seadra (U)	.20	.50
43	Slowbro (U)	.20	.50
44	Tentacruel (U)	.20	.50
45	Weezing (U)	.20	.50
46	Ekans (C)	.10	.25
47	Geodude (C)	.10	.25
48	Grimer (C)	.10	.25
49	Horsea (C)	.10	.25
50	Kabuto (C)	.10	.25
51	Krabby (C)	.10	.25
52	Omanyte (C)	.10	.25
53	Psyduck (C)	.10	.25
54	Shellder (C)	.10	.25
55	Slowpoke (C)	.10	.25
56	Tentacool (C)	.10	.25
57	Zubat (C)	.10	.25
58	Old Man Fuji (U)	.20	.50
59	Energy Search (C)	.10	.25
60	Gambler (C)	.10	.25
61	Recycle (C)	.10	.25
62	Mysterious Fossil (C)	.10	.25

Golem — 80 HP — Evolves from Graveler — Put Golem on the Stage 1 card
Stage 2
Megaton Pokémon. Length: 4' 7", Weight: 662 lbs.
Avalanche 60
Selfdestruct Does 20 damage to each Pokémon on each player's Bench. (Don't apply Weakness and Resistance for Benched Pokémon.) Golem does 100 damage to itself. 100
weakness / resistance / retreat cost
Its boulder-like body is extremely hard. It can easily withstand dynamite blasts without damage. LV. 76 #076

Base 2 Unlimited Wizards of the Coast

Complete Set (130)		45.00	70.00
Booster Box (36 ct)		40.00	60.00
Booster Pack (11 cards)		1.00	3.00
Common Card (not listed) (C)		.10	.25
Uncommon Card (not listed) (U)		.25	.50
Rare Card (not listed) (R)		.50	1.00
Grass Chopper Deck (60)		6.00	12.00
Hot Water Deck (60)		9.00	10.00
Lightning Bug Deck (60)		6.00	10.00
Psych Out Deck (60)		9.00	12.00
1	Alakazam (holo) (R)	2.00	4.00
2	Blastoise (holo) (R)	5.00	10.00
3	Chansey (holo) (R)	2.00	4.00
4	Charizard (holo) (R)	10.00	20.00
5	Clefable (holo) (R)	2.00	4.00
6	Clefairy (holo) (R)	2.00	4.00
7	Gyarados (holo) (R)	2.00	4.00
8	Hitmonchan (holo) (R)	2.00	4.00
9	Magneton (holo) (R)	2.00	4.00
10	Mewtwo (holo) (R)	2.00	4.00

#	Card		
11	Nidoking (holo) (R)	2.00	4.00
12	Nidoqueen (holo) (R)	2.00	4.00
13	Ninetales (holo) (R)	2.00	4.00
14	Pidgeot (holo) (R)	2.00	4.00
15	Poliwrath (holo) (R)	2.00	4.00
16	Raichu (holo) (R)	2.00	4.00
17	Scyther (holo) (R)	2.00	4.00
18	Venusaur (holo) (R)	4.00	8.00
19	Wigglytuff (holo) (R)	2.00	4.00
20	Zapdos (holo) (R)	2.00	4.00
21	Beedrill (R)	.50	1.00
22	Dragonair (R)	.50	1.00
23	Dugtrio (R)	.50	1.00
24	Electabuzz (R)	.50	1.00
25	Electrode (R)	.50	1.00
26	Kangaskhan (R)	.50	1.00
27	Mr. Mime (R)	.50	1.00
28	Pidgeotto (R)	.50	1.00
29	Pinsir (R)	.50	1.00
30	Snorlax (R)	.50	1.00
31	Venomoth (R)	.50	1.00
32	Victreebel (R)	.50	1.00
33	Arcanine (U)	.25	.50
34	Butterfree (U)	.25	.50
35	Charmeleon (U)	.25	.50
36	Dewgong (U)	.25	.50
37	Dodrio (U)	.25	.50
38	Dratini (U)	.25	.50
39	Exeggutor (U)	.25	.50
40	Farfetch'd (U)	.25	.50
41	Fearow (U)	.25	.50
42	Growlithe (U)	.25	.50
43	Haunter (U)	.25	.50
44	Ivysaur (U)	.25	.50
45	Jynx (U)	.25	.50
46	Kadabra (U)	.25	.50
47	Kakuna (U)	.25	.50
48	Lickitung (U)	.25	.50
49	Machoke (U)	.25	.50
50	Magikarp (U)	.25	.50
51	Magmar (U)	.25	.50
52	Marowak (U)	.25	.50
53	Nidorina (U)	.25	.50
54	Nidorino (U)	.25	.50
55	Parasect (U)	.25	.50
56	Persian (U)	.25	.50
57	Poliwhirl (U)	.25	.50
58	Raticate (U)	.25	.50

Charizard — 120 HP — Evolves from Charmeleon — Put Charizard on the Stage 1 card
Stage 2
Flame Pokémon. Length: 5' 7", Weight: 200 lbs.
Pokémon Power: Energy Burn As often as you like during your turn (before your attack), you may turn all Energy attached to Charizard into Energy for the rest of the turn. This power can't be used if Charizard is Asleep, Confused, or Paralyzed.
Fire Spin Discard 2 Energy cards attached to Charizard in order to use this attack. 100
weakness / resistance / retreat cost
Spits fire that is hot enough to melt boulders. Known to unintentionally cause forest fires. LV. 76 #006

#	Card		
59	Rhydon (U)	.25	.50
60	Seaking (U)	.25	.50
61	Seel (U)	.25	.50
62	Tauros (U)	.25	.50
63	Wartortle (U)	.25	.50

Gyarados — 100 HP — Evolves from Magikarp — Put Gyarados on the Basic Pokémon
Stage 1
Atrocious Pokémon. Length: 21' 4", Weight: 518 lbs.
Dragon Rage 50
Bubblebeam Flip a coin. If heads, the Defending Pokémon is now Paralyzed. 40
weakness / resistance / retreat cost
Rarely seen in the wild. Huge and vicious, it is capable of destroying entire cities in a rage. LV. 41 #130

#	Card		
64	Weepinbell (U)	.25	.50
65	Abra (C)	.10	.25
66	Bellsprout (C)	.10	.25
67	Bulbasaur (C)	.10	.25
68	Caterpie (C)	.10	.25
69	Charmander (C)	.10	.25
70	Cubone (C)	.10	.25
71	Diglett (C)	.10	.25
72	Doduo (C)	.10	.25
73	Drowzee (C)	.10	.25
74	Exeggcute (C)	.10	.25
75	Gastly (C)	.10	.25
76	Goldeen (C)	.10	.25
77	Jigglypuff (C)	.10	.25
78	Machop (C)	.10	.25
79	Magnemite (C)	.10	.25
80	Meowth (C)	.10	.25
81	Metapod (C)	.10	.25
82	Nidoran-F (C)	.10	.25
83	Nidoran-M (C)	.10	.25
84	Onix (C)	.10	.25
85	Paras (C)	.10	.25
86	Pidgey (C)	.10	.25
87	Pikachu (C)	.50	1.00
88	Poliwag (C)	.10	.25
89	Rattata (C)	.10	.25
90	Rhyhorn (C)	.10	.25
91	Sandshrew (C)	.10	.25
92	Spearow (C)	.10	.25
93	Squirtle (C)	.10	.25
94	Starmie (C)	.10	.25
95	Staryu (C)	.10	.25
96	Tangela (C)	.10	.25
97	Venonat (C)	.10	.25
98	Voltorb (C)	.10	.25
99	Vulpix (C)	.10	.25
100	Weedle (C)	.10	.25
101	Computer Search (R)	.50	1.00
102	Imposter Professor Oak (R)	.50	1.00
103	Item Finder (R)	.50	1.00
104	Lass (R)	.50	1.00
105	Pokemon Breeder (R)	.50	1.00
106	Pokemon Trader (R)	.50	1.00
107	Scoop Up (R)	.50	1.00
108	Super Energy Removal (R)	.50	1.00
109	Defender (U)	.25	.50
110	Energy Retrieval (U)	.25	.50
111	Full Heal (U)	.25	.50
112	Maintenance (U)	.25	.50
113	PlusPower (U)	.25	.50
114	Pokemon Center (U)	.25	.50
115	Pokedex (U)	.25	.50
116	Professor Oak (U)	.25	.50

117	Super Potion (U)	.25	.50
118	Bill (C)	.10	.25
119	Energy Removal (C)	.10	.25
120	Gust of Wind (C)	.10	.25
121	Poke Ball (C)	.10	.25
122	Potion (C)	.10	.25
123	Switch (C)	.10	.25
124	Double Colorless Energy (U)	.25	.50
125	Fighting Energy (C)	.10	.25
126	Fire Energy (C)	.10	.25
127	Grass Energy (C)	.10	.25
128	Lightning Energy (C)	.10	.25
129	Psychic Energy (C)	.10	.25
130	Water Energy (C)	.10	.25

Team Rocket 1st Edition Wizards of the Coast

	Complete Set (82)	50.00	75.00
	Complete Set w/Raichu (83)	55.00	80.00
	Booster Box (36 ct)	40.00	60.00
	Booster Pack (11 cards)	2.00	4.00
	Common Card (not listed) (C)	.10	.25
	Uncommon Card (not listed) (U)	.20	.50
	Rare Card (not listed) (R)	.50	1.00
1	Dark Alakazam (holo) (R)	4.00	7.00
2	Dark Arbok (holo) (R) (ERR)	3.00	6.00
3	Dark Blastoise (holo) (R)	3.00	6.00
4	Dark Charizard (holo) (R)	6.00	12.00
5	Dark Dragonite (holo) (R)	3.00	6.00
6	Dark Dugtrio (holo) (R)	2.00	4.00
7	Dark Golbat (holo) (R)	3.00	6.00
8	Dark Gyarados (holo) (R)	3.00	6.00

9	Dark Hypno (holo) (R)	2.00	4.00
10	Dark Machamp (holo) (R)	3.00	6.00
11	Dark Magneton (holo) (R)	2.00	4.00
12	Dark Slowbro (holo) (R)	2.00	4.00
13	Dark Vileplume (holo) (R)	3.00	6.00
14	Dark Weezing (holo) (R)	2.00	4.00
15	Here Comes Team Rocket (holo) (R)	2.00	4.00
16	Rocket's Sneak Attack (holo) (R)	3.00	6.00
17	Rainbow Energy (holo) (R)	3.00	6.00
18	Dark Alakazam (R)	.50	1.00
19	Dark Arbok (R) (ERR)	1.00	2.00
20	Dark Blastoise (R)	1.00	2.00
21	Dark Charizard (R)	3.00	6.00
22	Dark Dragonite (R)	1.00	2.00
23	Dark Dugtrio (R)	.50	1.00
24	Dark Golbat (R)	.50	1.00
25	Dark Gyarados (R)	.50	1.00
26	Dark Hypno (R)	.50	1.00
27	Dark Machamp (R)	.50	1.00

28	Dark Magneton (R)	.50	1.00
29	Dark Slowbro (R)	.50	1.00
30	Dark Vileplume (R)	.50	1.00
31	Dark Weezing (R)	.50	1.00
32	Dark Charmeleon (U)	.20	.50
33	Dark Dragonair (U)	.20	.50
34	Dark Electrode (U)	.20	.50
35	Dark Flareon (U)	.20	.50
36	Dark Gloom (U)	.20	.50
37	Dark Golduck (U)	.20	.50
38	Dark Jolteon (U)	.20	.50
39	Dark Kadabra (U)	.20	.50
40	Dark Machoke (U)	.20	.50
41	Dark Muk (U)	.20	.50
42	Dark Persian (U)	.20	.50
43	Dark Primeape (U)	.20	.50
44	Dark Rapidash (U) (ERR)	.75	1.75
45	Dark Vaporeon (U)	.20	.50
46	Dark Wartortle (U)	.20	.50
47	Magikarp (U)	.20	.50
48	Porygon (U)	.20	.50
49	Abra (C)	.10	.25
50	Charmander (C)	.10	.25
51	Dark Raticate (C)	.10	.25
52	Diglett (C)	.10	.25
53	Dratini (C)	.10	.25
54	Drowzee (C)	.10	.25
55	Eevee (C)	.10	.25
56	Ekans (C)	.10	.25
57	Grimer (C)	.10	.25
58	Koffing (C)	.10	.25
59	Machop (C)	.10	.25
60	Magnemite (C)	.10	.25
61	Mankey (C)	.10	.25
62	Meowth (C)	.10	.25
63	Oddish (C)	.10	.25
64	Ponyta (C)	.10	.25
65	Psyduck (C)	.10	.25
66	Rattata (C)	.10	.25
67	Slowpoke (C)	.10	.25
68	Squirtle (C)	.10	.25
69	Voltorb (C)	.10	.25
70	Zubat (C)	.10	.25
71	Here Comes Team Rocket (R)	2.00	4.00
72	Rocket's Sneak Attack (R)	.50	1.00
73	The Boss's Way (R)	.20	.50
74	Challenge (U)	.20	.50
75	Digger (U)	.20	.50
76	Imposter Oak's Revenge (U)	.20	.50
77	Nightly Garbage Run (U)	.20	.50
78	Gas Attack (C)	.10	.25
79	Sleep (C)	.10	.25
80	Rainbow Energy (R)	.50	1.00
81	Full Heal Energy (U)	.20	.50
82	Potion Energy (U)	.20	.50
83	Dark Raichu (holo) (R) (ERR)	2.00	5.00

Team Rocket Unlimited Wizards of the Coast

	Complete Set (82)	40.00	50.00
	Complete Set w/Raichu (83)	40.00	55.00
	Booster Box (36 ct)	35.00	50.00
	Booster Pack (11 cards)	1.00	2.00
	Common Card (not listed) (C)	.10	.25
	Uncommon Card (not listed) (U)	.20	.50
	Rare Card (not listed) (R)	.50	1.00
	Theme Deck (60 cards)	8.00	15.00
1	Dark Alakazam (holo) (R)	2.00	4.00
2	Dark Arbok (holo) (R) (ERR)	2.00	4.00
3	Dark Blastoise (holo) (R)	3.00	4.00
4	Dark Charizard (holo) (R)	3.00	6.00
5	Dark Dragonite (holo) (R)	2.00	4.00
6	Dark Dugtrio (holo) (R)	2.00	4.00
7	Dark Golbat (holo) (R)	2.00	4.00
8	Dark Gyarados (holo) (R)	2.00	4.00

9	Dark Hypno (holo) (R)	2.00	4.00
10	Dark Machamp (holo) (R)	2.00	4.00
11	Dark Magneton (holo) (R)	2.00	4.00
12	Dark Slowbro (holo) (R)	2.00	4.00
13	Dark Vileplume (holo) (R)	2.00	4.00
14	Dark Weezing (holo) (R)	2.00	4.00
15	Here Comes Team Rocket (holo) (R)	2.00	4.00
16	Rocket's Sneak Attack (holo) (R)	2.00	4.00
17	Rainbow Energy (holo) (R)	2.00	4.00
18	Dark Alakazam (R)	.50	1.00
19	Dark Arbok (R) (ERR)	.50	1.00
20	Dark Blastoise (R)	.50	1.00
21	Dark Charizard (R)	1.00	3.00
22	Dark Dragonite (R)	.50	1.00
23	Dark Dugtrio (R)	.50	1.00
24	Dark Golbat (R)	.50	1.00
25	Dark Gyarados (R)	.50	1.00
26	Dark Hypno (R)	.50	1.00
27	Dark Machamp (R)	.50	1.00
28	Dark Magneton (R)	.50	1.00
29	Dark Slowbro (R)	.50	1.00
30	Dark Vileplume (R)	.60	1.00
31	Dark Weezing (R)	.50	1.00
32	Dark Charmeleon (U)	.20	.50
33	Dark Dragonair (U)	.20	.50
34	Dark Electrode (U)	.20	.50
35	Dark Flareon (U)	.20	.50
36	Dark Gloom (U)	.20	.50
37	Dark Golduck (U)	.20	.50
38	Dark Jolteon (U)	.20	.50
39	Dark Kadabra (U)	.20	.50
40	Dark Machoke (U)	.20	.50

41	Dark Muk (U)	.20	.50
42	Dark Persian (U)	.20	.50
43	Dark Primeape (U)	.20	.50
44	Dark Rapidash (U) (ERR)	.50	1.00
45	Dark Vaporeon (U)	.20	.50
46	Dark Wartortle (U)	.20	.50
47	Magikarp (U)	.20	.50
48	Porygon (U)	.20	.50
49	Abra (C)	.10	.25
50	Charmander (C)	.10	.25
51	Dark Raticate (C)	.10	.25
52	Diglett (C)	.10	.25
53	Dratini (C)	.10	.25
54	Drowzee (C)	.10	.25
55	Eevee (C)	.10	.25
56	Ekans (C)	.10	.25
57	Grimer (C)	.10	.25
58	Koffing (C)	.10	.25
59	Machop (C)	.10	.25
60	Magnemite (C)	.10	.25
61	Mankey (C)	.10	.25
62	Meowth (C)	.10	.25
63	Oddish (C)	.10	.25
64	Ponyta (C)	.10	.25
65	Psyduck (C)	.10	.25
66	Rattata (C)	.10	.25
67	Slowpoke (C)	.10	.25
68	Squirtle (C)	.10	.25
69	Voltorb (C)	.10	.25

70	Zubat (C)	.10	.25
71	Here Comes Team Rocket (R)	.50	1.00
72	Rocket's Sneak Attack (R)	.50	1.00
73	The Boss's Way (U)	.20	.50
74	Challenge (U)	.20	.50
75	Digger (U)	.20	.50
76	Imposter Oak's Revenge (U)	.20	.50
77	Nightly Garbage Run (U)	.20	.50
78	Gas Attack (C)	.10	.25
79	Sleep (C)	.10	.25
80	Rainbow Energy (R)	.50	1.00
81	Full Heal Energy (U)	.20	.50
82	Potion Energy (U)	.20	.50
83	Dark Raichu (holo) (R) (ERR)	3.00	6.00

Gym Heroes 1st Edition Wizards of the Coast

Complete Set (132)	65.00	80.00
Unopened Box (36 ct)	45.00	70.00
Unopened Pack (11 cards)	2.00	4.00
Common Card (not listed) (C)	.10	.25
Uncommon Card (not listed) (U)	.20	.50

	Rare Card (not listed) (R)	.50	1.00
1	Blaine's Moltres (holo) (R)	3.00	7.00
2	Brock's Rhydon (holo) (R)	3.00	6.00
3	Erika's Clefable (holo) (R)	3.00	6.00
4	Erika's Dragonair (holo) (R)	3.00	6.00
5	Erika's Vileplume (holo) (R)	3.00	6.00
6	Lt. Surge's Electabuzz (holo) (R)	3.00	6.00
7	Lt. Surge's Fearow (holo) (R)	3.00	6.00
8	Lt. Surge's Magneton (holo) (R)	3.00	6.00
9	Misty's Seadra (holo) (R)	3.00	6.00
10	Misty's Tentacruel (holo) (R)	3.00	6.00
11	Rocket's Hitmonchan (holo) (R)	3.00	6.00
12	Rocket's Moltres (holo) (R)	3.00	6.00
13	Rocket's Scyther (holo) (R)	4.00	6.00
14	Sabrina's Gengar (holo) (R)	3.00	6.00
15	Brock (holo) (R)	3.00	6.00
16	Erika (holo) (R)	3.00	6.00
17	Lt. Surge (holo) (R)	3.00	6.00
18	Misty (holo) (R)	3.00	6.00
19	The Rocket's Trap (holo) (R)	3.00	6.00
20	Brock's Golem (R)	.50	1.00
21	Brock's Onix (R)	.50	1.00
22	Brock's Rhyhorn (R)	.50	1.00
23	Brock's Sandslash (R)	.50	1.00
24	Brock's Zubat (R)	.50	1.00
25	Erika's Clefairy (R)	.50	1.00
26	Erika's Victreebel (R)	.50	1.00
27	Lt. Surge's Electabuzz (R)	.50	1.00
28	Lt. Surge's Raichu (R)	.50	1.00
29	Misty's Cloyster (R)	.50	1.00
30	Misty's Goldeen (R)	.50	1.00
31	Misty's Poliwrath (R)	.50	1.00
32	Misty's Tentacool (R)	.50	1.00
33	Rocket's Snorlax (R)	.50	1.00
34	Sabrina's Venomoth (R)	.50	1.00
35	Blaine's Growlithe (U)	.20	.50
36	Blaine's Kangaskhan (U)	.20	.50
37	Blaine's Magmar (U)	.20	.50
38	Brock's Geodude (U)	.20	.50
39	Brock's Golbat (U)	.20	.50
40	Brock's Graveler (U)	.20	.50
41	Brock's Lickitung (U)	.20	.50
42	Erika's Dratini (U)	.20	.50
43	Erika's Exeggcute (U)	.20	.50
44	Erika's Exeggutor (U)	.20	.50
45	Erika's Gloom (U)	.20	.50
46	Erika's Gloom (U)	.20	.50
47	Erika's Oddish (U)	.20	.50

48	Erika's Weepinbell (U)	.20	.50
49	Erika's Weepinbell (U)	.20	.50
50	Lt. Surge's Magnemite (U)	.20	.50
51	Lt. Surge's Raticate (U)	.20	.50
52	Lt. Surge's Spearow (U)	.20	.50

53	Misty's Poliwhirl (U)	.20	.50
54	Misty's Psyduck (U)	.20	.50
55	Misty's Seaking (U)	.20	.50
56	Misty's Starmie (U)	.20	.50
57	Misty's Tentacool (U)	.20	.50
58	Sabrina's Haunter (U)	.20	.50
59	Sabrina's Jynx (U)	.20	.50
60	Sabrina's Slowbro (U)	.20	.50
61	Blaine's Charmander (C)	.10	.25
62	Blaine's Growlithe (C)	.10	.25
63	Blaine's Ponyta (C)	.10	.25
64	Blaine's Tauros (C)	.10	.25
65	Blaine's Vulpix (C)	.10	.25
66	Brock's Geodude (C)	.10	.25
67	Brock's Mankey (C)	.10	.25
68	Brock's Mankey (C)	.10	.25
69	Brock's Onix (C)	.10	.25
70	Brock's Ryhorn (C)	.10	.25
71	Brock's Sandshrew (C)	.10	.25
72	Brock's Sandshrew (C)	.10	.25
73	Brock's Vulpix (C)	.10	.25
74	Brock's Zubat (C)	.10	.25
75	Erika's Bellsprout (C)	.10	.25
76	Erika's Bellsprout (C)	.10	.25
77	Erika's Exeggcute (C)	.10	.25
78	Erika's Oddish (C)	.10	.25
79	Erika's Tangela (C)	.10	.25
80	Lt. Surge's Magnemite (C)	.10	.25
81	Lt. Surge's Pikachu (C)	.50	1.25
82	Lt. Surge's Rattata (C)	.10	.25
83	Lt. Surge's Spearow (C)	.10	.25
84	Lt. Surge's Voltorb (C)	.10	.25
85	Misty's Goldeen (C)	.10	.25
86	Misty's Horsea (C)	.10	.25
87	Misty's Poliwag (C)	.10	.25
88	Misty's Seel (C)	.10	.25
89	Misty's Shellder (C)	.10	.25
90	Misty's Staryu (C)	.10	.25
91	Sabrina's Abra (C)	.10	.25
92	Sabrina's Drowzee (C)	.10	.25
93	Sabrina's Gastly (C)	.10	.25
94	Sabrina's Mr. Mime (C)	.10	.25
95	Sabrina's Slowpoke (C)	.10	.25
96	Sabrina's Venonat (C)	.10	.25
97	Blaine's Quiz #1 (C)	.50	1.00
98	Brock (R)	.50	1.00
99	Charity (R)	.50	1.00
100	Erika (R)	.50	1.00
101	Lt. Surge (R)	.50	1.00
102	Misty (R)	.50	1.00
103	No Removal Gym (R)	.50	1.00
104	The Rocket's Gym (R)	.50	1.00
105	Blaine's Last Resort (U)	.20	.50
106	Brock's Training Method (U)	.20	.50

❏ 107	Celadon City Gym (U)	.20	.50
❏ 108	Cerulean City Gym (U)	.20	.50
❏ 109	Erika's Maids (U)	.20	.50
❏ 110	Erika's Perfume (U)	.20	.50
❏ 111	Good Manners (U)	.20	.50
❏ 112	Lt. Surge's Treaty (U)	.20	.50
❏ 113	Minion of Team Rocket (U)	.20	.50
❏ 114	Misty's Wrath (U)	.20	.50
❏ 115	Pewter City Gym (U)	.20	.50
❏ 116	Recall (U)	.20	.50
❏ 117	Sabrina's ESP (U)	.20	.50
❏ 118	Secret Mission (U)	.20	.50
❏ 119	Tickling Machine (U)	.20	.50
❏ 120	Vermilion City Gym (U)	.20	.50
❏ 121	Blaine's Gamble (C)	.10	.25
❏ 122	Energy Flow (C)	.10	.25
❏ 123	Misty's Duel (C)	.10	.25
❏ 124	Narrow Gym (C)	.10	.25
❏ 125	Sabrina's Gaze (C)	.10	.25
❏ 126	Trash Exchange (C)	.10	.25
❏ 127	Fighting Energy (C)	.10	.25
❏ 128	Fire Energy (C)	.10	.25
❏ 129	Grass Energy (C)	.10	.25
❏ 130	Lightning Energy (C)	.10	.25
❏ 131	Psychic Energy (C)	.10	.25
❏ 132	Water Energy (C)	.10	.25

Gym Heroes Unlimited Wizards of the Coast

Complete Set (132)	40.00	55.00
Unopened Box (36 ct)	38.00	55.00
Unopened Pack (11 cards)	1.00	2.50
Common Card (not listed) (C)	.10	.25
Uncommon Card (not listed) (U)	.20	.50
Rare Card (not listed) (R)	.50	1.00

❏ 1	Blaine's Moltres (holo) (R)	2.00	4.00
❏ 2	Brock's Rhydon (holo) (R)	2.00	4.00
❏ 3	Erika's Clefable (holo) (R)	2.00	4.00
❏ 4	Erika's Dragonair (holo) (R)	2.00	4.00
❏ 5	Erika's Vileplume (holo) (R)	2.00	4.00
❏ 6	Lt. Surge's Electabuzz (holo) (R)	2.00	4.00
❏ 7	Lt. Surge's Fearow (holo) (R)	2.00	4.00
❏ 8	Lt. Surge's Magneton (holo) (R)	2.00	4.00
❏ 9	Misty's Seadra (holo) (R)	2.00	4.00
❏ 10	Misty's Tentacruel (holo) (R)	2.00	4.00
❏ 11	Rocket's Hitmonchan (holo) (R)	2.00	4.00
❏ 12	Rocket's Moltres (holo) (R)	2.00	4.00
❏ 13	Rocket's Scyther (holo) (R)	2.00	4.00
❏ 14	Sabrina's Gengar (holo) (R)	2.00	4.00
❏ 15	Brock (holo) (R)	2.00	4.00
❏ 16	Erika (holo) (R)	2.00	4.00
❏ 17	Lt. Surge (holo) (R)	2.00	4.00

❏ 18	Misty (holo) (R)	2.00	4.00
❏ 19	The Rocket's Trap (holo) (T)	2.00	4.00
❏ 20	Brock's Golem (R)	.50	1.00
❏ 21	Brock's Onix (R)	.50	1.00
❏ 22	Brock's Rhyhorn (R)	.50	1.00
❏ 23	Brock's Sandslash (R)	.50	1.00
❏ 24	Brock's Zubat (R)	.50	1.00

❏ 25	Erika's Clefairy (R)	.50	1.00
❏ 26	Erika's Victreebel (R)	.50	1.00
❏ 27	Lt. Surge's Electabuzz (R)	.50	1.00
❏ 28	Lt. Surge's Raichu (R)	.50	1.00
❏ 29	Misty's Cloyster (R)	.50	1.00
❏ 30	Misty's Goldeen (R)	.50	1.00
❏ 31	Misty's Poliwrath (R)	.50	1.00
❏ 32	Misty's Tentacool (R)	.50	1.00
❏ 33	Rocket's Snorlax (R)	.50	1.00
❏ 34	Sabrina's Venomoth (R)	.50	1.00
❏ 35	Blaine's Growlithe (U)	.20	.50
❏ 36	Blaine's Kangaskhan (U)	.20	.50
❏ 37	Blaine's Magmar (U)	.20	.50
❏ 38	Brock's Geodude (U)	.20	.50
❏ 39	Brock's Golbat (U)	.20	.50
❏ 40	Brock's Graveler (U)	.20	.50
❏ 41	Brock's Lickitung (U)	.20	.50
❏ 42	Erika's Dratini (U)	.20	.50
❏ 43	Erika's Exeggcute (U)	.20	.50
❏ 44	Erika's Exeggutor (U)	.20	.50
❏ 45	Erika's Gloom (U)	.20	.50
❏ 46	Erika's Gloom (U)	.20	.50
❏ 47	Erika's Oddish (U)	.20	.50
❏ 48	Erika's Weepinbell (U)	.20	.50
❏ 49	Erika's Weepinbell (U)	.20	.50
❏ 50	Lt. Surge's Magnemite (U)	.20	.50
❏ 51	Lt. Surge's Raticate (U)	.20	.50
❏ 52	Lt. Surge's Spearow (U)	.20	.50
❏ 53	Misty's Poliwhirl (U)	.20	.50
❏ 54	Misty's Psyduck (U)	.20	.50
❏ 55	Misty's Seaking (U)	.20	.50
❏ 56	Misty's Starmie (U)	.20	.50
❏ 57	Misty's Tentacool (U)	.20	.50
❏ 58	Sabrina's Haunter (U)	.20	.50
❏ 59	Sabrina's Jynx (U)	.20	.50
❏ 60	Sabrina's Slowbro (U)	.20	.50
❏ 61	Blaine's Charmander (C)	.10	.25
❏ 62	Blaine's Growlithe (C)	.10	.25
❏ 63	Blaine's Ponyta (C)	.10	.25
❏ 64	Blaine's Tauros (C)	.10	.25
❏ 65	Blaine's Vulpix (C)	.10	.25
❏ 66	Brock's Geodude (C)	.10	.25
❏ 67	Brock's Mankey (C)	.10	.25
❏ 68	Brock's Mankey (C)	.10	.25
❏ 69	Brock's Onix (C)	.10	.25

❏ 70	Brock's Ryhorn (C)	.10	.25
❏ 71	Brock's Sandshrew (C)	.10	.25
❏ 72	Brock's Sandshrew (C)	.10	.25
❏ 73	Brock's Vulpix (C)	.10	.25
❏ 74	Brock's Zubat (C)	.10	.25
❏ 75	Erika's Bellsprout (C)	.10	.25
❏ 76	Erika's Bellsprout (C)	.10	.25
❏ 77	Erika's Exeggcute (C)	.10	.25
❏ 78	Erika's Oddish (C)	.10	.25
❏ 79	Erika's Tangela (C)	.10	.25
❏ 80	Lt. Surge's Magnemite (C)	.10	.25
❏ 81	Lt. Surge's Pikachu (C)	.25	.50
❏ 82	Lt. Surge's Rattata (C)	.10	.25
❏ 83	Lt. Surge's Spearow (C)	.10	.25
❏ 84	Lt. Surge's Voltorb (C)	.10	.25
❏ 85	Misty's Goldeen (C)	.10	.25
❏ 86	Misty's Horsea (C)	.10	.25
❏ 87	Misty's Poliwag (C)	.10	.25
❏ 88	Misty's Seel (C)	.10	.25
❏ 89	Misty's Shellder (C)	.10	.25
❏ 90	Misty's Staryu (C)	.10	.25
❏ 91	Sabrina's Abra (C)	.10	.25
❏ 92	Sabrina's Drowzee (C)	.10	.25
❏ 93	Sabrina's Gastly (C)	.10	.25
❏ 94	Sabrina's Mr. Mime (C)	.10	.25
❏ 95	Sabrina's Slowpoke (C)	.10	.25

❏ 96	Sabrina's Venonat (C)	.10	.25
❏ 97	Blaine's Quiz #1 (R)	.50	1.00
❏ 98	Brock (R)	.50	1.00
❏ 99	Charity (R)	.50	1.00
❏ 100	Erika (R)	.50	1.00
❏ 101	Lt. Surge (R)	.50	1.00
❏ 102	Misty (R)	.50	1.00
❏ 103	No Removal Gym (R)	.50	1.00
❏ 104	The Rocket's Gym (R)	.50	1.00
❏ 105	Blaine's Last Resort (U)	.20	.50
❏ 106	Brock's Training Method (U)	.20	.50
❏ 107	Celadon City Gym (U)	.20	.50
❏ 108	Cerulean City Gym (U)	.20	.50
❏ 109	Erika's Maids (U)	.20	.50
❏ 110	Erika's Perfume (U)	.20	.50
❏ 111	Good Manners (U)	.20	.50
❏ 112	Lt. Surge's Treaty (U)	.20	.50
❏ 113	Minion of Team Rocket (U)	.20	.50
❏ 114	Misty's Wrath (U)	.20	.50
❏ 115	Pewter City Gym (U)	.20	.50
❏ 116	Recall (U)	.20	.50
❏ 117	Sabrina's ESP (U)	.20	.50
❏ 118	Secret Mission (U)	.20	.50
❏ 119	Tickling Machine (U)	.20	.50
❏ 120	Vermilion City Gym (U)	.20	.50
❏ 121	Blaine's Gamble (C)	.10	.25
❏ 122	Energy Flow (C)	.10	.25

#	Card		
123	Misty's Duel (C)	.10	.25
124	Narrow Gym (C)	.10	.25
125	Sabrina's Gaze (C)	.10	.25
126	Trash Exchange (C)	.10	.25
127	Fighting Energy (C)	.10	.25
128	Fire Energy (C)	.10	.25
129	Grass Energy (C)	.10	.25
130	Lightning Energy (C)	.10	.25
131	Psychic Energy (C)	.10	.25
132	Water Energy (C)	.10	.25

Gym Challenge 1st Edition Wizards of the Coast

	Complete set (132)	65.00	90.00
	Unopened Box (36 ct.)	50.00	70.00
	Unopened Pack (11 cards)	2.00	4.00
	Common Card (not listed) (C)	.10	.25
	Uncommon Card (not listed) (U)	.20	.50
	Rare Card (not listed) (R)	.50	1.00
1	Blaine's Arcanine (holo) (R)	4.00	8.00
2	Blaine's Charizard (holo) (R)	6.00	12.00
3	Brock's Ninetales (holo) (R)	3.00	6.00
4	Erika's Venusaur (holo) (R)	3.00	6.00
5	Giovanni's Gyarados (holo) (R)	3.00	6.00
6	Giovanni's Machamp (holo) (R)	3.00	6.00
7	Giovanni's Nidoking (holo) (R)	3.00	6.00
8	Giovanni's Persian (holo) (R)	3.00	6.00
9	Koga's Beedrill (holo) (R)	3.00	6.00

10	Koga's Ditto (holo) (R)	3.00	6.00
11	Lt. Surge's Raichu (holo) (R)	4.00	8.00
12	Misty's Golduck (holo) (R)	3.00	6.00
13	Misty's Gyarados (holo) (R)	3.00	6.00
14	Rocket's Mewtwo (holo) (R)	4.00	8.00
15	Rocket's Zapdos (holo) (R)	3.00	7.00
16	Sabrina's Alakazam (holo) (R)	3.00	6.00
17	Blaine (holo) (R)	3.00	6.00
18	Giovanni (holo) (R)	3.00	6.00
19	Koga (holo) (R)	3.00	6.00
20	Sabrina (holo) (R)	3.00	6.00
21	Blaine's Ninetales (R)	.50	1.00
22	Brock's Dugtrio (R)	.50	1.00
23	Giovanni's Nidoqueen (R)	.50	1.00
24	Giovanni's Pinsir (R)	.50	1.00
25	Koga's Arbok (R)	.50	1.00
26	Koga's Muk (R)	.50	1.00
27	Koga's Pidgeotto (R)	.50	1.00
28	Lt. Surge's Jolteon (R)	.50	1.00
29	Sabrina's Gengar (R)	.50	1.00
30	Sabrina's Golduck (R)	.50	1.00
31	Blaine's Charmeleon (U)	.20	.50
32	Blaine's Dodrio (U)	.20	.50

33	Blaine's Rapidash (U)	.20	.50
34	Brock's Graveler (U)	.20	.50
35	Brock's Primeape (U)	.20	.50
36	Brock's Sandslash (U)	.20	.50
37	Brock's Vulpix (U)	.20	.50
38	Erika's Bellsprout (U)	.20	.50
39	Erika's Bulbasaur (U)	.20	.50
40	Erika's Clefairy (U)	.20	.50
41	Erika's Ivysaur (U)	.20	.50
42	Giovanni's Machoke (U)	.20	.50
43	Giovanni's Meowth (U)	.20	.50
44	Giovanni's Nidorina (U)	.20	.50
45	Giovanni's Nidorino (U)	.20	.50
46	Koga's Golbat (U)	.20	.50
47	Koga's Kakuna (U)	.20	.50
48	Koga's Koffing (U)	.20	.50
49	Koga's Pidgey (U)	.20	.50
50	Koga's Weezing (U)	.20	.50
51	Lt. Surge's Eevee (U)	.20	.50
52	Lt. Surge's Electrode (U)	.20	.50
53	Lt. Surge's Raticate (U)	.20	.50
54	Misty's Dewgong (U)	.20	.50
55	Sabrina's Haunter (U)	.20	.50
56	Sabrina's Hypno (U)	.20	.50
57	Sabrina's Jynx (U)	.20	.50
58	Sabrina's Kadabra (U)	.20	.50
59	Sabrina's Mr. Mime (U)	.20	.50
60	Blaine's Charmander (C)	.10	.25
61	Blaine's Doduo (C)	.10	.25
62	Blaine's Growlithe (C)	.10	.25
63	Blaine's Mankey (C)	.10	.25
64	Blaine's Ponyta (C)	.10	.25
65	Blaine's Rhyhorn (C)	.10	.25
66	Blaine's Vulpix (C)	.10	.25
67	Brock's Diglett (C)	.10	.25
68	Brock's Geodude (C)	.10	.25
69	Erika's Jigglypuff (C)	.10	.25
70	Erika's Oddish (C)	.10	.25
71	Erika's Paras (C)	.10	.25
72	Giovanni's Machop (C)	.10	.25
73	Giovanni's Magikarp (C)	.10	.25
74	Giovanni's Meowth (C)	.10	.25
75	Giovanni's Nidoran (Fem) (C)	.10	.25
76	Giovanni's Nidoran (Male) (C)	.10	.25
77	Koga's Ekans (C)	.10	.25
78	Koga's Grimer (C)	.10	.25
79	Koga's Koffing (C)	.10	.25
80	Koga's Pidgey (C)	.10	.25
81	Koga's Tangela (C)	.10	.25
82	Koga's Weedle (C)	.10	.25
83	Koga's Zubat (C)	.10	.25
84	Lt. Surge's Pikachu (C)	.25	.50
85	Lt. Surge's Rattata (C)	.10	.25

86	Lt. Surge's Voltorb (C)	.10	.25
87	Misty's Horsea (C)	.10	.25
88	Misty's Magikarp (C)	.10	.25
89	Misty's Poliwag (C)	.10	.25
90	Misty's Psyduck (C)	.10	.25
91	Misty's Seel (C)	.10	.25
92	Misty's Staryu (C)	.10	.25
93	Sabrina's Abra (C)	.10	.25
94	Sabrina's Abra (C)	.10	.25
95	Sabrina's Drowsee (C)	.10	.25
96	Sabrina's Gastly (C)	.10	.25
97	Sabrina's Gastly (C)	.10	.25
98	Sabrina's Porygon (C)	.10	.25
99	Sabrina's Psyduck (C)	.10	.25
100	Blaine (R)	.50	1.00
101	Brock's Protection (R)	.50	1.00
102	Chaos Gym (R)	.50	1.00
103	Erika's Kindess (R)	.50	1.00
104	Giovanni (R)	.50	1.00
105	Giovanni's Last Resort (R)	.50	1.00
106	Koga (R)	.50	1.00
107	Lt. Surge's Secret Plan (R)	.50	1.00
108	Misty's Wish (R)	.50	1.00
109	Resistance Gym (R)	.50	1.00
110	Sabrina (R)	.50	1.00
111	Blaine's Quiz #2 (U)	.20	.50
112	Blaine's Quiz #3 (U)	.20	.50
113	Cinnabar City Gym (U)	.20	.50
114	Fuchsia City Gym (U)	.20	.50
115	Koga's Ninja Trick (U)	.20	.50
116	Master Ball (U)	.20	.50

117	Max Revive (U)	.20	.50
118	Misty's Tears (U)	.20	.50
119	Rocket's Minefield Gym (U)	.20	.50
120	Rocket's secret Experiment (U)	.20	.50
121	Sabrina's Psychic Control (U)	.20	.50
122	Saffron City Gym (U)	.20	.50
123	Viridian City Gym (U)	.20	.50
124	Fervor (C)	.10	.25
125	Transparent Walls (C)	.10	.25
126	Warp Point (C)	.10	.25
127	Fighting Energy (C)	.10	.25
128	Fire Energy (C)	.10	.25
129	Grass Energy (C)	.10	.25
130	Lightning Energy (C)	.10	.25
131	Psychic Energy (C)	.10	.25
132	Water Energy (C)	.10	.25

Gym Challenge Unlimited Wizards of the Coast

	Complete set (132)	40.00	55.00
	Unopened Box (36 ct)	40.00	55.00

	Unopened Pack (11 cards)	1.50	3.00
	Common Card (not listed) (C)	.10	.20
	Uncommon Card (not listed) (U)	.20	.50
	Rare Card (not listed) (R)	.50	1.00
❏ 1	Blaine's Arcanine (holo) (R)	2.00	4.00
❏ 2	Blaine's Charizard (holo) (R)	5.00	10.00
❏ 3	Brock's Ninetales (holo) (R)	2.00	4.00
❏ 4	Erika's Venusaur (holo) (R)	2.00	4.00
❏ 5	Giovanni's Gyarados (holo) (R)	2.00	4.00
❏ 6	Giovanni's Machamp (holo) (R)	2.00	4.00
❏ 7	Giovanni's Nidoking (holo) (R)	2.00	4.00
❏ 8	Giovanni's Persian (holo) (R)	2.00	4.00
❏ 9	Koga's Beedrill (holo) (R)	2.00	4.00
❏ 10	Koga's Ditto (holo) (R)	2.00	4.00
❏ 11	Lt. Surge's Raichu (holo) (R)	2.00	4.00
❏ 12	Misty's Golduck (holo) (R)	2.00	4.00
❏ 13	Misty's Gyarados (holo) (R)	2.00	4.00
❏ 14	Rocket's Mewtwo (holo) (R)	2.00	4.00
❏ 15	Rocket's Zapdos (holo) (R)	2.00	4.00
❏ 16	Sabrina's Alakazam (holo) (R)	2.00	4.00
❏ 17	Blaine (holo) (R)	2.00	4.00
❏ 18	Giovanni (holo) (R)	2.00	4.00
❏ 19	Koga (holo) (R)	2.00	4.00
❏ 20	Sabrina (holo) (R)	2.00	4.00
❏ 21	Blaine's Ninetales (R)	.50	1.00
❏ 22	Brock's Dugtrio (R)	.50	1.00
❏ 23	Giovanni's Nidoqueen (R)	.50	1.00
❏ 24	Koga's Pinsir (R)	.50	1.00
❏ 25	Koga's Arbok (R)	.50	1.00
❏ 26	Koga's Muk (R)	.50	1.00
❏ 27	Koga's Pidgeotto (R)	.50	1.00
❏ 28	Lt. Surge's Jolteon (R)	.50	1.00
❏ 29	Sabrina's Gengar (R)	.50	1.00

❏ 30	Sabrina's Golduck (R)	.50	1.00
❏ 31	Blaine's Charmeleon (U)	.20	.50
❏ 32	Blaine's Dodrio (U)	.20	.50
❏ 33	Blaine's Rapidash (U)	.20	.50
❏ 34	Brock's Graveler (U)	.20	.50
❏ 35	Brock's Primeape (U)	.20	.50
❏ 36	Brock's Sandslash (U)	.20	.50
❏ 37	Brock's Vulpix (U)	.20	.50
❏ 38	Erika's Bellsprout (U)	.20	.50
❏ 39	Erika's Bulbasaur (U)	.20	.50
❏ 40	Erika's Clefairy (U)	.20	.50
❏ 41	Erika's Ivysaur (U)	.20	.50
❏ 42	Giovanni's Machoke (U)	.20	.50
❏ 43	Giovanni's Meowth (U)	.20	.50
❏ 44	Giovanni's Nidorina (U)	.20	.50
❏ 45	Giovanni's Nidorino (U)	.20	.50
❏ 46	Koga's Golbat (U)	.20	.50
❏ 47	Koga's Kakuna (U)	.20	.50
❏ 48	Koga's Koffing (U)	.20	.50
❏ 49	Koga's Pidgey (U)	.20	.50

❏ 50	Koga's Weezing (U)	.20	.50
❏ 51	Lt. Surge's Eevee (U)	.20	.60
❏ 52	Lt. Surge's Electrode (U)	.20	.50
❏ 53	Lt. Surge's Raticate (U)	.20	.50
❏ 54	Misty's Dewgong (U)	.20	.50
❏ 55	Sabrina's Haunter (U)	.20	.50
❏ 56	Sabrina's Hypno (U)	.20	.50
❏ 57	Sabrina's Jynx (U)	.20	.50
❏ 58	Sabrina's Kadabra (U)	.20	.50
❏ 59	Sabrina's Mr. Mime (U)	.20	.50
❏ 60	Blaine's Charmander (C)	.10	.20
❏ 61	Blaine's Doduo (C)	.10	.20
❏ 62	Blaine's Growlithe (C)	.10	.20
❏ 63	Blaine's Mankey (C)	.10	.20
❏ 64	Blaine's Ponyta (C)	.10	.20
❏ 65	Blaine's Rhyhorn (C)	.10	.20
❏ 66	Blaine's Vulpix (C)	.10	.20
❏ 67	Brock's Diglett (C)	.10	.20
❏ 68	Brock's Geodude (C)	.10	.20
❏ 69	Erika's Jigglypuff (C)	.10	.20
❏ 70	Erika's Oddish (C)	.10	.20
❏ 71	Erika's Paras (C)	.10	.20
❏ 72	Giovanni's Machop (C)	.10	.20
❏ 73	Giovanni's Magikarp (C)	.10	.20
❏ 74	Giovanni's Meowth (C)	.10	.20
❏ 75	Giovanni's Nidoran (Fem) (C)	.10	.20
❏ 76	Giovanni's Nidoran (Male) (C)	.10	.20
❏ 77	Koga's Ekans (C)	.10	.20
❏ 78	Koga's Grimer (C)	.10	.20
❏ 79	Koga's Koffing (C)	.10	.20
❏ 80	Koga's Pidgey (C)	.10	.20
❏ 81	Koga's Tangela (C)	.10	.20
❏ 82	Koga's Weedle (C)	.10	.20
❏ 83	Koga's Zubat (C)	.10	.20
❏ 84	Lt. Surge's Pikachu (C)	.25	.50
❏ 85	Lt. Surge's Rattata (C)	.10	.20
❏ 86	Lt. Surge's Voltorb (C)	.10	.20
❏ 87	Misty's Horsea (C)	.10	.20
❏ 88	Misty's Magikarp (C)	.10	.20
❏ 89	Misty's Poliwag (C)	.10	.20
❏ 90	Misty's Psyduck (C)	.10	.20
❏ 91	Misty's Seel (C)	.10	.20
❏ 92	Misty's Staryu (C)	.10	.20
❏ 93	Sabrina's Abra (C)	.10	.20
❏ 94	Sabrina's Abra (C)	.10	.20
❏ 95	Sabrina's Drowsee (C)	.10	.20
❏ 96	Sabrina's Gastly (C)	.10	.20
❏ 97	Sabrina's Gastly (C)	.10	.20
❏ 98	Sabrina's Porygon (C)	.10	.20
❏ 99	Sabrina's Psyduck (C)	.10	.20
❏ 100	Blaine (R)	.10	.20
❏ 101	Brock's Protection (R)	.50	1.00

❏ 102	Chaos Gym (R)	.50	1.00
❏ 103	Erika's Kindness (T)	.50	1.00
❏ 104	Giovanni (R)	.50	1.00
❏ 105	Giovanni's Last Resort (R)	.50	1.00
❏ 106	Koga (R)	.50	1.00
❏ 107	Lt. Surge's Secret Plan (R)	.50	1.00
❏ 108	Misty's Wish (R)	.50	1.00
❏ 109	Resistance Gym (R)	.50	1.00
❏ 110	Sabrina (R)	.50	1.00
❏ 111	Blaine's Quiz #2 (U)	.20	.50
❏ 112	Blaine's Quiz #3 (U)	.20	.50
❏ 113	Cinnabar City Gym (U)	.20	.50
❏ 114	Fuchsia City Gym (U)	.20	.50
❏ 115	Koga's Ninja Trick (U)	.20	.50
❏ 116	Master Ball (U)	.20	.50
❏ 117	Max Revive (U)	.20	.50
❏ 118	Misty's Tears (U)	.20	.50
❏ 119	Rocket's Minefield Gym (U)	.20	.50
❏ 120	Rocket's secret Experiment (U)	.20	.50
❏ 121	Sabrina's Psychic Control (U)	.20	.50
❏ 122	Saffron City Gym (U)	.20	.50
❏ 123	Viridian City Gym (U)	.20	.50
❏ 124	Fervor (C)	.10	.20
❏ 125	Transparent Walls (C)	.10	.20
❏ 126	Warp Point (C)	.10	.20
❏ 127	Fighting Energy (C)	.10	.20
❏ 128	Fire Energy (C)	.10	.20
❏ 129	Grass Energy (C)	.10	.20
❏ 130	Lightning Energy (C)	.10	.20
❏ 131	Psychic Energy (C)	.10	.20
❏ 132	Water Energy (C)	.10	.20

Neo Genesis 1st Edition Wizards of the Coast

	Complete Set (111)	75.00	100.00
	Booster Box (36 ct)	60.00	90.00
	Booster Pack (11 cards)	2.00	4.00
	Common Card (not listed) (C)	.10	.25
	Uncommon Card (not listed) (U)	.20	.50
	Rare Card (not listed) (R)	.50	1.00
❏ 1	Ampharos (holo) (R)	3.00	6.00
❏ 2	Azumarill (holo) (R)	3.00	6.00
❏ 3	Bellossom (holo) (R)	3.00	6.00
❏ 4	Feraligatr Lv.56 (holo) (R)	3.00	6.00
❏ 5	Feraligatr Lv.69 (holo) (R)	4.00	8.00
❏ 6	Heracross (holo) (R)	3.00	6.00
❏ 7	Jumpluff (holo) (R)	3.00	6.00
❏ 8	Kingdra (holo) (R)	3.00	6.00
❏ 9	Lugia (holo) (R)	18.00	30.00
❏ 10	Meganium Lv.54 (holo) (R)	4.00	8.00
❏ 11	Meganium Lv.57 (holo) (R)	3.00	6.00
❏ 12	Pichu (holo) (R)	5.00	10.00

Ampharos 80 HP
STAGE 2 | Evolves from Flaaffy | Put Ampharos on the Stage 1 card
Stage 2 Pokémon

Light Pokémon. Length: 4' 7", Weight: 136 lbs.

Gigaspark Flip a coin. If heads, the Defending Pokémon is now Paralyzed and this attack does 10 damage to each of your opponent's Benched Pokémon. (Don't apply Weakness and Resistance for Benched Pokémon.) — 40

weakness / resistance / retreat cost

The tail's tip shines brightly and can be seen from far away. It acts as a beacon for lost people. LV. 40 #181

Illus. Ken Sugimori ©1995-2000 Nintendo, Creatures, GAMEFREAK. 1/111

#	Card		
☐ 13	Skarmory (holo) (R)	3.00	6.00
☐ 14	Slowking (holo) (R)	3.00	6.00
☐ 15	Steelix (holo) (R)	3.00	6.00
☐ 16	Togetic (holo) (R)	3.00	6.00
☐ 17	Typhlosion Lv.55 (holo) (R)	3.00	6.00
☐ 18	Typhlosion Lv.57 (holo) (R)	4.00	8.00
☐ 19	Metal Energy (holo) (R)	3.00	6.00
☐ 20	Cleffa (R)	.50	1.00
☐ 21	Donphan (R)	.50	1.00
☐ 22	Elekid (R)	.50	1.00
☐ 23	Magby (R)	.50	1.00
☐ 24	Murkrow (R)	.50	1.00
☐ 25	Sneasel (R)	.50	1.00
☐ 26	Aipom (U)	.20	.50
☐ 27	Ariados (U)	.20	.50
☐ 28	Bayleef Lv.22 (U)	.20	.50
☐ 29	Bayleef Lv.39 (U)	.20	.50
☐ 30	Clefairy (U)	.20	.50
☐ 31	Croconaw Lv.34 (U)	.20	.50
☐ 32	Croconaw Lv.41 (U)	.20	.50
☐ 33	Electabuzz (U)	.20	.50
☐ 34	Flaaffy (U)	.20	.50
☐ 35	Furret (U)	.20	.50
☐ 36	Gloom (U)	.20	.50
☐ 37	Granbull (U)	.20	.50
☐ 38	Lanturn (U)	.20	.50
☐ 39	Ledian (U)	.20	.50
☐ 40	Magmar (U)	.20	.50
☐ 41	Miltank (U)	.20	.50
☐ 42	Noctowl (U)	.20	.50
☐ 43	Phanpy (U)	.20	.50
☐ 44	Piloswine (U)	.20	.50
☐ 45	Quagsire (U)	.20	.50
☐ 46	Quilava Lv.28 (U)	.20	.50
☐ 47	Quilava Lv.35 (U)	.20	.50
☐ 48	Seadra (U)	.20	.50
☐ 49	Skiploom (U)	.20	.50
☐ 50	Sunflora (U)	.20	.50
☐ 51	Togepi (U)	1.00	2.00
☐ 52	Xatu (U)	.20	.50
☐ 53	Chikorita Lv.12 (C)	.10	.25
☐ 54	Chikorita Lv.19 (C)	.10	.25
☐ 55	Chinchou (C)	.10	.25
☐ 56	Cyndaquil Lv.14 (C)	.10	.25
☐ 57	Cyndaquil Lv.21 (C)	.10	.25
☐ 58	Girafarig (C)	.10	.25
☐ 59	Gligar (C)	.10	.25
☐ 60	Hoothoot (C)	.10	.25
☐ 61	Hoppip (C)	.10	.25
☐ 62	Horsea (C)	.10	.25
☐ 63	Ledyba (C)	.10	.25
☐ 64	Mantine (C)	.10	.25
☐ 65	Mareep (C)	.10	.25

#	Card		
☐ 66	Marill (C)	.10	.25
☐ 67	Natu (C)	.10	.25
☐ 68	Oddish (C)	.10	.25
☐ 69	Onix (C)	.10	.25
☐ 70	Pikachu (C)	.50	1.00
☐ 71	Sentret (C)	.10	.25
☐ 72	Shuckle (C)	.10	.25
☐ 73	Slowpoke (C)	.10	.25
☐ 74	Snubbull (C)	.10	.25
☐ 75	Spinarak (C)	.10	.25
☐ 76	Stantler (C)	.10	.25
☐ 77	Sudowoodo (C)	.10	.25
☐ 78	Sunkern (C)	.10	.25
☐ 79	Swinub (C)	.10	.25
☐ 80	Totodile Lv.13 (C)	.10	.25
☐ 81	Totodile Lv.20 (C)	.10	.25
☐ 82	Wooper (C)	.10	.25
☐ 83	Arcade Game (R)	.50	1.00
☐ 84	Ecogym (R)	.50	1.00
☐ 85	Energy Charge (R)	.50	1.00
☐ 86	Focus Band (R)	.50	1.00
☐ 87	Mary (R)	.50	1.00
☐ 88	PokeGear (R)	.50	1.00

Electabuzz 70 HP
Basic Pokémon

Electric Pokémon. Length: 3' 7", Weight: 66 lbs.

Punch — 20

Swift This attack's damage isn't affected by Weakness, Resistance, Pokémon Powers, or any other effects on the Defending Pokémon. — 30

weakness / resistance / retreat cost

Electricity runs across the surface of its body. In darkness, its entire body glows a whitish-blue. LV. 38 #125

Illus. Shin-ichi Yoshida ©1995-2000 Nintendo, Creatures, GAMEFREAK. 33/111

#	Card		
☐ 89	Super Energy Retrieval (R)	.50	1.00
☐ 90	Time Capsule (R)	.50	1.00
☐ 91	Bill's Teleporter (U)	.20	.50
☐ 92	Card-Flip Game (U)	.20	.50
☐ 93	Gold Berry (U)	.20	.50
☐ 94	Miracle Berry (U)	.20	.50
☐ 95	New Pokedex (U)	.20	.50
☐ 96	Professor Elm (U)	.20	.50
☐ 97	Sprout Tower (U)	.20	.50
☐ 98	Super Scoop Up (U)	.20	.50
☐ 99	Berry (C)	.10	.25
☐ 100	Double Gust (C)	.10	.25
☐ 101	Moo-Moo Milk (C)	.10	.25
☐ 102	Pokemon March (C)	.10	.25
☐ 103	Super Rod (C)	.10	.25
☐ 104	Darkness Energy (R)	.50	1.00
☐ 105	Recycle Energy (R)	.50	1.00
☐ 106	Fighting Energy	.10	.25
☐ 107	Fire Energy	.10	.25
☐ 108	Grass Energy	.10	.25
☐ 109	Lightning Energy	.10	.25
☐ 110	Psychic Energy	.10	.25
☐ 111	Water Energy	.10	.25

Neo Genesis Unlimited Wizards of the Coast

Complete Set (111)		45.00	60.00

Booster Box (36 ct)		40.00	65.00
Booster Pack (11 cards)		1.50	2.50
Common Card (not listed) (C)		.10	.20
Uncommon Card (not listed) (U)		.20	.50
Rare Card (not listed) (R)		.50	1.00
Hotfoot Deck (60 cards)		4.00	10.00
Cold Fusion Deck (60 cards)		4.00	10.00
☐ 1	Ampharos (holo) (R)	2.00	4.00
☐ 2	Azumarill (holo) (R)	2.00	4.00
☐ 3	Bellossom (holo) (R)	2.00	4.00
☐ 4	Feraligatr Lv.56 (holo) (R)	3.00	6.00
☐ 5	Feraligatr Lv.69 (holo) (R)	3.00	6.00
☐ 6	Heracross (holo) (R)	2.00	4.00
☐ 7	Jumpluff (holo) (R)	2.00	4.00
☐ 8	Kingdra (holo) (R)	2.00	4.00
☐ 9	Lugia (holo) (R)	8.00	16.00
☐ 10	Meganium Lv.54 (holo) (R)	2.00	4.00
☐ 11	Meganium Lv.57 (holo) (R)	2.00	4.00
☐ 12	Pichu (holo) (R)	3.00	6.00
☐ 13	Skarmory (holo) (R)	2.00	4.00
☐ 14	Slowking (holo) (R)	2.00	4.00
☐ 15	Steelix (holo) (R)	2.00	4.00
☐ 16	Togetic (holo) (R)	2.00	4.00
☐ 17	Typhlosion Lv.55 (holo) (R)	2.00	5.00
☐ 18	Typhlosion Lv.57 (holo) (R)	2.00	5.00
☐ 19	Metal Energy (holo) (R)	2.00	4.00
☐ 20	Cleffa (R)	.50	1.00
☐ 21	Donphan (R)	.50	1.00
☐ 22	Elekid (R)	.50	1.00
☐ 23	Magby (R)	.50	1.00

Togetic 60 HP
STAGE 1 | Evolves from Togepi | Put Togetic on the Basic Pokémon
Stage 1 Pokémon

Happiness Pokémon. Length: 2' 0", Weight: 7 lbs.

Super Metronome Flip a coin. If heads, choose an attack of 1 of your opponent's Pokémon. Super Metronome copies that attack except for its Energy cost. (You must still do anything else in order to use that attack.) (No matter what type the Defending Pokémon is, Togetic's type is still ☐.) Togetic performs that attack. (Togetic can make that attack even if it does not have the appropriate number or type of Energy attached to it, necessary to make the attack.)

Fly Flip a coin. If heads, during your opponent's next turn, prevent all effects of attacks, including damage, done to Togetic; if tails, this attack does nothing (not even damage). — 30

weakness / resistance / retreat cost

They say that it will appear before kindhearted, caring people and shower them with happiness. LV. 31 #176

Illus. Ken Sugimori ©1995-2000 Nintendo, Creatures, GAMEFREAK. 16/111

#	Card		
☐ 24	Murkrow (R)	.50	1.00
☐ 25	Sneasel (R)	.50	1.00
☐ 26	Aipom (U)	.20	.50
☐ 27	Ariados (U)	.20	.50
☐ 28	Bayleef Lv.22 (U)	.20	.50
☐ 29	Bayleef Lv.39 (U)	.20	.50
☐ 30	Clefairy (U)	.20	.50
☐ 31	Croconaw Lv.34 (U)	.20	.50
☐ 32	Croconaw Lv.41 (U)	.20	.50
☐ 33	Electabuzz (U)	.20	.50
☐ 34	Flaaffy (U)	.20	.50
☐ 35	Furret (U)	.20	.50
☐ 36	Gloom (U)	.20	.50
☐ 37	Granbull (U)	.20	.50
☐ 38	Lanturn (U)	.20	.50
☐ 39	Ledian (U)	.20	.50
☐ 40	Magmar (U)	.20	.50
☐ 41	Miltank (U)	.20	.50
☐ 42	Noctowl (U)	.20	.50
☐ 43	Phanpy (U)	.20	.50
☐ 44	Piloswine (U)	.20	.50

#	Name	Lo	Hi
45	Quagsire (U)	.20	.50
46	Quilava Lv.28 (U)	.20	.50
47	Quilava Lv.35 (U)	.20	.50
48	Seadra (U)	.20	.50
49	Skiploom (U)	.20	.50
50	Sunflora (U)	.20	.50
51	Togepi (U)	.25	.75
52	Xatu (U)	.20	.50
53	Chikorita Lv.12 (C)	.10	.20
54	Chikorita Lv.19 (C)	.10	.20
55	Chinchou (C)	.10	.20
56	Cyndaquil Lv.14 (C)	.10	.20
57	Cyndaquil Lv.21 (C)	.10	.20
58	Girafarig (C)	.10	.20
59	Gligar (C)	.10	.20
60	Hoothoot (C)	.10	.20
61	Hoppip (C)	.10	.20
62	Horsea (C)	.10	.20
63	Ledyba (C)	.10	.20
64	Mantine (C)	.10	.20
65	Mareep (C)	.10	.20
66	Marill (C)	.10	.20
67	Natu (C)	.10	.20
68	Oddish (C)	.10	.20
69	Onix (C)	.10	.20
70	Pikachu (C)	.10	.25
71	Sentret (C)	.10	.20
72	Shuckle (C)	.10	.20
73	Slowpoke (C)	.10	.20
74	Snubbull (C)	.10	.20
75	Spinarak (C)	.10	.20
76	Stantler (C)	.10	.20

#	Name	Lo	Hi
77	Sudowoodo (C)	.10	.20
78	Sunkern (C)	.10	.20
79	Swinub (C)	.10	.20
80	Totodile Lv.13 (C)	.10	.20
81	Totodile Lv.20 (C)	.10	.20
82	Wooper (C)	.10	.20
83	Arcade Game (R)	.50	1.00
84	Ecogym (R)	.50	1.00
85	Energy Charge (R)	.50	1.00
86	Focus Band (R)	.50	1.00
87	Mary (R)	.50	1.00
88	PokeGear (R)	.50	1.00
89	Super Energy Retrieval (R)	.50	1.00
90	Time Capsule (R)	.50	1.00
91	Bill's Teleporter (U)	.20	.50
92	Card-Flip Game (U)	.20	.50
93	Gold Berry (U)	.20	.50
94	Miracle Berry (U)	.20	.50
95	New Pokedex (U)	.20	.50

#	Name	Lo	Hi
96	Professor Elm (U)	.20	.50
97	Sprout Tower (U)	.20	.50
98	Super Scoop Up (U)	.20	.50
99	Berry (C)	.10	.20
100	Double Gust (C)	.10	.20
101	Moo-Moo Milk (C)	.10	.20
102	Pokemon March (C)	.10	.20

#	Name	Lo	Hi
103	Super Rod (C)	.10	.20
104	Darkness Energy (R)	.50	1.00
105	Recycle Energy (R)	.50	1.00
106	Fighting Energy	.10	.20
107	Fire Energy	.10	.20
108	Grass Energy	.10	.20
109	Lightning Energy	.10	.20
110	Psychic Energy	.10	.20
111	Water Energy	.10	.20

Neo Discovery 1st Edition Wizards of the Coast

#	Name	Lo	Hi
	Complete Set (75)	75.00	120.00
	Booster Box (36 ct.)	60.00	100.00
	Booster Pack (11 cards)	3.00	5.00
	Common Card (not listed)	.10	.25
	Uncommon Card (not listed)	.20	.50
	Rare Card (not listed)	.50	1.00
1	Espeon (holo) (R)	3.00	6.00
2	Forretress (holo) (R)	3.00	6.00
3	Hitmontop (holo) (R)	3.00	6.00
4	Houndoom (holo) (R)	3.00	6.00
5	Houndour (holo) (R)	3.00	7.00
6	Kabutops (holo) (R)	3.00	6.00
7	Magnemite (holo) (R)	3.00	7.00
8	Politoed (holo) (R)	3.00	6.00
9	Poliwrath (holo) (R)	3.00	6.00
10	Scizor (holo) (R)	3.00	6.00
11	Smeargle (holo) (R)	3.00	6.00
12	Tyranitar (holo) (R)	3.00	7.00
13	Umbreon (holo) (R)	3.00	6.00
14	Unown A (holo) (R)	4.00	8.00
15	Ursaring (holo) (R)	3.00	6.00
16	Wobbuffet (holo) (R)	3.00	6.00
17	Yanma (holo) (R)	3.00	6.00
18	Beedrill (R)	.50	1.00
19	Butterfree (R)	.50	1.00
20	Espeon (R)	.50	1.00
21	Forretress (R)	.50	1.00
22	Hitmontop (R)	.50	1.00
23	Houndoom (R)	.50	1.00
24	Houndour (R)	.50	1.00
25	Kabutops (R)	.50	1.00

#	Name	Lo	Hi
26	Magnemite (R)	.50	1.00
27	Politoed (R)	.50	1.00
28	Poliwrath (R)	.50	1.00
29	Scizor (R)	.50	1.00
30	Smeargle (R)	.50	1.00
31	Tyranitar (R)	.50	1.00
32	Umbreon (R)	.50	1.00
33	Unown A (R)	.50	1.00
34	Ursaring (R)	.50	1.00
35	Wobbuffet (R)	.50	1.00
36	Yanma (R)	.50	1.00
37	Corsola (U)	.20	.50
38	Eevee (U)	.20	.50
39	Houndour (U)	.20	.50
40	Igglybuff (U)	.20	.50
41	Kakuna (U)	.20	.50
42	Metapod (U)	.20	.50
43	Omastar (U)	.20	.50
44	Poliwhirl (U)	.20	.50
45	Pupitar (U)	.20	.50
46	Scyther (U)	.20	.50
47	Unown D (U)	.20	.50
48	Unown F (U)	.20	.50
49	Unown M (U)	.20	.50
50	Unown N (U)	.20	.50

#	Name	Lo	Hi
51	Unown U (U)	.20	.50
52	Xatu (U)	.20	.50
53	Caterpie (C)	.10	.25
54	Dunsparce (C)	.10	.25
55	Hoppip (C)	.10	.25
56	Kabuto (C)	.10	.25
57	Larvitar (C)	.10	.25
58	Mareep (C)	.10	.25
59	Natu (C)	.10	.25
60	Omanyte (C)	.10	.25
61	Pineco (C)	.10	.25
62	Poliwag (C)	.10	.25
63	Sentret (C)	.10	.25
64	Spinarak (C)	.10	.25
65	Teddiursa (C)	.10	.25
66	Tyrogue (C)	.10	.25
67	Unown E (C)	.10	.25
68	Unown I (C)	.10	.25
69	Unown O (C)	.10	.25
70	Weedle (C)	.10	.25
71	Wooper (C)	.10	.25
72	Trainer: Fossil Egg (U)	.20	.50
73	Trainer: Hyper Devolution Spray (U)	.20	.50
74	Trainer: Ruin Wall (U)	.20	.50
75	Trainer: Energy Ark (C)	.10	.25

Neo Discovery Unlimited Wizards of the Coast

Complete Set (75)	45.00	65.00	
Booster Box (36 ct.)	50.00	75.00	
Booster Pack (11 cards)	2.00	4.00	
Common Card (not listed) (C)	.10	.20	
Uncommon Card (not listed) (U)	.20	.50	
Rare Card (not listed) (R)	.50	1.00	
Brainwave Deck	4.00	10.00	
Wallop Deck	4.00	10.00	
❑ 1 Espeon (holo) (R)	2.00	4.00	
❑ 2 Forretress (holo) (R)	2.00	4.00	
❑ 3 Hitmontop (holo) (R)	2.00	4.00	
❑ 4 Houndoom (holo) (R)	2.00	4.00	
❑ 5 Houndour (holo) (R)	2.00	4.00	
❑ 6 Kabutops (holo) (R)	2.00	4.00	
❑ 7 Magnemite (holo) (R)	2.00	4.00	
❑ 8 Politoed (holo) (R)	2.00	4.00	
❑ 9 Poliwrath (holo) (R)	2.00	4.00	
❑ 10 Scizor (holo) (R)	2.00	4.00	
❑ 11 Smeargle (holo) (R)	2.00	4.00	
❑ 12 Tyranitar (holo) (R)	2.00	5.00	
❑ 13 Umbreon (holo) (R)	2.00	4.00	
❑ 14 Unown A (holo) (R)	2.00	4.00	
❑ 15 Ursaring (holo) (R)	2.00	4.00	
❑ 16 Wobbuffet (holo) (R)	2.00	4.00	
❑ 17 Yanma (holo) (R)	2.00	4.00	
❑ 18 Beedrill (R)	.50	1.00	

Hitmontop 60 HP — Basic Pokémon

Handstand Pokémon. Length: 4' 3", Weight: 106 lbs.

Detect Flip a coin. If heads, during your opponent's next turn, prevent all effects of attacks, including damage, done to Hitmontop.

Triple Kick Flip 3 coins. This attack does 30 damage times the number of heads. 30x

❑ 19 Butterfree (R)	.50	1.00
❑ 20 Espeon (R)	.50	1.00
❑ 21 Forretress (R)	.50	1.00
❑ 22 Hitmontop (R)	.50	1.00
❑ 23 Houndoom (R)	.50	1.00
❑ 24 Houndour (R)	.50	1.00
❑ 25 Kabutops (R)	.50	1.00
❑ 26 Magnemite (R)	.50	1.00
❑ 27 Politoed (R)	.50	1.00
❑ 28 Poliwrath (R)	.50	1.00
❑ 29 Scizor (R)	.50	1.00
❑ 30 Smeargle (R)	.50	1.00
❑ 31 Tyranitar (R)	.50	1.00
❑ 32 Umbreon (R)	.50	1.00
❑ 33 Unown A (R)	.50	1.00
❑ 34 Ursaring (R)	.50	1.00
❑ 35 Wobbuffet (R)	.50	1.00
❑ 36 Yanma (R)	.50	1.00
❑ 37 Corsola (U)	.20	.50
❑ 38 Eevee (U)	.20	.50
❑ 39 Houndour (U)	.20	.50
❑ 40 Igglybuff (U)	.20	.50

❑ 41 Kakuna (U)	.20	.50
❑ 42 Metapod (U)	.20	.50
❑ 43 Omastar (U)	.20	.50
❑ 44 Poliwhirl (U)	.20	.50
❑ 45 Pupitar (U)	.20	.50
❑ 46 Scyther (U)	.20	.50
❑ 47 Unown D (U)	.20	.50
❑ 48 Unown F (U)	.20	.50
❑ 49 Unown M (U)	.20	.50
❑ 50 Unown N (U)	.20	.50
❑ 51 Unown U (U)	.20	.50
❑ 52 Xatu (U)	.20	.50
❑ 53 Caterpie (C)	.10	.20
❑ 54 Dunsparce (C)	.10	.20
❑ 55 Hoppip (C)	.10	.20
❑ 56 Kabuto (C)	.10	.20
❑ 57 Larvitar (C)	.10	.20
❑ 58 Mareep (C)	.10	.20
❑ 59 Natu (C)	.10	.20
❑ 60 Omanyte (C)	.10	.20
❑ 61 Pineco (C)	.10	.20
❑ 62 Poliwag (C)	.10	.20
❑ 63 Sentret (C)	.10	.20
❑ 64 Spinarak (C)	.10	.20
❑ 65 Teddiursa (C)	.10	.20
❑ 66 Tyrogue (C)	.10	.20
❑ 67 Unown E (C)	.10	.20
❑ 68 Unown I (C)	.10	.20
❑ 69 Unown O (C)	.10	.20
❑ 70 Weedle (C)	.10	.20
❑ 71 Wooper (C)	.10	.20
❑ 72 Trainer: Fossil Egg (U)	.20	.50
❑ 73 Trainer: Hyper Devolution Spray (U)	.20	.50
❑ 74 Trainer: Ruin Wall (U)	.20	.50
❑ 75 Trainer: Energy Ark (C)	.10	.20

Neo Revelation 1st Edition Wizards of the Coast

Complete Set (66)	80.00	125.00
Booster Box (36 ct.)	75.00	100.00
Booster Pack (11 cards)	3.00	5.00
Common Card (not listed)	.10	.25
Uncommon Card (not listed)	.20	.50
Rare Card (not listed)	.50	1.00

Ho-oh 90 HP — Basic Pokémon

Rainbow Pokémon. Length: 12' 6", Weight: 439 lbs.

Stoke You may search your deck for 5 in Energy card and attach it to Ho-oh. Shuffle your deck afterward.

Sacred Fire Flip a coin. If heads, choose 1 of your opponent's Pokémon. This attack does 40 damage to that Pokémon. Don't apply Weakness and Resistance.

Dive Bomb Flip a coin. If tails, this attack does nothing. 90

❑ 1 Ampharos (holo) (R)	3.00	6.00
❑ 2 Blissey (holo) (R)	3.00	6.00
❑ 3 Celebi (holo) (R)	4.00	8.00
❑ 4 Crobat (holo) (R)	3.00	6.00
❑ 5 Delibird (holo) (R)	3.00	6.00
❑ 6 Entei (holo) (R)	4.00	8.00

❑ 7 Ho-oh (holo) (R)	10.00	20.00
❑ 8 Houndoom (holo) (R)	3.00	6.00
❑ 9 Jumpluff (holo) (R)	3.00	6.00
❑ 10 Magneton (holo) (R)	3.00	6.00
❑ 11 Misdreavus (holo) (R)	4.00	8.00
❑ 12 Porygon 2 (holo) (R)	3.00	6.00
❑ 13 Raikou (holo) (R)	3.00	6.00
❑ 14 Suicune (holo) (R)	4.00	8.00
❑ 15 Aerodactyl (R)	.50	1.00
❑ 16 Celebi (R)	1.00	2.00
❑ 17 Entei (R)	1.00	2.00
❑ 18 Ho-oh (R)	.50	1.00
❑ 19 Kingdra (R)	.50	1.00
❑ 20 Lugia (R)	.50	1.00
❑ 21 Raichu (R)	.50	1.00
❑ 22 Raikou (R)	.50	1.00
❑ 23 Skarmory (R)	.50	1.00
❑ 24 Sneasel (R)	.50	1.00
❑ 25 Starmie (R)	.50	1.00
❑ 26 Sudowoodo (R)	.50	1.00
❑ 27 Suicune (R)	.50	1.00
❑ 28 Flaaffy (U)	.20	.50
❑ 29 Golbat (U)	.20	.50
❑ 30 Graveler (U)	.20	.50
❑ 31 Jynx (U)	.20	.50
❑ 32 Lanturn (U)	.20	.50
❑ 33 Magcargo (U)	.20	.50
❑ 34 Octillery (U)	.20	.50
❑ 35 Parasect (U)	.20	.50
❑ 36 Piloswine (U)	.20	.50

Geodude 40 HP — Basic Pokémon

Rock Pokémon. Length: 1' 4", Weight: 44 lbs.

Knuckle Punch 20

It uses its arms to steadily climb steep mountain paths. It swings its fists around if angered. LV. 14 #74

❑ 37 Seaking (U)	.20	.50
❑ 38 Stantler (U)	.20	.50
❑ 39 Unown B (U)	.20	.50
❑ 40 Unown Y (U)	.20	.50
❑ 41 Aipom (C)	.10	.25
❑ 42 Chinchou (C)	.10	.25
❑ 43 Farfetch'd (C)	.10	.25
❑ 44 Geodude (C)	.10	.25
❑ 45 Goldeen (C)	.10	.25
❑ 46 Murkrow (C)	.10	.25
❑ 47 Paras (C)	.10	.25
❑ 48 Quagsire (C)	.10	.25
❑ 49 Qwilfish (C)	.10	.25
❑ 50 Remoraid (C)	.10	.25
❑ 51 Shuckle (C)	.10	.25
❑ 52 Skiploom (C)	.10	.25
❑ 53 Slugma (C)	.10	.25
❑ 54 Smoochum (C)	.10	.25
❑ 55 Snubbull (C)	.10	.25
❑ 56 Staryu (C)	.10	.25
❑ 57 Swinub (C)	.10	.25

58	Unown K (C)	.10	.25
59	Zubat (C)	.10	.25
60	Balloon Berry (U)	.20	.50
61	Healing Fiold (U)	.20	.50
62	Pokemon Breeder Fields (U)	.20	.50
63	Rocket's Hideout (U)	.20	.50
64	Old Rod (C)	.10	.25
65	Shining Gyarados (holo) (R)	10.00	20.00
66	Shining Magikarp (holo) (R)	5.00	10.00

Neo Revelation Unlimited Wizards of the Coast

	Complete Set (66)	45.00	70.00
	Booster Box (36 ct.)	60.00	75.00
	Booster Pack (11 cards)	2.00	4.00
	Common Card (not listed) (C)	.10	.20
	Uncommon Card (not listed) (U)	.20	.50
	Rare Card (not listed) (R)	.50	1.00
1	Ampharos (holo) (R)	2.00	4.00
2	Blissey (holo) (R)	3.00	4.00
3	Celebi (holo) (R)	5.00	8.00
4	Crobat (holo) (R)	2.00	4.00
5	Delibird (holo) (R)	2.00	4.00
6	Entei (holo) (R)	3.00	6.00
7	Ho-oh (holo) (R)	3.00	6.00
8	Houndoom (holo) (R)	2.00	4.00
9	Jumpluff (holo) (R)	2.00	4.00
10	Magneton (holo) (R)	2.00	4.00
11	Misdreavus (holo) (R)	2.00	4.00
12	Porygon 2 (holo) (R)	2.00	4.00
13	Raikou (holo) (R)	2.00	4.00

14	Suicune (holo) (R)	2.00	4.00
15	Aerodactyl (R)	.50	1.00
16	Celebi (R)	.50	1.00
17	Entei (R)	.50	1.00
18	Ho-oh (R)	.50	1.00
19	Kingdra (R)	.50	1.00
20	Lugia (R)	.50	1.00
21	Raichu (R)	.50	1.00
22	Raikou (R)	.50	1.00
23	Skarmory (R)	.50	1.00
24	Sneasel (R)	.50	1.00
25	Starmie (R)	.50	1.00
26	Sudowoodo (R)	.50	1.00
27	Suicune (R)	.50	1.00
28	Flaaffy (U)	.20	.50
29	Golbat (U)	.20	.50
30	Graveler (U)	.20	.50
31	Jynx (U)	.20	.50
32	Lantum (U)	.20	.50

33	Magcargo (U)	.20	.50
34	Octillery (U)	.20	.50
35	Parasect (U)	.20	.50
36	Piloswine (U)	.20	.50
37	Seaking (U)	.20	.50
38	Stantler (U)	.20	.50
39	Unown B (U)	.20	.50
40	Unown Y (U)	.20	.50
41	Aipom (C)	.10	.20
42	Chinchou (C)	.10	.20
43	Farfetch'd (C)	.10	.20
44	Geodude (C)	.10	.20
45	Goldeen (C)	.10	.20
46	Murkrow (C)	.10	.20
47	Paras (C)	.10	.20
48	Quagsire (C)	.10	.20
49	Qwilfish (C)	.10	.20
50	Remoraid (C)	.10	.20
51	Shuckle (C)	.10	.20
52	Skiploom (C)	.10	.20
53	Slugma (C)	.10	.20
54	Smoochum (C)	.10	.20
55	Snubbull (C)	.10	.20
56	Staryu (C)	.10	.20
57	Swinub (C)	.10	.20
58	Unown K (C)	.10	.20
59	Zubat (C)	.10	.20
60	Balloon Berry (U)	.20	.50
61	Healing Field (U)	.20	.50
62	Pokemon Breeder Fields (U)	.20	.50
63	Rocket's Hideout (U)	.20	.50
64	Old Rod (C)	.10	.20
65	Shining Gyarados (holo) (R)	4.00	10.00
66	Shining Magikarp (holo) (R)	4.00	8.00

Neo Destiny 1st Edition Wizards of the Coast

	Complete Set (113)	90.00	125.00
	Booster Box (36 ct.)	70.00	100.00
	Booster Pack (11 cards)	3.00	5.00
	Common Cards (not listed) (C)	.10	.20
	Uncommon Cards (not listed) (U)	.20	.50
	Rare Cards (not listed) (R)		
1	Dark Ampharos (holo) (R)	3.00	6.00
2	Dark Crobat (holo) (R)	3.00	6.00
3	Dark Donphan (holo) (R)	3.00	6.00
4	Dark Espeon (holo) (R)	5.00	10.00
5	Dark Feraligatr (holo) (R)	4.00	10.00
6	Dark Gengar (holo) (R)	3.00	6.00
7	Dark Houndoom (holo) (R)	3.00	7.00
8	Dark Porygon2 (holo) (R)	3.00	6.00

9	Dark Scizor (holo) (R)	3.00	6.00
10	Dark Typhlosion (holo) (R)	3.00	6.00
11	Dark Iyranitar (holo) (R)	4.00	8.00
12	Light Arcanine (holo) (R)	3.00	6.00
13	Light Azumarill (holo) (R)	3.00	6.00
14	Light Dragonite (holo) (R)	3.00	6.00
15	Light Togetic (holo) (R)	3.00	6.00
16	Miracle Energy (holo) (R)	3.00	6.00
17	Dark Ariados (R)	.50	1.00
18	Dark Magcargo (R)	.50	1.00
19	Dark Omastar (R)	.50	1.00
20	Dark Slowking (R)	.50	1.00
21	Dark Ursaring (R)	.50	1.00
22	Light Dragonite (R)	.50	1.00
23	Light Lanturn (R)	.50	1.00
24	Light Ledian (R)	.50	1.00
25	Light Machamp (R)	.50	1.00
26	Light Piloswine (R)	.50	1.00
27	Unown G (R)	.50	1.00
28	Unown H (R)	.50	1.00
29	Unown W (R)	.50	1.00
30	Unown X (R)	.50	1.00
31	Chansey (U)	.20	.50
32	Dark Croconaw (U)	.20	.50
33	Dark Exeggutor (U)	.20	.50

34	Dark Flaaffy (U)	.20	.50
35	Dark Forretress (U)	.20	.50
36	Dark Haunter (U)	.20	.50
37	Dark Omanyte (U)	.20	.50
38	Dark Pupitar (U)	.20	.50
39	Dark Quilava (U)	.20	.50
40	Dark Wigglytuff (U)	.20	.50
41	Heracross (U)	.20	.50
42	Hitmonlee (U)	.20	.50
43	Houndour (U)	.20	.50
44	Jigglypuff (U)	.20	.50
45	Light Dewgong (U)	.20	.50
46	Light Flareon (U)	.20	.50
47	Light Golduck (U)	.20	.50
48	Light Jolteon (U)	.20	.50
49	Light Machoke (U)	.20	.50
50	Light Ninetales (U)	.20	.50
51	Light Slowbro (U)	.20	.50
52	Light Vaporeon (U)	.20	.50
53	Light Venomoth (U)	.20	.50
54	Light Wigglytuff (U)	.20	.50
55	Scyther (U)	.20	.50
56	Togepi (U)	.75	1.50
57	Unown C (U)	.20	.50
58	Unown P (U)	.20	.50
59	Unown Q (U)	.20	.50

❏ 60	Unown Z (U)	.20	.50
❏ 61	Cyndaquil (C)	.10	.20
❏ 62	Dark Octillery (C)	.10	.20
❏ 63	Dratini (C)	.10	.20
❏ 64	Exeggcute (C)	.10	.20
❏ 65	Gastly (C)	.10	.20
❏ 66	Girafarig (C)	.10	.20
❏ 67	Gligar (C)	.10	.20
❏ 68	Growlithe (C)	.10	.20
❏ 69	Hitmonchan (C)	.10	.20
❏ 70	Larvitar (C)	.10	.20
❏ 71	Ledyba (C)	.10	.20
❏ 72	Light Sunflora (C)	.10	.20
❏ 73	Machop (C)	.10	.20
❏ 74	Mantine (C)	.10	.20
❏ 75	Mareep (C)	.10	.20
❏ 76	Phanpy (C)	.10	.20
❏ 77	Pineco (C)	.10	.20
❏ 78	Porygon (C)	.10	.20
❏ 79	Psyduck (C)	.10	.20
❏ 80	Remoraid (C)	.10	.20
❏ 81	Seel (C)	.10	.20
❏ 82	Slugma (C)	.10	.20
❏ 83	Sunkern (C)	.10	.20
❏ 84	Swinub (C)	.10	.20
❏ 85	Totodile (C)	.10	.20
❏ 86	Unown L (C)	.10	.20
❏ 87	Unown S (C)	.10	.20

Machop — 40 HP — Basic Pokémon
Superpower Pokémon. Length: 2' 7", Weight: 43 lbs.
Chop — 10
Punch — 20
When bored, this super-strong Pokémon trains by lifting rocks. LV. 16 #066

❏ 88	Unown T (C)	.10	.20
❏ 89	Unown V (C)	.10	.20
❏ 90	Venonat (C)	.10	.20
❏ 91	Vulpix (C)	.10	.20
❏ 92	Broken Ground Gym (R)	.50	1.00
❏ 93	EXP.ALL (R)	.50	1.00
❏ 94	Impostor Prof.Oak's Invent.(R)	.50	1.00
❏ 95	Radio Tower (R)	.50	1.00
❏ 96	Thought Wave Machine (R)	.50	1.00
❏ 97	Counterattack Claws (U)	.20	.50
❏ 98	Energy Amplifier (U)	.20	.50
❏ 99	Energy Stadium (U)	.20	.50
❏ 100	Lucky Stadium (U)	.20	.50
❏ 101	Pigmented Lens (U)	.20	.50
❏ 102	Pokemon Personality Test (U)	.20	.50
❏ 103	Team Rockets Evil Deeds (U)	.20	.50
❏ 104	Heal Powder (C)	.10	.20
❏ 105	Mail from Bill (C)	.10	.20
❏ 106	Shining Celebi (holo) (UR)	12.00	22.00
❏ 107	Shining Charizard (holo) (UR)	20.00	30.00
❏ 108	Shining Kabutops (holo) (UR)	7.50	15.00
❏ 109	Shining Mewtwo (holo) (UR)	10.00	20.00
❏ 110	Shining Noctowl (holo) (UR)	7.50	15.00

❏ 111	Shining Raichu (holo) (UR)	10.00	20.00
❏ 112	Shining Steelix (holo) (UR)	7.50	15.00
❏ 113	Shining Tyranitar (holo) (UR)	7.50	15.00

Neo Destiny Unlimited Wizards of the Coast

	Complete Set (113)	60.00	100.00
	Booster Box (36 ct.)	50.00	80.00
	Booster Pack (11 cards)	2.00	3.50
	Common Card (not listed) (C)	.10	.20
	Uncommon Card (not listed) (U)	.20	.50
	Rare Cards (not listed) (R)	.50	1.00
❏ 1	Dark Ampharos (holo) (R)	2.00	4.00
❏ 2	Dark Crobat (holo) (R)	2.00	4.00
❏ 3	Dark Donphan (holo) (R)	2.00	4.00
❏ 4	Dark Espeon (holo) (R)	2.00	4.00
❏ 5	Dark Feraligatr (holo) (R)	2.00	4.00
❏ 6	Dark Gengar (holo) (R)	2.00	4.00
❏ 7	Dark Houndoom (holo) (R)	2.00	4.00
❏ 8	Dark Porygon2 (holo) (R)	2.00	4.00
❏ 9	Dark Scizor (holo) (R)	2.00	4.00
❏ 10	Dark Typhlosion (holo) (R)	2.00	4.00
❏ 11	Dark Tyranitar (holo) (R)	2.00	4.00
❏ 12	Light Arcanine (holo) (R)	2.00	4.00
❏ 13	Light Azumarill (holo) (R)	2.00	4.00
❏ 14	Light Dragonite (holo) (R)	2.00	4.00
❏ 15	Light Togetic (holo) (R)	2.00	4.00
❏ 16	Miracle Energy (holo) (R)	2.00	4.00
❏ 17	Dark Ariados (R)	.50	1.00
❏ 18	Dark Magcargo (R)	.50	1.00
❏ 19	Dark Omastar (R)	.50	1.00
❏ 20	Dark Slowking (R)	.50	1.00
❏ 21	Dark Ursaring (R)	.50	1.00
❏ 22	Light Dragonite (R)	.50	1.00
❏ 23	Light Lanturn (R)	.50	1.00
❏ 24	Light Ledian (R)	.50	1.00
❏ 25	Light Machamp (R)	.50	1.00
❏ 26	Light Piloswine (R)	.50	1.00
❏ 27	Unown G (R)	.50	1.00
❏ 28	Unown H (R)	.50	1.00
❏ 29	Unown W (R)	.50	1.00
❏ 30	Unown X (R)	.50	1.00
❏ 31	Chansey (U)	.20	.50
❏ 32	Dark Croconaw (U)	.20	.50
❏ 33	Dark Exeggutor (U)	.20	.50

STAGE 1 — Evolves from Jigglypuff — Put Light Wigglytuff on the Basic Pokémon
Light Wigglytuff — 80 HP — Stage 1 Pokémon
Balloon Pokémon. Length: 3' 3", Weight: 26 lbs.
Evolution Song
Body Slam — Flip a coin. If heads, the Defending Pokémon is now Paralyzed. — 20
54/105

❏ 34	Dark Flaaffy (U)	.20	.50
❏ 35	Dark Forretress (U)	.20	.50
❏ 36	Dark Haunter (U)	.20	.50
❏ 37	Dark Omanyte (U)	.20	.50

❏ 38	Dark Pupitar (U)	.20	.50
❏ 39	Dark Quilava (U)	.20	.50
❏ 40	Dark Wigglytuff (U)	.20	.50
❏ 41	Heracross (U)	.20	.50
❏ 42	Hitmonlee (U)	.20	.50
❏ 43	Houndour (U)	.20	.50
❏ 44	Jigglypuff (U)	.20	.50
❏ 45	Light Dewgong (U)	.20	.50
❏ 46	Light Flareon (U)	.20	.50
❏ 47	Light Golduck (U)	.20	.50
❏ 48	Light Jolteon (U)	.20	.50
❏ 49	Light Machoke (U)	.20	.50
❏ 50	Light Ninetales (U)	.20	.50
❏ 51	Light Slowbro (U)	.20	.50
❏ 52	Light Vaporeon (U)	.20	.50
❏ 53	Light Venomoth (U)	.20	.50
❏ 54	Light Wigglytuff (U)	.20	.50
❏ 55	Scyther (U)	.20	.50
❏ 56	Togepi (U)	.50	1.00
❏ 57	Unown C (U)	.20	.50
❏ 58	Unown P (U)	.20	.50
❏ 59	Unown Q (U)	.20	.50
❏ 60	Unown Z (U)	.20	.50
❏ 61	Cyndaquil (C)	.10	.20
❏ 62	Dark Octillery (C)	.10	.20
❏ 63	Dratini (C)	.10	.20
❏ 64	Exeggcute (C)	.10	.20
❏ 65	Gastly (C)	.10	.20
❏ 66	Girafarig (C)	.10	.20
❏ 67	Gligar (C)	.10	.20

Vulpix — 50 HP — Basic Pokémon
Fox Pokémon. Length: 2' 0", Weight: 22 lbs.
Ember — Discard 1 Energy card attached to Vulpix in order to use this attack. — 30
As it grows older, its several tall changes color and splits into as different tails. Its body radiates a faint warmth. LV. 19 #037

❏ 68	Growlithe (C)	.10	.20
❏ 69	Hitmonchan (C)	.10	.20
❏ 70	Larvitar (C)	.10	.20
❏ 71	Ledyba (C)	.10	.20
❏ 72	Light Sunflora (C)	.10	.20
❏ 73	Machop (C)	.10	.20
❏ 74	Mantine (C)	.10	.20
❏ 75	Mareep (C)	.10	.20
❏ 76	Phanpy (C)	.10	.20
❏ 77	Pineco (C)	.10	.20
❏ 78	Porygon (C)	.10	.20
❏ 79	Psyduck (C)	.10	.20
❏ 80	Remoraid (C)	.10	.20
❏ 81	Seel (C)	.10	.20
❏ 82	Slugma (C)	.10	.20
❏ 83	Sunkern (C)	.10	.20
❏ 84	Swinub (C)	.10	.20
❏ 85	Totodile (C)	.10	.20
❏ 86	Unown L (C)	.10	.20
❏ 87	Unown S (C)	.10	.20
❏ 88	Unown T (C)	.10	.20

❏ 89	Unown V (C)	.10	.20
❏ 90	Venonat (C)	.10	.20
❏ 91	Vulpix (C)	.10	.20
❏ 92	Broken Ground Gym (R)	.50	1.00
❏ 93	EXP.ALL (R)	.50	1.00
❏ 94	Impostor Prof.Oak's Invent.(R)	.50	1.00
❏ 95	Radio Tower (R)	.50	1.00
❏ 96	Thought Wave Machine (R)	.50	1.00
❏ 97	Counterattack Claws (U)	.20	.50
❏ 98	Energy Amplifier (U)	.20	.50
❏ 99	Energy Stadium (U)	.20	.50
❏ 100	Lucky Stadium (U)	.20	.50
❏ 101	Pigmented Lens (U)	.20	.50
❏ 102	Pokemon Personality Test (U)	.20	.50
❏ 103	Team Rockets Evil Deeds (U)	.20	.50
❏ 104	Heal Powder (C)	.10	.20
❏ 105	Mail from Bill (C)	.10	.20
❏ 106	Shining Celebi (holo) (UR)	7.00	15.00
❏ 107	Shining Charizard (holo) (UR)	12.00	20.00
❏ 108	Shining Kabutops (holo) (UR)	6.00	12.00
❏ 109	Shining Mewtwo (holo) (UR)	7.00	15.00
❏ 110	Shining Noctowl (holo) (UR)	5.00	10.00
❏ 111	Shining Raichu (holo) (UR)	5.00	12.00
❏ 112	Shining Steelix (holo) (UR)	5.00	12.00
❏ 113	Shining Tyranitar (holo) (UR)	7.00	15.00

Legendary Collection

Complete set (110)	65.00	95.00
Booster Box (36 ct.)	60.00	90.00
Booster Pack (11 cards)	2.00	3.50
Common Cards (not listed) (C)	.10	.20
Uncommon cards (not listed) (U)	.20	.50
Rare Cards (not listed) (R)	.50	1.00
Reverse Holo set (110)	90.00	150.00
Reverse Holofoil 2X Regular Version		
Box Topper 2X Regular Version		

❏ 1	Alakazam (holo) (R)	3.00	6.00
❏ 2	Articuno (holo) (R)	2.00	4.00
❏ 3	Charizard (holo) (R)	8.00	17.00
❏ 4	Dark Blastoise (holo) (R)	4.00	8.00
❏ 5	Dark Dragonite (holo) (R)	3.00	6.00
❏ 6	Dark Persian (holo) (R)	3.00	6.00
❏ 7	Dark Raichu (holo) (R)	3.00	6.00
❏ 8	Dark Slowbro (holo) (R)	2.00	4.00
❏ 9	Dark Vaporeon (holo) (R)	2.00	4.00
❏ 10	Flareon (holo) (R)	2.00	4.00
❏ 11	Gengar (holo) (R)	2.00	4.00
❏ 12	Gyarados (holo) (R)	2.00	4.00
❏ 13	Hitmonlee (holo) (R)	2.00	4.00
❏ 14	Jolteon (holo) (R)	2.00	4.00

❏ 15	Machamp (holo) (R)	2.00	4.00
❏ 16	Muk (holo) (R)	2.00	4.00
❏ 17	Ninetales (holo) (R)	2.00	4.00
❏ 18	Venusaur (holo) (R)	2.00	4.00
❏ 19	Zapdos (holo) (R)	2.00	4.00
❏ 20	Beedrill (R)	.50	1.00
❏ 21	Butterfree (R)	.50	1.00

❏ 22	Electrode (R)	.50	1.00
❏ 23	Exeggutor (R)	.50	1.00
❏ 24	Golem (R)	.50	1.00
❏ 25	Hypno (R)	.50	1.00
❏ 26	Jynx (R)	.50	1.00
❏ 27	Kabutops (R)	.50	1.00
❏ 28	Magneton (R)	.50	1.00
❏ 29	Mewtwo (R)	.50	1.00
❏ 30	Moltres (R)	.50	1.00
❏ 31	Nidoking (R)	.50	1.00
❏ 32	Nidoqueen (R)	.50	1.00
❏ 33	Pidgeot (R)	.50	1.00
❏ 34	Pidgeotto (R)	.50	1.00
❏ 35	Rhyhorn (R)	.50	1.00
❏ 36	Arcanine (U)	.20	.50
❏ 37	Charmeleon (U)	.20	.50
❏ 38	Dark Dragonair (U)	.20	.50
❏ 39	Dark Wartortle (U)	.20	.50
❏ 40	Dewgong (U)	.20	.50
❏ 41	Dodrio (U)	.20	.50
❏ 42	Fearow (U)	.20	.50
❏ 43	Golduck (U)	.20	.50
❏ 44	Graveler (U)	.20	.50
❏ 45	Growlithe (U)	.20	.50
❏ 46	Haunter (U)	.20	.50
❏ 47	Ivysaur (U)	.20	.50
❏ 48	Kabuto (U)	.20	.50
❏ 49	Kadabra (U)	.20	.50
❏ 50	Kakuna (U)	.20	.50
❏ 51	Machoke (U)	.20	.50
❏ 52	Magikarp (U)	.20	.50
❏ 53	Meowth (U)	.20	.50
❏ 54	Metapod (U)	.20	.50
❏ 55	Nidorina (U)	.20	.50
❏ 56	Nidorino (U)	.20	.50
❏ 57	Omanyte (U)	.20	.50
❏ 58	Omastar (U)	.20	.50
❏ 59	Primeape (U)	.20	.50
❏ 60	Rapidash (U)	.20	.50
❏ 61	Raticate (U)	.20	.50
❏ 62	Sandslash (U)	.20	.50
❏ 63	Seadra (U)	.20	.50
❏ 64	Snorlax (U)	.20	.50
❏ 65	Tauros (U)	.20	.50

❏ 66	Tentacruel (U)	.20	.50
❏ 67	Abra (C)	.10	.20
❏ 68	Bulbasaur (C)	.10	.20
❏ 69	Caterpie (C)	.10	.20
❏ 70	Charmander (C)	.10	.20
❏ 71	Doduo (C)	.10	.20
❏ 72	Dratini (C)	.10	.20
❏ 73	Drowzee (C)	.10	.20
❏ 74	Eevee (C)	.10	.20
❏ 75	Exeggcute (C)	.10	.20
❏ 76	Gastly (C)	.10	.20
❏ 77	Geodude (C)	.10	.20
❏ 78	Grimer (C)	.10	.20
❏ 79	Machop (C)	.10	.20
❏ 80	Magnemite (C)	.10	.20
❏ 81	Mankey (C)	.10	.20
❏ 82	Nidoran (F) (C)	.10	.20
❏ 83	Nidoran (M) (C)	.10	.20
❏ 84	Onix (C)	.10	.20
❏ 85	Pidgey (C)	.10	.20
❏ 86	Pikachu (C)	.50	1.00
❏ 87	Ponyta (C)	.10	.20
❏ 88	Psyduck (C)	.10	.20
❏ 89	Rattata (C)	.10	.20
❏ 90	Rhyhorn (C)	.10	.20
❏ 91	Sandshrew (C)	.10	.20
❏ 92	Seel (C)	.10	.20
❏ 93	Slowpoke (C)	.10	.20
❏ 94	Spearow (C)	.10	.20
❏ 95	Squirtle (C)	.10	.20
❏ 96	Tentacool (C)	.10	.20
❏ 97	Voltorb (C)	.10	.20
❏ 98	Vulpix (C)	.10	.20
❏ 99	Weedle (C)	.10	.20
❏ 100	Full Heal Energy (U)	.20	.50
❏ 101	Potion Energy (U)	.20	.50
❏ 102	Pokemon Breeder (R)	.50	1.00
❏ 103	Pokemon Trader (R)	.50	1.00
❏ 104	Scoop Up (R)	.50	1.00
❏ 105	Boss's Way (U)	.20	.50
❏ 106	Challenge! (U)	.20	.50
❏ 107	Energy Retrieval (U)	.20	.50
❏ 108	Bill (C)	.10	.20
❏ 109	Mysterious Fossil (C)	.10	.20
❏ 110	Potion (C)	.10	.20

Legendary Collection REVERSE FOIL

Complete set (110)	90.00	175.00
Reverse Holofoil 2X Regular Version		

Expedition Base Set

Complete Set (165)	75.00	120.00
Booster Box (36 packs)	60.00	80.00
Booster Pack (11 cards)	2.50	3.50
Common Cards (not listed) (C)	.10	.20
Uncommon Cards (not listed) (U)	.20	.50
Rare Cards (not listed) (R)	.50	1.00
Electric Garden Theme Deck	6.00	10.00
Box Toppers 1.5x regular		
Reverse Holofoils 2x regular		

❏ 1	Alakazam (holo) (R)	3.00	6.00
❏ 2	Ampharos (holo) (R)	2.00	4.00
❏ 3	Arbok (holo) (R)	2.00	4.00
❏ 4	Blastoise (holo) (R)	4.00	8.00
❏ 5	Butterfree (holo) (R)	2.00	4.00
❏ 6	Charizard (holo) (R)	12.50	25.00
❏ 7	Clefable (holo) (R)	2.00	4.00
❏ 8	Cloyster (holo) (R)	2.00	4.00
❏ 9	Dragonite (holo) (R)	2.00	4.00
❏ 10	Dugtrio (holo) (R)	2.00	4.00
❏ 11	Fearow (holo) (R)	2.00	4.00
❏ 12	Feraligatr (holo) (R)	2.00	4.00
❏ 13	Gengar (holo) (R)	2.00	4.00

❏ 14	Golem (holo) (R)	2.00	4.00
❏ 15	Kingler (holo) (R)	2.00	4.00
❏ 16	Machamp (holo) (R)	2.00	4.00
❏ 17	Magby (holo) (R)	2.00	4.00
❏ 18	Meganium (holo) (R)	2.00	4.00
❏ 19	Mew (holo) (R)	4.00	7.00
❏ 20	Mewtwo (holo) (R)	2.00	5.00
❏ 21	Ninetales (holo) (R)	2.00	4.00
❏ 22	Pichu (holo) (R)	2.00	4.00
❏ 23	Pidgeot (holo) (R)	2.00	4.00
❏ 24	Poliwrath (holo) (R)	2.00	4.00
❏ 25	Raichu (holo) (R)	2.00	4.00
❏ 26	Rapidash (holo) (R)	2.00	4.00
❏ 27	Skarmony (holo) (R)	2.00	4.00
❏ 28	Typhlosion (holo) (R)	2.00	4.00
❏ 29	Tyranitar (holo) (R)	2.00	4.00
❏ 30	Venusaur (holo) (R)	2.00	4.00
❏ 31	Vileplume (holo) (R)	2.00	4.00
❏ 32	Weezing (holo) (R)	2.00	4.00
❏ 33	Alakazam (R)	.50	1.00
❏ 34	Ampharos (R)	.50	1.00
❏ 35	Arbok (R)	.50	1.00
❏ 36	Blastoise (R)	.50	1.00
❏ 37	Blastoise (R)	.50	1.00
❏ 38	Butterfree (R)	.50	1.00
❏ 39	Charizard (R)	1.00	2.00
❏ 40	Charizard (R)	3.00	6.00
❏ 41	Clefable (R)	.50	1.00
❏ 42	Cloyster (R)	.50	1.00

❏ 43	Dragonite (R)	.50	1.00
❏ 44	Dugtrio (R)	.50	1.00
❏ 45	Fearow (R)	.50	1.00
❏ 46	Feraligatr (R)	.50	1.00
❏ 47	Feraligatr (R)	.50	1.00
❏ 48	Gengar (R)	.50	1.00
❏ 49	Golem (R)	.50	1.00
❏ 50	Kingler (R)	.50	1.00
❏ 51	Machamp (R)	.50	1.00
❏ 52	Magby (R)	.50	1.00
❏ 53	Meganium (R)	.50	1.00
❏ 54	Meganium (R)	.50	1.00
❏ 55	Mew (R)	.50	1.00
❏ 56	Mewtwo (R)	.50	1.00
❏ 57	Ninetales (R)	.50	1.00
❏ 58	Pichu (R)	.50	1.00
❏ 59	Pidgeot (R)	.50	1.00
❏ 60	Poliwrath (R)	.50	1.00
❏ 61	Raichu (R)	.50	1.00
❏ 62	Rapidash (R)	.50	1.00
❏ 63	Skarmony (R)	.50	1.00
❏ 64	Typhlosion (R)	.50	1.00
❏ 65	Typhlosion (R)	.50	1.00
❏ 66	Tyranitar (R)	.50	1.00
❏ 67	Venusaur (R)	.50	1.00
❏ 68	Venusaur (R)	.50	1.00
❏ 69	Vileplume (R)	.50	1.00
❏ 70	Weezing (R)	.50	1.00
❏ 71	Bayleef (U)	.20	.50
❏ 72	Chansey (U)	.20	.50
❏ 73	Charmeleon (U)	.20	.50
❏ 74	Croconaw (U)	.20	.50
❏ 75	Dragonair (U)	.20	.50
❏ 76	Electabuzz (U)	.20	.50
❏ 77	Flaafy (U)	.20	.50
❏ 78	Gloom (U)	.20	.50
❏ 79	Graveler (U)	.20	.50
❏ 80	Haunter (U)	.20	.50
❏ 81	Hitmonlee (U)	.20	.50
❏ 82	Ivysaur (U)	.20	.50
❏ 83	Jynx (U)	.20	.50
❏ 84	Kadabra (U)	.20	.50
❏ 85	Machoke (U)	.20	.50
❏ 86	Magmar (U)	.20	.50
❏ 87	Metapod (U)	.20	.50
❏ 88	Pidgeotto (U)	.20	.50
❏ 89	Poliwhirl (U)	.20	.50
❏ 90	Pupitar (U)	.20	.50
❏ 91	Quilava (U)	.20	.50
❏ 92	Wartortle (U)	.20	.50
❏ 93	Abra (C)	.10	.20
❏ 94	Bulbasaur (C)	.10	.20

❏ 95	Bulbasaur (C)	.10	.20
❏ 96	Caterpie (C)	.10	.20
❏ 97	Charmander (C)	.10	.20
❏ 98	Charmander (C)	.10	.20
❏ 99	Chikorita (C)	.10	.20
❏ 100	Chikorita (C)	.10	.20
❏ 101	Clefairy (C)	.10	.20
❏ 102	Corsola (C)	.10	.20
❏ 103	Cubone (C)	.10	.20
❏ 104	Cyndaquil (C)	.10	.20
❏ 105	Cyndaquil (C)	.10	.20
❏ 106	Diglett (C)	.10	.20
❏ 107	Dratini (C)	.10	.20
❏ 108	Ekans (C)	.10	.20
❏ 109	Gastly (C)	.10	.20
❏ 110	Geodude (C)	.10	.20
❏ 111	Goldeen (C)	.10	.20
❏ 112	Hoppip (C)	.10	.20
❏ 113	Houndour (C)	.10	.20
❏ 114	Koffing (C)	.10	.20
❏ 115	Krabby (C)	.10	.20
❏ 116	Larvitar (C)	.10	.20
❏ 117	Machop (C)	.10	.20
❏ 118	Magikarp (C)	.10	.20
❏ 119	Mareep (C)	.10	.20
❏ 120	Marill (C)	.10	.20
❏ 121	Meowth (C)	.10	.20
❏ 122	Oddish (C)	.10	.20
❏ 123	Pidgey (C)	.10	.20
❏ 124	Pikachu (C)	.50	1.00
❏ 125	Poliwag (C)	.10	.20
❏ 126	Ponyta (C)	.10	.20
❏ 127	Qwilfish (C)	.10	.20
❏ 128	Rattata (C)	.10	.20
❏ 129	Shellder (C)	.10	.20
❏ 130	Spearow (C)	.10	.20
❏ 131	Squirtle (C)	.10	.20
❏ 132	Squirtle (C)	.10	.20
❏ 133	Tauros (C)	.10	.20
❏ 134	Totodile (C)	.10	.20
❏ 135	Totodile (C)	.10	.20
❏ 136	Vulpix (C)	.10	.20
❏ 137	Bill's Maintenance (C)	.10	.20
❏ 138	Copycat (C)	.10	.20
❏ 139	Dual Ball (C)	.10	.20
❏ 140	Energy Removal 2 (U)	.20	.50
❏ 141	Energy Restore (U)	.20	.50
❏ 142	Mary's Impulse (U)	.20	.50
❏ 143	Master Ball (U)	.20	.50
❏ 144	Multi Technical (U)	.20	.50
❏ 145	Pokémon Nurse (U)	.20	.50

#	Card	Low	High
146	Pokemon Reversal (U)	.20	.50
147	Power Charge (U)	.20	.50
148	Professor Elm's (U)	.20	.50
149	Professor Oak's (U)	.20	.50
150	Strength Charm (U)	.20	.50
151	Super Scoop Up (U)	.20	.50
152	Warp Point (U)	.20	.50
153	Energy Search (C)	.10	.20
154	Full Heal (C)	.10	.20
155	Moo-moo Milk (C)	.10	.20
156	Potion (C)	.10	.20
157	Switch (C)	.10	.20
158	Darkness Energy (R)	.50	1.00
159	Metal Energy (R)	.50	1.00
160	Fire Energy	.10	.20
161	Rock Energy	.10	.20
162	Grass Energy	.10	.20
163	Lightning Energy	.10	.20
164	Psychic Energy	.10	.20
165	Water Energy	.10	.20

Expedition REVERSE FOIL

		Low	High
Complete Set (165)		90.00	175.00
Reverse Holofoils 2x regular			

Aquapolis

		Low	High
Complete set (186)		100.00	150.00
Booster Box (36 ct.)		75.00	100.00
Booster Pack (11 cards)		3.00	3.75
Common Cards (not listed) (C)		.10	.20
Uncommon Cards (not listed) (U)		.20	.50
Rare Cards (not listed) (R)		.50	1.00
Theme Decks		8.00	12.00
Reverse Set (151)		150.00	275.00
Reverse Holofoil 2x Regular version			
Box Toppers 2x Regular version			

#	Card	Low	High
1	Ampharos (R)	.50	1.00
2	Arcanine (R)	.50	1.00
3	Ariados (R)	.50	1.00
4	Azumarill (R)	.50	1.00
5	Bellossom (R)	.50	1.00
6	Blissey (R)	1.00	2.00
7	Donphan (R)	.50	1.00
8	Electrode (R)	.50	1.00
9	Elekid (R)	.50	1.00
10	Entei (R)	2.00	4.00
11	Espeon (R)	1.00	3.00
12	Exeggutor (R)	.50	1.00
13	Exeggutor (R)	.50	1.00
14	Houndoom (R)	.50	1.00
15	Houndoom (R)	.50	1.00
16	Hypno (R)	.50	1.00
17	Jumpluff (R)	.50	1.00
18	Jynx (R)	.50	1.00
19	Kingdra (R)	.50	1.00
20	Lanturn (R)	.50	1.00
21	Lanturn (R)	.50	1.00
22	Magneton (R)	.50	1.00
23	Muk (R)	.50	1.00
24	Nidoking (R)	.50	1.00
25	Ninetales (R)	.50	1.00
26	Octillery (R)	.50	1.00
27	Parasect (R)	.50	1.00
28	Porygon2 (R)	.50	1.00
29	Primeape (R)	.50	1.00
30	Quagsire (R)	.50	1.00
31	Rapidash (R)	.50	1.00
32	Scizor (R)	.50	1.00
33	Slowbro (H)	.50	1.00
34	Slowking (R)	.50	1.00
35	Steelix (R)	.50	1.00
36	Sudowoodo (R)	.50	1.00
37	Suicune (R)	2.00	4.00
38	Tentacruel (R)	.50	1.00
39	Togetic (R)	.50	1.00
40	Tyranitar (R)	.50	1.00
41	Umbreon (R)	.50	1.00
42	Victreebel (R)	.50	1.00
43	Vileplume (R)	.50	1.00
44	Zapdos (R)	.50	1.00
45	Bellsprout (U)	.20	.50
46	Dodrio (U)	.20	.50
47	Flaaffy (U)	.20	.50
48	Furret (U)	.20	.50
49	Gloom (U)	.20	.50
50A	Golduck (U)	.20	.50
50B	Golduck (U)	.20	.50
51	Growlithe (U)	.20	.50
52	Magnemite (U)	.20	.50
53	Marill (U)	.20	.50
54	Marowak (U)	.20	.50
55	Nidorino (U)	.20	.50
56	Pupitar (U)	.20	.50
57	Scyther (U)	.20	.50
58	Seadra (U)	.20	.50
59	Seaking (U)	.20	.50
60	Skiploom (U)	.20	.50
61	Smoochum (U)	.20	.50
62	Spinarak (U)	.20	.50
63	Tyrogue (U)	.20	.50
64	Voltorb (U)	.20	.50
65	Weepingbell (U)	.20	.50
66	Wooper (U)	.20	.50
67	Aipom (C)	.10	.20
68	Bellsprout (C)	.10	.20
69	Chansey (C)	.10	.20
70	Chinchou (C)	.10	.20
71	Chinchou (C)	.10	.20
72	Cubone (C)	.10	.20
73	Doduo (C)	.10	.20
74A	Drowzee (C)	.10	.20
74B	Drowzee (C)	.10	.20
75	Eevee (C)	.10	.20
76	Exeggcute (C)	.10	.20
77	Exeggcute (C)	.10	.20
78	Goldeen (C)	.10	.20
79	Grimer (C)	.10	.20
80	Growlithe (C)	.10	.20
81	Hitmonchan (C)	.10	.20
82	Hitmontop (C)	.10	.20
83	Hoppip (C)	.10	.20
84	Horsea (C)	.10	.20
85	Horsea (C)	.10	.20
86	Houndour (C)	.10	.20
87	Houndour (C)	.10	.20
88	Kangaskhan (C)	.10	.20
89	Larvitar (C)	.10	.20
90	Lickitung (C)	.10	.20
91	Magnemite (C)	.10	.20
92	Mankey (C)	.10	.20
93	Mareep (C)	.10	.20
94	Miltank (C)	.10	.20
95A	Mr. Mime (C)	.10	.20
95B	Mr. Mime (C)	.10	.20
96	Nidoran (C)	.10	.20
97	Oddish (C)	.10	.20
98	Onix (C)	.10	.20
99	Paras (C)	.10	.20
100	Phanpy (C)	.10	.20
101	Pinsir (C)	.10	.20
102	Ponyta (C)	.10	.20
103A	Porygon (C)	.10	.20
103B	Porygon (C)	.10	.20
104	Psyduck (C)	.10	.20
105	Remoraid (C)	.10	.20
106	Scyther (C)	.10	.20
107	Sentret (C)	.10	.20
108	Slowpoke (C)	.10	.20
109	Smeargle (C)	.10	.20
110	Sneasel (C)	.10	.20
111	Spinarak (C)	.10	.20
112	Tangela (C)	.10	.20
113	Tentacool (C)	.10	.20

❑ 114	Togepi (C)	.10	.25
❑ 115	Voltorb (C)	.10	.20
❑ 116	Vulpix (C)	.10	.20
❑ 117	Wooper (C)	.10	.20
❑ 118	Apricorn Forest (R)	.50	1.00
❑ 119	Darkness Cube (U)	.20	.50
❑ 120	Energy Switch (U)	.20	.50
❑ 121	Fighting Cube 01 (U)	.20	.50
❑ 122	Fire Cube 01 (U)	.20	.50
❑ 123	Forest Guardian (U)	.20	.50
❑ 124	Grass Cube 01 (U)	.20	.50
❑ 125	Healing Berry (U)	.20	.50
❑ 126	Juggler (U)	.20	.50
❑ 127	Lightning Cube 01 (U)	.20	.50
❑ 128	Memory Berry (U)	.20	.50
❑ 129	Metal Cube 01 (U)	.20	.50
❑ 130	Pokemon Fan Club (U)	.20	.50
❑ 131	Pokemon Park (U)	.20	.50
❑ 132	Psychic Cube 01 (U)	.20	.50
❑ 133	Seer (U)	.20	.50
❑ 134	Super Energy Removal 2 (U)	.20	.50
❑ 135	Time Shard (U)	.20	.50
❑ 136	Town Volunteers (U)	.20	.50
❑ 137	Traveling Salesman (U)	.20	.50
❑ 138	Undersea Ruins (U)	.20	.50
❑ 139	Power Plant (U)	.20	.50
❑ 140	Water Cube 1 (U)	.20	.50
❑ 141	Weakness Guard (U)	.20	.50

❑ 142	Darkness Energy (R)	.50	1.00
❑ 143	Metal Energy (R)	.50	1.00
❑ 144	Rainbow Energy (R)	.50	1.00
❑ 145	Boost Energy (U)	.20	.50
❑ 146	Crystal Energy (U)	.20	.50
❑ 147	Warp Energy (U)	.20	.50
❑ 148	Kingdra (holo) (R)	4.00	10.00
❑ 149	Lugia (holo) (R)	10.00	20.00
❑ 150	Nidoking (holo) (R)	4.00	10.00
❑ H1	Ampharos (holo) (R)	2.00	4.00
❑ H2	Arcanine (holo) (R)	2.00	4.00
❑ H3	Ariados (holo) (R)	2.00	4.00
❑ H4	Azumarill (holo) (R)	3.00	7.00
❑ H5	Bellossom (holo) (R)	2.00	4.00
❑ H6	Blissey (holo) (R)	2.00	4.00
❑ H7	Electrode (holo) (R)	2.00	4.00
❑ H8	Entei (holo) (R)	2.00	5.00
❑ H9	Espeon (holo) (R)	2.00	4.00
❑ H10	Exeggutor (holo) (R)	2.00	4.00
❑ H11	Houndoom (holo) (R)	2.00	4.00
❑ H12	Hypno (holo) (R)	2.00	4.00
❑ H13	Jumpluff (holo) (R)	2.00	4.00
❑ H14	Kingdra (holo) (R)	2.00	4.00

❑ H15	Lanturn (holo) (R)	2.00	4.00
❑ H16	Magneton (holo) (R)	2.00	4.00
❑ H17	Muk (holo) (R)	2.00	4.00
❑ H18	Nidoking (holo) (R)	2.00	4.00
❑ H19	Ninetales (holo) (R)	2.00	4.00
❑ H20	Octillery (holo) (R)	2.00	4.00
❑ H21	Scizor (holo) (R)	2.00	4.00
❑ H22	Slowking (holo) (R)	2.00	4.00
❑ H23	Steelix (holo) (R)	2.00	4.00
❑ H24	Sudowoodo (holo) (R)	2.00	4.00
❑ H25	Suicune (holo) (R)	2.00	4.00
❑ H26	Tentacruel (holo) (R)	2.00	4.00
❑ H27	Togetic (holo) (R)	2.00	4.00
❑ H28	Tyranitar (holo) (R)	2.00	4.00
❑ H29	Umbreon (holo) (R)	4.00	10.00
❑ H30	Victreebel (holo) (R)	2.00	4.00
❑ H31	Vileplume (holo) (R)	2.00	4.00
❑ H32	Zapdos (holo) (R)	2.00	4.00

Aquapolis REVERSE FOIL

Complete set (186)	150.00	250.00
Reverse Holofoil 2x Regular version		

Sky Ridge

Regular Set (150)	50.00	100.00
Complete Set (182)	100.00	175.00
Booster Box (36 packs)	75.00	90.00
Booster Pack (11 cards)	3.00	5.00
Common cards (not listed) (C)	.10	.20
Uncommon cards (not listed) (U)	.20	.50
Rare Cards (not listed) (R)	.50	1.00
Jumbo Box Toppers 1.5X Regular		
Reverse Holofoils 2X Regular		
❑ 1 Aerodactyl (R)	.50	1.00
❑ 2 Alakazam (R)	.50	1.00
❑ 3 Arcanine (R)	.50	1.00
❑ 4 Articuno (R)	.50	1.00
❑ 5 Beedrill (R)	.50	1.00
❑ 6 Crobat (R)	.50	1.00
❑ 7 Dewgong (R)	.50	1.00
❑ 8 Flareon (R)	.50	1.00
❑ 9 Forretress (R)	.50	1.00
❑ 10 Gengar (R)	.50	1.00
❑ 11 Gyarados (R)	.50	1.00
❑ 12 Houndoom (R)	.50	1.00
❑ 13 Jolteon (R)	.50	1.00

❑ 14	Kabutops (R)	.50	1.00
❑ 15	Ledian (R)	.50	1.00
❑ 16	Machamp (R)	.50	1.00
❑ 17	Magcargo (R)	.50	1.00
❑ 18	Magcargo (R)	.50	1.00

❑ 19	Magneton (R)	.50	1.00
❑ 20	Magneton (R)	.50	1.00
❑ 21	Moltres (R)	.50	1.00
❑ 22	Nidoqueen (R)	.50	1.00
❑ 23	Omastar (R)	.50	1.00
❑ 24	Piloswine (R)	.50	1.00
❑ 25	Politoed (R)	.50	1.00
❑ 26	Poliwrath (R)	.50	1.00
❑ 27	Raichu (R)	.50	1.00
❑ 28	Raikou (R)	.50	1.00
❑ 29	Rhydon (R)	.50	1.00
❑ 30	Starmie (R)	.50	1.00
❑ 31	Steelix (R)	.50	1.00
❑ 32	Umbreon (R)	.50	1.00
❑ 33	Vaporeon (R)	.50	1.00
❑ 34	Wigglytuff (R)	.50	1.00
❑ 35	Xatu (R)	.50	1.00
❑ 36	Electrode (U)	.20	.50
❑ 37	Kabuto (U)	.20	.50
❑ 38	Machoke (U)	.20	.50
❑ 39	Misdreavus (U)	.20	.50
❑ 40	Noctowl (U)	.20	.50
❑ 41	Omanyte (U)	.20	.50
❑ 42	Persian (U)	.20	.50
❑ 43	Piloswine (U)	.20	.50
❑ 44	Starmie (U)	.20	.50
❑ 45	Wobbuffet (U)	.20	.50
❑ 46	Abra (C)	.10	.20
❑ 47	Buried Fossil (C)	.10	.20
❑ 48	Cleffa (C)	.10	.20

❑ 49	Delibird (C)	.10	.20
❑ 50	Diglett (C)	.10	.20
❑ 51	Ditto (C)	.10	.20
❑ 52	Dugtrio (C)	.10	.20
❑ 53	Dunsparce (C)	.10	.20
❑ 54	Eevee (C)	.10	.20
❑ 55	Farfetch'd (C)	.10	.20
❑ 56	Forretress (C)	.10	.20
❑ 57	Gastly (C)	.10	.20
❑ 58	Girafarig (C)	.10	.20
❑ 59	Gligar (C)	.10	.20
❑ 60	Golbat (C)	.10	.20
❑ 61	Granbull (C)	.10	.20
❑ 62	Growlithe (C)	.10	.20
❑ 63	Haunter (C)	.10	.20
❑ 64	Heracross (C)	.10	.20
❑ 65	Hoothoot (C)	.10	.20
❑ 66	Houndour (C)	.10	.20
❑ 67	Igglybuff (C)	.10	.20
❑ 68	Jigglypuff (C)	.10	.20
❑ 69	Kadabra (C)	.10	.20

❏ 70	Kakuna (C)	.10	.20
❏ 71	Lapras (C)	.10	.20
❏ 72	Ledyba (C)	.10	.20
❏ 73	Ledyba (L)	.10	.20
❏ 74	Machop (C)	.10	.20
❏ 75	Magikarp (C)	.10	.20
❏ 76	Magnemite (C)	.10	.20
❏ 77	Mantine (C)	.10	.20
❏ 78	Meowth (C)	.10	.20
❏ 79	Murkrow (C)	.10	.20
❏ 80	Natu (C)	.10	.20
❏ 81	Nidoran F (C)	.10	.20
❏ 82	Nidoran F (C)	.10	.20
❏ 83	Nidorina (C)	.10	.20
❏ 84	Pikachu (C)	.10	.50
❏ 85	Pineco (C)	.10	.20
❏ 86	Pineco (C)	.10	.20
❏ 87	Poliwag (C)	.10	.20
❏ 88	Poliwhirl (C)	.10	.20
❏ 89	Raticate (C)	.10	.20
❏ 90	Rattata (C)	.10	.20
❏ 91	Rhyhorn (C)	.10	.20
❏ 92	Sandshrew (C)	.10	.20
❏ 93	Sandslash (C)	.10	.20
❏ 94	Seel (C)	.10	.20
❏ 95	Seel (C)	.10	.20
❏ 96	Shuckle (C)	.10	.20
❏ 97	Skarmory (C)	.10	.20
❏ 98	Slugma (C)	.10	.20
❏ 99	Slugma (C)	.10	.20
❏ 100	Snorlax (C)	.10	.20
❏ 101	Snubbull (C)	.10	.20

❏ 102	Stantler (C)	.10	.20
❏ 103	Staryu (C)	.10	.20
❏ 104	Staryu (C)	.10	.20
❏ 105	Sunflora (C)	.10	.20
❏ 106	Sunkern (C)	.10	.20
❏ 107	Swinub (C)	.10	.20
❏ 108	Swinub (C)	.10	.20
❏ 109	Teddiursa (C)	.10	.20
❏ 110	Ursaring (C)	.10	.20
❏ 111	Venomoth (C)	.10	.20
❏ 112	Venonat (C)	.10	.20
❏ 113	Voltorb (C)	.10	.20
❏ 114	Weedle (C)	.10	.20
❏ 115	Weedle (C)	.10	.20
❏ 116	Yanma (C)	.10	.20
❏ 117	Zubat (C)	.10	.20
❏ 118	Zubat (C)	.10	.20
❏ 119	Ancient Ruins (U)	.20	.50
❏ 120	Relic Hunter (U)	.20	.50

❏ 121	Apricorn (U)	.20	.50
❏ 122	Cyrstal Shard (U)	.20	.50
❏ 123	Desert Shaman (U)	.20	.50
❏ 124	Fast Ball (U)	.20	.50
❏ 125	Fisherman (U)	.20	.50
❏ 126	Friend Ball (U)	.20	.50
❏ 127	Hyper Potion (U)	.20	.50

❏ 128	Lure Ball (U)	.20	.50
❏ 129	Miracle Sphere (Alpha) (U)	.20	.50
❏ 130	Miracle Sphere (Beta) (U)	.20	.50
❏ 131	Miracle Sphere (Gamma)(U)	.20	.50
❏ 132	Mirage Stadium (U)	.20	.50
❏ 133	Mystery Plate (Alpha) (U)	.20	.50
❏ 134	Mystery Plate (Beta) (U)	.20	.50
❏ 135	Mystery Plate (Gamma) (U)	.20	.50
❏ 136	Mystery Plate (Delta) (U)	.20	.50
❏ 137	Mystery Zone (U)	.20	.50
❏ 138	Oracle (U)	.20	.50
❏ 139	Star Piece (U)	.20	.50
❏ 140	Underground Expedition (U)	.20	.50
❏ 141	Underground Lake (U)	.20	.50
❏ 142	Bounce Energy (U)	.20	.50
❏ 143	Cyclone Energy (U)	.20	.50
❏ 144	Retro Energy (U)	.20	.50
❏ 145	Celebi (holo) (R)	10.00	20.00
❏ 146	Charizard (holo) (R)	20.00	40.00
❏ 147	Crobat (holo) (R)	7.00	14.00
❏ 148	Golem (holo) (R)	4.00	8.00
❏ 149	Ho-oh (holo) (R)	3.00	6.00
❏ 150	Kabutops (holo) (R)	7.00	14.00
❏ H1	Alakazam (holo) (R)	2.00	4.00
❏ H2	Arcanine (holo) (R)	2.00	4.00
❏ H3	Articuno (holo) (R)	2.00	4.00
❏ H4	Beedrill (holo) (R)	2.00	4.00
❏ H5	Crobat (holo) (R)	2.00	4.00
❏ H6	Dewgong (holo) (R)	2.00	4.00
❏ H7	Flareon (holo) (R)	2.00	4.00
❏ H8	Forretress (holo) (R)	2.00	4.00
❏ H9	Gengar (holo) (R)	2.00	4.00
❏ H10	Gyarados (holo) (R)	2.00	4.00
❏ H11	Houndoom (holo) (R)	2.00	4.00
❏ H12	Jolteon (holo) (R)	2.00	4.00
❏ H13	Kabutops (holo) (R)	3.00	6.00
❏ H14	Ledian (holo) (R)	2.00	4.00
❏ H15	Machamp (holo) (R)	2.00	4.00
❏ H16	Magcargo (holo) (R)	2.00	4.00
❏ H17	Magcargo (holo) (R)	2.00	4.00
❏ H18	Magneton (holo) (R)	2.00	4.00
❏ H19	Magneton (holo) (R)	2.00	4.00
❏ H20	Moltres (holo) (R)	2.00	4.00
❏ H21	Nidoqueen (holo) (R)	2.00	4.00

❏ H22	Piloswine (holo) (R)	2.00	4.00
❏ H23	Politoed (holo) (R)	2.00	4.00
❏ H24	Poliwrath (holo) (R)	2.00	4.00
❏ H25	Raichu (holo) (R)	2.00	4.00
❏ H26	Raikou (holo) (R)	2.00	4.00
❏ H27	Rhydon (holo) (R)	2.00	4.00
❏ H28	Starmie (holo) (R)	2.00	4.00
❏ H29	Steelix (holo) (R)	2.00	4.00
❏ H30	Umbreon (holo) (R)	2.00	4.00
❏ H31	Vaporeon (holo) (R)	2.00	4.00
❏ H32	Xatu (holo) (R)	2.00	4.00

Skyridge REVERSE FOIL

Regular Set (150)		
Complete Set (182)	125.00	225.00
COMPLETE SET		
Reverse Holofoils 2X Regular		

EX Ruby & Sapphire

Complete Set (109)	75.00	130.00
Booster Box (36 ct.)	70.00	85.00
Booster Pack (9 cards)	3.00	4.00
Common Card (not listed) (C)	.10	.20
Uncommon Cards (not listed) (U)	.20	.50
Rare Cards (not listed) (R)	.50	1.00
Ruby Theme Deck	10.00	15.00
Sapphire Theme Deck	10.00	15.00
Reverse Holofoils 2X Regular		

❏ 1	Aggron (holo) (R)	2.00	4.00
❏ 2	Beautifly (holo) (R)	2.00	4.00
❏ 3	Blaziken (holo) (R)	4.00	10.00
❏ 4	Camerupt (holo) (R)	2.00	4.00
❏ 5	Delcatty (holo) (R)	3.00	6.00
❏ 6	Dustox (holo) (R)	2.00	4.00
❏ 7	Gardevoir (holo) (R)	2.00	4.00
❏ 8	Hariyama (holo) (R)	2.00	4.00
❏ 9	Manectric (holo) (R)	2.00	4.00
❏ 10	Mightyena (holo) (R)	2.00	4.00
❏ 11	Sceptile (holo) (R)	2.00	4.00
❏ 12	Slaking (holo) (R)	2.00	4.00
❏ 13	Swampert (holo) (R)	2.00	4.00
❏ 14	Wailord (holo) (R)	3.00	7.00
❏ 15	Blaziken (R)	.50	1.00
❏ 16	Breloom (R)	.50	1.00
❏ 17	Donphan (R)	.50	1.00
❏ 18	Nosepass (R)	.50	1.00
❏ 19	Pelipper (R)	.50	1.00
❏ 20	Sceptile (R)	.50	1.00
❏ 21	Seaking (R)	.50	1.00
❏ 22	Sharpedo (R)	.50	1.00
❏ 23	Swampert (R)	.50	1.00

❏ 24	Weezing (R)	.50	1.00
❏ 25	Aron (U)	.20	.50
❏ 26	Cascoon (U)	.20	.50
❏ 27	Combusken (U)	.20	.50
❏ 28	Combusken (U)	.20	.50
❏ 29	Delcatty (U)	.20	.50
❏ 30	Electrike (U)	.20	.50
❏ 31	Grovyle (U)	.20	.50
❏ 32	Grovyle (U)	.20	.50
❏ 33	Hariyama (U)	.20	.50
❏ 34	Kirlia (U)	.20	.50
❏ 35	Kirlia (U)	.20	.50
❏ 36	Lairon (U)	.20	.50
❏ 37	Lairon (U)	.20	.50
❏ 38	Linoone (U)	.20	.50
❏ 39	Manectric (U)	.20	.50
❏ 40	Marshtomp (U)	.20	.50
❏ 41	Marshtomp (U)	.20	.50
❏ 42	Mightyena (U)	.20	.50
❏ 43	Silcoon (U)	.20	.50
❏ 44	Skitty (U)	.20	.50
❏ 45	Slakoth (U)	.20	.50
❏ 46	Swellow (U)	.20	.50
❏ 47	Vigoroth (U)	.20	.50
❏ 48	Wailmer (U)	.20	.50
❏ 49	Aron (C)	.10	.20
❏ 50	Aron (C)	.10	.20
❏ 51	Carvanha (C)	.10	.20

Makuhita — 50 HP
BASIC
Fake Out — 10
Flip a coin. If heads, the Defending Pokémon is now Paralyzed.

❏ 52	Electrike (C)	.10	.20
❏ 53	Electrike (C)	.10	.20
❏ 54	Koffing (C)	.10	.20
❏ 55	Goldeen (C)	.10	.20
❏ 56	Makuhita (C)	.10	.20
❏ 57	Makuhita (C)	.10	.20
❏ 58	Makuhita (C)	.10	.20
❏ 59	Mudkip (C)	.10	.20
❏ 60	Mudkip (C)	.10	.20
❏ 61	Numel (C)	.10	.20
❏ 62	Phanpy (C)	.10	.20
❏ 63	Poochyena (C)	.10	.20
❏ 64	Poochyena (C)	.10	.20
❏ 65	Poochyena (C)	.10	.20
❏ 66	Ralts (C)	.10	.20
❏ 67	Ralts (C)	.10	.20
❏ 68	Ralts (C)	.10	.20
❏ 69	Shroomish (C)	.10	.20
❏ 70	Skitty (C)	.10	.20
❏ 71	Skitty (C)	.10	.20
❏ 72	Tailow (C)	.10	.20
❏ 73	Torchic (C)	.10	.20
❏ 74	Torchic (C)	.10	.20

❏ 75	Treecko (C)	.10	.20
❏ 76	Treecko (C)	.10	.20
❏ 77	Wingull (C)	.10	.20
❏ 78	Wurmple (C)	.10	.20
❏ 79	Zigzagoon (C)	.10	.20
❏ 80	Trainer: Energy Removal 2 (U)	.20	.50
❏ 81	Trainer: Energy Restore (U)	.20	.50
❏ 82	Trainer: Energy Switch (U)	.20	.50
❏ 83	Trainer: Lady Outing (U)	.20	.50
❏ 84	Trainer: Lum Berry (U)	.20	.50
❏ 85	Trainer: Oran Berry (U)	.20	.50
❏ 86	Trainer: Poke Ball (U)	.20	.50
❏ 87	Trainer: Pokemon Reversal (U)	.20	.50
❏ 88	Trainer: PokeNav (U)	.20	.50
❏ 89	Trainer: Professor Birch (U)	.20	.50
❏ 90	Trainer: Energy Search (C)	.10	.20
❏ 91	Trainer: Potion (C)	.10	.20
❏ 92	Trainer: Switch (C)	.10	.20
❏ 93	Darkness Energy (R)	.50	1.00
❏ 94	Metal Energy (R)	.50	1.00
❏ 95	Rainbow Energy (R)	.50	1.00
❏ 96	Chansey ex (holo) (R)	4.00	8.00
❏ 97	Electabuzz ex (holo) (R)	4.00	8.00
❏ 98	Hitmonchan ex (holo) (R)	5.00	10.00
❏ 99	Lapras ex (holo) (R)	4.00	10.00
❏ 100	Magmar ex (holo) (R)	4.00	10.00
❏ 101	Mewtwo ex (holo) (R)	7.50	15.00
❏ 102	Scyther ex (holo) (R)	7.50	15.00
❏ 103	Sneasel ex (holo) (R)	4.00	8.00
❏ 104	Grass Energy (C)	.10	.20
❏ 105	Fighting Energy (C)	.10	.20
❏ 106	Water Energy (C)	.10	.20
❏ 107	Psychic Energy (C)	.10	.20
❏ 108	Fire Energy (C)	.10	.20
❏ 109	Lightning Energy (C)	.10	.20

EX Ruby & Sapphire REVERSE FOIL

COMPLETE SET	125.00	225.00
Reverse Holofoils 2X Regular		

EX Sandstorm

Complete Set (100)	90.00	150.00
Booster Box (36 ct.)	65.00	90.00
Booster Pack (9 Cards)	3.00	4.00
Common Cards (not listed) (C)	.10	.20
Uncommon Cards (not listed) (U)	.20	.50
Rare Cards (not listed) (R)	.50	1.00
Reverse Foils (value 2x regular cards)		
❏ 1 Armaldo (holo) (R)	2.00	4.00
❏ 2 Cacturne (holo) (R)	2.00	4.00
❏ 3 Cradily (holo) (R)	2.00	4.00

Cacnea — 50 HP
BASIC
Poison Sting — 10
Flip a coin. If heads, the Defending Pokémon is now Poisoned.

❏ 4	Dusclops (holo) (R)	2.00	4.00
❏ 5	Flareon (holo) (R)	2.00	4.00
❏ 6	Jolteon (holo) (R)	2.00	4.00
❏ 7	Ludicolo (holo) (R)	2.00	4.00
❏ 8	Lunatone (holo) (R)	2.00	4.00
❏ 9	Mawile (holo) (R)	2.00	4.00
❏ 10	Sableye (holo) (R)	2.00	4.00
❏ 11	Seviper (holo) (R)	2.00	4.00
❏ 12	Shiftry (holo) (R)	2.00	4.00
❏ 13	Solrock (holo) (R)	2.00	4.00
❏ 14	Zangoose (holo) (R)	2.00	4.00
❏ 15	Arcanine (R)	.50	1.00
❏ 16	Espeon (R)	.50	1.00
❏ 17	Golduck (R)	.50	1.00
❏ 18	Kecleon (R)	.50	1.00
❏ 19	Omastar (R)	.50	1.00
❏ 20	Pichu (R)	.50	1.00
❏ 21	Sandslash (R)	.50	1.00
❏ 22	Shiftry (R)	.50	1.00
❏ 23	Steelix (R)	.50	1.00
❏ 24	Umbreon (R)	.50	1.00
❏ 25	Vaporeon (R)	.50	1.00
❏ 26	Wobbuffet (R)	.50	1.00
❏ 27	Anorith (U)	.20	.50
❏ 28	Anorith (U)	.20	.50
❏ 29	Arbok (U)	.20	.50
❏ 30	Azumarill (U)	.20	.50
❏ 31	Azuril (U)	.20	.50
❏ 32	Baltoy (U)	.20	.50
❏ 33	Breloom (U)	.20	.50

Aggron ex — 150 HP
STAGE 2 — Evolves from Lairon
Rend — 30
If the Defending Pokémon has any damage counters on it, this attack does 30 damage plus 30 more damage.
Metal Surge — 50
Does 20 damage to each of your opponent's Benched Pokémon. (Don't apply Weakness and Resistance for Benched Pokémon.)

❏ 34	Delcatty (U)	.20	.50
❏ 35	Electabuzz (U)	.20	.50
❏ 36	Elekid (U)	.20	.50
❏ 37	Fearow (U)	.20	.50
❏ 38	Illumise (U)	.20	.50
❏ 39	Kabuto (U)	.20	.50
❏ 40	Kirlia (U)	.20	.50
❏ 41	Lairon (U)	.20	.50
❏ 42	Lileep (U)	.20	.50
❏ 43	Lileep (U)	.20	.50
❏ 44	Linoone (U)	.20	.50
❏ 45	Lombre (U)	.20	.50
❏ 46	Lombre (U)	.20	.50
❏ 47	Murkrow (U)	.20	.50
❏ 48	Nuzleaf (U)	.20	.50
❏ 49	Nuzleaf (U)	.20	.50
❏ 50	Peliper (U)	.20	.50
❏ 51	Quilava (U)	.20	.50
❏ 52	Vigoroth (U)	.20	.50
❏ 53	Volbeat (U)	.20	.50
❏ 54	Wynaut (U)	.20	.50

❏ 55	Xatu (U)	.20	.50
❏ 56	Aron (C)	.10	.20
❏ 57	Cacnea (C)	.10	.20
❏ 58	Cacnea (U)	.10	.20
❏ 59	Cyndaquil (C)	.10	.20
❏ 60	Dunsparce (C)	.10	.20
❏ 61	Duskull (C)	.10	.20
❏ 62	Duskull (C)	.10	.20
❏ 63	Eevee (C)	.10	.20
❏ 64	Ekans (C)	.10	.20
❏ 65	Growlithe (C)	.10	.20
❏ 66	Lotad (C)	.10	.20
❏ 67	Lotad (C)	.10	.20
❏ 68	Marill (C)	.10	.20
❏ 69	Natu (C)	.10	.20
❏ 70	Omanyte (C)	.10	.20
❏ 71	Onix (C)	.10	.20
❏ 72	Pikachu (C)	.25	.50
❏ 73	Psyduck (C)	.10	.20
❏ 74	Ralts (C)	.10	.20
❏ 75	Sandshrew (C)	.10	.20
❏ 76	Seedot (C)	.10	.20
❏ 77	Seedot (C)	.10	.20
❏ 78	Shroomish (C)	.10	.20
❏ 79	Skitty (C)	.10	.20
❏ 80	Slakoth (C)	.10	.20
❏ 81	Spearow (C)	.10	.20
❏ 82	Trapinch (C)	.10	.20
❏ 83	Wailmer (C)	.10	.20
❏ 84	Wingull (C)	.10	.20
❏ 85	Zigzagoon (C)	.10	.20
❏ 86	Double Full Heal (U)	.20	.50
❏ 87	Lanette's Net Search (U)	.20	.50
❏ 88	Rare Candy (U)	.20	.50
❏ 89	Wally's Training (U)	.20	.50
❏ 90	Claw Fossil (C)	.10	.20
❏ 91	Mysterious Fossil (C)	.10	.20
❏ 92	Root Fossil (C)	.10	.20
❏ 93	Multi Energy (R)	.50	1.00
❏ 94	Aerodactyl ex (holo) (R)	5.00	10.00
❏ 95	Aggron ex (holo) (R)	7.50	15.00
❏ 96	Gardevoir ex (holo) (R)	6.00	14.00
❏ 97	Kabutops ex (holo) (R)	6.00	13.00
❏ 98	Raichu ex (holo) (R)	12.50	25.00
❏ 99	Typhlosion ex (holo) (R)	10.00	20.00
❏ 100	Wailord ex (holo) (R)	30.00	50.00

EX Sandstorm Reverse Foil

COMPLETE SET (100)	150.00	250.00
Reverse Foils (value 2x regular cards)		

EX Dragon

Complete Set (100)	125.00	170.00
Booster Box (36 ct.)	80.00	100.00
Booster Pack (9 cards)	4.00	5.00
Common Cards (not listed)	.10	.20
Uncommon Cards (not listed)	.20	.50
Rare Cards (not listed) (R)	.50	1.00
FireFang Deck	8.00	12.00
WindBlast Deck	8.00	12.00
Reversed Foils (value 2x regular cards)		
❏ 1	Absol (holo) (R)	2.00	4.00
❏ 2	Altaria (holo) (R)	2.00	4.00
❏ 3	Crawdaunt (holo) (R)	2.00	4.00
❏ 4	Flygon (holo) (R)	2.00	4.00
❏ 5	Golem (holo) (R)	2.00	4.00
❏ 6	Grumpig (holo) (R)	2.00	4.00
❏ 7	Minun (holo) (R)	2.00	4.00
❏ 8	Plusle (holo) (R)	2.00	4.00
❏ 9	Roselia (holo) (R)	2.00	4.00
❏ 10	Salamence (holo) (R)	2.00	4.00
❏ 11	Shedinja (holo) (R)	2.00	4.00
❏ 12	Torkoal (holo) (R)	2.00	4.00

❏ 13	Crawdaunt (R)	.50	1.00
❏ 14	Dragonair (R)	.50	1.00
❏ 15	Flygon (R)	.50	1.00
❏ 16	Girafarig (R)	.50	1.00
❏ 17	Magneton (R)	.50	1.00
❏ 18	Ninjask (R)	.50	1.00
❏ 19	Salamence (R)	.50	1.00
❏ 20	Shelgon (R)	.50	1.00
❏ 21	Skarmory (R)	.50	1.00
❏ 22	Vibrava (R)	.50	1.00
❏ 23	Bagon (U)	.20	.50
❏ 24	Camerupt (U)	.20	.50
❏ 25	Combusken (U)	.20	.50
❏ 26	Dratini (U)	.20	.50
❏ 27	Flaaffy (U)	.20	.50
❏ 28	Forretress (U)	.20	.50
❏ 29	Graveler (U)	.20	.50
❏ 30	Graveler (U)	.20	.50
❏ 31	Grovyle (U)	.20	.50
❏ 32	Gyarados (U)	.20	.50
❏ 33	Horsea (U)	.20	.50
❏ 34	Houndoom (U)	.20	.50
❏ 35	Magneton (U)	.20	.50
❏ 36	Marshtomp (U)	.20	.50
❏ 37	Meditite (U)	.20	.50
❏ 38	Ninjask (U)	.20	.50
❏ 39	Seadra (U)	.20	.50
❏ 40	Seadra (U)	.20	.50
❏ 41	Shelgon (U)	.20	.50
❏ 42	Shelgon (U)	.20	.50
❏ 43	Shuppet (U)	.20	.50
❏ 44	Snorunt (U)	.20	.50

❏ 45	Swellow (U)	.20	.50
❏ 46	Vibrava (U)	.20	.50
❏ 47	Vibrava (U)	.20	.50
❏ 48	Whiscash (U)	.20	.50
❏ 49	Bagon (C)	.10	.20
❏ 50	Bagon (C)	.10	.20
❏ 51	Barboach (C)	.10	.20
❏ 52	Corphish (C)	.10	.20
❏ 53	Corphish (C)	.10	.20
❏ 54	Corphish (C)	.10	.20
❏ 55	Geodude (C)	.10	.20
❏ 56	Geodude (C)	.10	.20
❏ 57	Grimer (C)	.10	.20
❏ 58	Horsea (C)	.10	.20
❏ 59	Houndour (C)	.10	.20
❏ 60	Magikarp (C)	.10	.20
❏ 61	Magnemite (C)	.10	.20
❏ 62	Magnemite (C)	.10	.20
❏ 63	Magnemite (C)	.10	.20
❏ 64	Mareep (C)	.10	.20
❏ 65	Mudkip (C)	.10	.20
❏ 66	Nincada (C)	.10	.20
❏ 67	Nincada (C)	.10	.20
❏ 68	Nincada (C)	.10	.20
❏ 69	Numel (C)	.10	.20
❏ 70	Numel (C)	.10	.20
❏ 71	Pineco (C)	.10	.20
❏ 72	Slugma (C)	.10	.20
❏ 73	Spoink (C)	.10	.20
❏ 74	Spoink (C)	.10	.20
❏ 75	Swablu (C)	.10	.20
❏ 76	Taillow (C)	.10	.20
❏ 77	Torchic (C)	.10	.20
❏ 78	Trapinch (C)	.10	.20
❏ 79	Trapinch (C)	.10	.20
❏ 80	Treecko (C)	.10	.20
❏ 81	Wurmple (C)	.10	.20
❏ 82	Balloon Berry (C)	.10	.20
❏ 83	Buffer Piece (C)	.10	.20
❏ 84	Energy Recycle System (C)	.10	.20
❏ 85	High Pressure System (C)	.10	.20
❏ 86	Low Pressure System (C)	.10	.20
❏ 87	Mr. Briney's Compassion (C)	.10	.20
❏ 88	TV Reporter (C)	.10	.20
❏ 88R	TV Reporter (Rev. Foil)	30.00	60.00
❏ 89	Ampharos ex (holo) (R)	6.00	12.00
❏ 90	Dragonite ex (holo) (R)	15.00	30.00
❏ 91	Golem ex (holo) (R)	10.00	20.00
❏ 92	Kingdra ex (holo) (R)	4.00	8.00
❏ 93	Latias ex (holo) (R)	10.00	20.00
❏ 94	Latios ex (holo) (R)	10.00	20.00
❏ 95	Magcargo ex (holo) (R)	4.00	8.00
❏ 96	Muk ex (holo) (R)	4.00	8.00
❏ 97	Rayquaza ex (holo) (R)	10.00	20.00
❏ 98	Charmander (holo) (R)	4.00	8.00
❏ 99	Charmeleon (holo) (R)	4.00	8.00
❏ 100	Charizard (holo) (R)	20.00	40.00

EX Dragon REVERSE FOIL

COMPLETE SET(100)	200.00	300.00
Reversed Foils (value 2x regular cards)		

EX Team Magma Vs Team Aqua

Complete Set (97)	85.00	175.00
Complete Set with Rev. Foils (185)	175.00	275.00
Booster Box (36 ct)	60.00	80.00
Booster Pack (9 cards)	3.00	3.50
Team Aqua Deck	9.00	12.00
Team Magma Deck	9.00	12.00
Common Cards (not listed) (C)	.10	.20
Uncommon Cards (not listed) (U)	.20	.50
Rare Cards (not listed) (R)	.50	1.00
Reversed Foils (value 2x regular cards)		

TEAM AQUA'S Cacturne 80 HP

STAGE 1

Dark Bind 10
You may discard a ⚫ Energy card attached to Team Aqua's Cacturne. If you do, the Defending Pokémon is now Paralyzed.

Poison Barb 40
The Defending Pokémon is now Poisoned.

❏ 1	Team Aqua's Cacturne (holo) (R)	2.00	4.00
❏ 2	Team Aqua's Crawdaunt (holo) (R)	2.00	4.00
❏ 3	Team Aqua's Kyogre (holo) (R)	3.00	6.00
❏ 4	Team Aqua's Manectric (holo) (R)	2.00	4.00
❏ 5	Team Aqua's Sharpedo (holo) (R)	3.00	6.00
❏ 6	Team Aqua's Walrein (holo) (R)	2.00	4.00
❏ 7	Team Magma's Aggron (holo) (R)	3.00	4.00
❏ 8	Team Magma's Claydol (holo) (R)	2.00	4.00
❏ 9	Team Magma's Groudon (holo) (R)	4.00	8.00
❏ 10	Team Magma's Houndoom (holo) (R)	2.00	4.00
❏ 11	Team Magma's Rhydon (holo) (R)	2.00	4.00
❏ 12	Team Magma's Torkoal (holo) (R)	2.00	4.00
❏ 13	Raichu (R)	1.00	2.00
❏ 14	Team Aqua's Crawdaunt (R)	.50	1.00
❏ 15	Team Aqua's Mightyena (R)	.50	1.00
❏ 16	Team Aqua's Sealeo (R)	.50	1.00
❏ 17	Team Aqua's Seviper (R)	.50	1.00
❏ 18	Team Aqua's Sharpedo (R)	.50	1.00
❏ 19	Team Magma's Camerupt (R)	.50	1.00
❏ 20	Team Magma's Lairon (R)	.50	1.00
❏ 21	Team Magma's Mightyena (R)	.50	1.00
❏ 22	Team Magma's Rhydon (R)	.50	1.00
❏ 23	Team Magma's Zangoose (R)	.50	1.00
❏ 24	Team Aqua's Cacnea (U)	.20	.50
❏ 25	Team Aqua's Carvanha (U)	.20	.50
❏ 26	Team Aqua's Corphish (U)	.20	.50
❏ 27	Team Aqua's Electrike (U)	.20	.50
❏ 28	Team Aqua's Lantura (U)	.20	.50
❏ 29	Team Aqua's Manectric (U)	.20	.50
❏ 30	Team Aqua's Mightyena (U)	.20	.50
❏ 31	Team Aqua's Sealeo (U)	.20	.50

TEAM MAGMA's Rhydon 80 HP

STAGE 1

Second Strike 20+
If the Defending Pokémon already has at least 2 damage counters on it, this attack does 20 damage plus 20 more damage.

Land Crush 60
Flip a coin. If tails, discard an Energy card attached to Team Magma's Rhydon.

❏ 32	Team Magma's Baltoy (U)	.20	.50
❏ 33	Team Magma's Claydol (U)	.20	.50
❏ 34	Team Magma's Houndoom (U)	.20	.50
❏ 35	Team Magma's Houndour (U)	.20	.50
❏ 36	Team Magma's Lairon (U)	.20	.50
❏ 37	Team Magma's Mightyena (U)	.20	.50
❏ 38	Team Magma's Rhyhorn (U)	.20	.50
❏ 39	Bulbasaur (C)	.10	.20
❏ 40	Cubone (C)	.10	.20
❏ 41	Jigglypuff (C)	.10	.20
❏ 42	Meowth (C)	.10	.20
❏ 43	Pikachu (C)	.10	.20
❏ 44	Psyduck (C)	.10	.20
❏ 45	Slowpoke (C)	.10	.20
❏ 46	Squirtle (C)	.10	.20
❏ 47	Team Aqua's Carvanha (C)	.10	.20
❏ 48	Team Aqua's Carvanha (C)	.10	.20
❏ 49	Team Aqua's Chinchou (C)	.10	.20
❏ 50	Team Aqua's Corphish (C)	.10	.20
❏ 51	Team Aqua's Corphish (C)	.10	.20
❏ 52	Team Aqua's Electrike (C)	.10	.20
❏ 53	Team Aqua's Electrike (C)	.10	.20
❏ 54	Team Aqua's Poochyena (C)	.10	.20
❏ 55	Team Aqua's Poochyena (C)	.10	.20
❏ 56	Team Aqua's Spheal (C)	.10	.20
❏ 57	Team Aqua's Spheal (C)	.10	.20
❏ 58	Team Magma's Aron (C)	.10	.20
❏ 59	Team Magma's Aron (C)	.10	.20
❏ 60	Team Magma's Baltoy (C)	.10	.20
❏ 61	Team Magma's Baltoy (C)	.10	.20

Meowth 50 HP

BASIC

Plunder 10
Before doing damage, discard all Trainer cards attached to the Defending Pokémon (before they affect the damage).

Scratch 20

❏ 62	Team Magma's Houndour (C)	.10	.20
❏ 63	Team Magma's Houndour (C)	.10	.20
❏ 64	Team Magma's Numel (C)	.10	.20
❏ 65	Team Magma's Poochyena (C)	.10	.20
❏ 66	Team Magma's Poochyena (C)	.10	.20
❏ 67	Team Magma's Rhyhorn (C)	.10	.20
❏ 68	Team Magma's Rhyhorn (C)	.10	.20
❏ 69	Team Aqua Schemer (U)	.20	.50
❏ 70	Team Magma Schemer (U)	.20	.50
❏ 71	Archie (U)	.20	.50
❏ 72	Dual Ball (U)	.20	.50
❏ 73	Maxie (U)	.20	.50
❏ 74	Strength Charm (U)	.20	.50
❏ 75	Team Aqua Ball (U)	.20	.50
❏ 76	Team Aqua Belt (U)	.20	.50
❏ 77	Team Aqua Conspirator (U)	.20	.50
❏ 78	Team Aqua Hideout (U)	.20	.50
❏ 79	Team Aqua Technical Machine 01 (U)	.20	.50
❏ 80	Team Magma Ball (U)	.20	.50
❏ 81	Team Magma Belt (U)	.20	.50
❏ 82	Team Magma Conspirator (U)	.20	.50
❏ 83	Team Magma Hideout (U)	.20	.50
❏ 84	Team Magma Tech. Machine 01 (U)	.20	.50
❏ 85	Warp Point (U)	.20	.50
❏ 86	Aqua Energy (U)	.20	.50
❏ 87	Magma Energy (U)	.20	.50
❏ 88	Double Rainbow Energy (R)	.50	1.00
❏ 89	Blaziken ex (holo) (R)	12.50	25.00
❏ 90	Cradily ex (holo) (R)	7.00	15.00
❏ 91	Entei ex (holo) (R)	12.00	20.00
❏ 92	Raikou ex (holo) (R)	10.00	20.00
❏ 93	Sceptile ex (holo) (R)	10.00	20.00
❏ 94	Suicune ex (holo) (R)	10.00	20.00
❏ 95	Swampert ex (holo) (R)	10.00	20.00
❏ 96	Absol (holo) (R)	6.00	10.00
❏ 97	Jirachi (holo) (R)	7.50	15.00

EX Team Magma vs Team Aqua REVERSE FOIL

COMPLETE SET (97)	150.00	250.00
Reversed Foils (value 2x regular cards)		

2004 EX Hidden Legends

Complete Set (102)	125.00	190.00
Booster Box (36 ct)	65.00	85.00
Booster Pack (9 cards)	3.00	4.00
Common Cards (Not Listed) (C)	.10	.20
Uncommon Cards (Not Listed) (U)	.20	.50
Rare Cards (not listed) (R)	.50	1.00
Forrest Guardian Deck	8.00	15.00
Wish Maker Deck	8.00	15.00
Reverse Foil Cards (2x value of regular cards)		

❏ 1	Banette (Holo) (R)	5.00	8.00
❏ 2	Claydol (Holo) (R)	4.00	8.00
❏ 3	Crobat (Holo) (R)	4.00	7.00
❏ 4	Dark Celebi (Holo) (R)	5.00	11.00
❏ 5	Electrode (Holo) (R)	4.00	7.00

Corsola 70 HP

BASIC

Coral Glow
Draw a number of cards up to the number of your opponent's Basic Pokémon in play. (You can't have more than 10 cards in your hand in this way.)

Surf 40

❏ 6	Exploud (Holo) (R)	4.00	8.00
❏ 7	Heracross (Holo) (R)	4.00	7.00
❏ 8	Jirachi (Holo) (R)	4.00	8.00
❏ 9	Machamp (Holo) (R)	4.00	8.00
❏ 10	Medicham (Holo) (R)	4.00	8.00
❏ 11	Metagross (Holo) (R)	5.00	9.00
❏ 12	Milotic (Holo) (R)	5.00	10.00
❏ 13	Pinsir (Holo) (R)	3.00	7.00
❏ 14	Shiftry (Holo) (R)	3.00	6.50
❏ 15	Walrein (Holo) (R)	4.00	7.00
❏ 16	Bellossom (R)	.50	1.00
❏ 17	Chimecho (R)	.50	1.00
❏ 18	Gorebyss (R)	.50	1.00

❏ 19	Huntail (R)	.50	1.00
❏ 20	Masquerian (R)	.50	1.00
❏ 21	Metang (R)	.50	1.00
❏ 22	Ninetales (R)	.50	1.00
❏ 23	Rain Castform (R)	.50	1.00
❏ 24	Relicanth (R)	.50	1.00
❏ 25	Snow-cloud Castform (R)	.50	1.00
❏ 26	Sunny Castform (R)	.50	1.00
❏ 27	Tropius (R)	.50	1.00
❏ 28	Beldum (U)	.20	.50
❏ 29	Beldum (U)	.20	.50
❏ 30	Castform (U)	.20	.50
❏ 31	Claydol (U)	.20	.50
❏ 32	Corsola (U)	.20	.50
❏ 33	Dodrio (U)	.20	.50
❏ 34	Glalie (U)	.20	.50
❏ 35	Gloom (U)	.20	.50
❏ 36	Golbat (U)	.20	.50
❏ 37	Igglybuff (U)	.20	.50
❏ 38	Lanturn (U)	.20	.50
❏ 39	Loudred (U)	.20	.50
❏ 40	Luvdisc (U)	.20	.50
❏ 41	Machoke (U)	.20	.50
❏ 42	Medicham (U)	.20	.50
❏ 43	Metang (U)	.20	.50
❏ 44	Metang (U)	.20	.50
❏ 45	Nuzleaf (U)	.20	.50
❏ 46	Rhydon (U)	.20	.50
❏ 47	Sealeo (U)	.20	.50
❏ 48	Spinda (U)	.20	.50
❏ 49	Starmie (U)	.20	.50
❏ 50	Swalot (U)	.20	.50

❏ 51	Tentacruel (U)	.20	.50
❏ 52	Baltoy (C)	.10	.20
❏ 53	Baltoy (C)	.10	.20
❏ 54	Beldum (C)	.10	.20
❏ 55	Chikorita (C)	.10	.20
❏ 56	Chinchou (C)	.10	.20
❏ 57	Chinchou (C)	.10	.20
❏ 58	Clamperl (C)	.10	.20
❏ 59	Cyndaquil (C)	.10	.20
❏ 60	Doduo (C)	.10	.20
❏ 61	Feebas (C)	.10	.20
❏ 62	Gulpin (C)	.10	.20
❏ 63	Jigglypuff (C)	.10	.20
❏ 64	Machop (C)	.10	.20
❏ 65	Meditite (C)	.10	.20
❏ 66	Meditite (C)	.10	.20
❏ 67	Minun (C)	.10	.20
❏ 68	Oddish (C)	.10	.20
❏ 69	Plusle (C)	.10	.20

❏ 70	Rhyhorn (C)	.10	.20
❏ 71	Seedot (C)	.10	.20
❏ 72	Shuppet (C)	.10	.20
❏ 73	Snorunt (C)	.10	.20
❏ 74	Spheal (C)	.10	.20
❏ 75	Staryu (C)	.10	.20
❏ 76	Surskit (C)	.10	.20

❏ 77	Tentacool (C)	.10	.20
❏ 78	Togepi (C)	.10	.20
❏ 79	Totodile (C)	.10	.20
❏ 80	Voltorb (C)	.10	.20
❏ 81	Vulpix (C)	.10	.20
❏ 82	Whismur (C)	.10	.20
❏ 83	Zubat (C)	.10	.20
❏ 84	Ancient Technical Machine [Ice] (U)	.20	.50
❏ 85	Ancient Technical Machine [Rock] (U)	.20	.50
❏ 86	Ancient Technical Machine [Steel] (U)	.20	.50
❏ 87	Ancient Tomb (U)	.20	.50
❏ 88	Desert Ruins (U)	.20	.50
❏ 89	Island Cave (U)	.20	.50
❏ 90	Life Herb (U)	.20	.50
❏ 91	Magnetic Storm (U)	.20	.50
❏ 92	Steven's Advice (U)	.20	.50
❏ 93	Groudon ex (Holo) (R)	8.00	15.00
❏ 94	Kyogre ex (Holo) (R)	8.00	15.00
❏ 95	Metagross ex (Holo) (R)	9.00	18.00
❏ 96	Ninetales ex (Holo) (R)	7.00	14.00
❏ 97	Regice ex (Holo) (R)	10.00	20.00
❏ 98	Regirock ex (Holo) (R)	7.50	15.00
❏ 99	Registeel ex (Holo) (R)	10.00	20.00
❏ 100	Vileplume ex (Holo) (R)	7.50	15.00
❏ 101	Wigglytuff ex (Holo) (R)	6.00	12.00
❏ 102	Groudon (Holo) (R)	6.00	12.00

2004 EX Hidden Legends REVERSE FOIL

Complete Set	150.00	250.00
COMPLETE SET (116)	150.00	250.00
Reverse Foil Cards (2x value of regular cards)		

2004 EX Fire Red

Complete Set (116)	100.00	220.00
Booster Box (36 packs)	80.00	100.00
Booster Pack (9 cards)	3.00	4.00
Common Cards (Not Listed)	.10	.20
Uncommon Cards (Not Listed)	.20	.50
Rare Cards (Not Listed)	1.00	2.00
Theme Deck	10.00	17.00
Reverse Foil Cards (2x value of regular cards)		
❏ 1 Beedrill (Holo) (R)	2.00	4.00
❏ 2 Butterfree (Holo) (R)	2.00	4.00

❏ 3	Dewgong (Holo) (R)	2.00	4.00
❏ 4	Ditto (Holo) (R)	2.00	4.00
❏ 5	Exeggutor (Holo) (R)	2.00	4.00
❏ 6	Kangaskhan (Holo) (R)	2.00	4.00
❏ 7	Marowak (Holo) (R)	2.00	4.00
❏ 8	Nidoking (Holo) (R)	2.00*	4.00
❏ 9	Nidoqueen (Holo) (R)	2.00	4.00
❏ 10	Pidgeot (Holo) (R)	2.00	4.00
❏ 11	Poliwrath (Holo) (R)	2.00	4.00
❏ 12	Raichu (Holo) (R)	3.00	6.00
❏ 13	Rapidash (Holo) (R)	2.00	4.00
❏ 14	Slowbro (Holo) (R)	2.00	4.00
❏ 15	Snorlax (Holo) (R)	2.00	4.00
❏ 16	Tauros (Holo) (R)	2.00	4.00
❏ 17	Victreebel (Holo) (R)	2.00	4.00
❏ 18	Arcanine (Holo) (R)	3.00	6.00
❏ 19	Chansey (Holo) (R)	2.00	4.00
❏ 20	Cloyster (Holo) (R)	2.00	4.00
❏ 21	Dodrio (Holo) (R)	2.00	4.00
❏ 22	Dugtrio (Holo) (R)	2.00	4.00
❏ 23	Farfetch'd (Holo) (R)	2.00	4.00
❏ 24	Fearow (Holo) (R)	2.00	4.00
❏ 25	Hypno (Holo) (R)	2.00	4.00
❏ 26	Kingler (Holo) (R)	2.00	4.00
❏ 27	Magneton (Holo) (R)	2.00	4.00

❏ 28	Primeape (Holo) (R)	2.00	4.00
❏ 29	Scyther (Holo) (R)	2.00	4.00
❏ 30	Tangela (Holo) (R)	2.00	4.00
❏ 31	Charmeleon (U)	.20	.50
❏ 32	Drowzee (U)	.20	.50
❏ 33	Exeggcute (U)	.20	.50
❏ 34	Haunter (U)	.20	.50
❏ 35	Ivysaur (U)	.20	.50
❏ 36	Kakuna (U)	.20	.50
❏ 37	Lickitung (U)	.20	.50
❏ 38	Mankey (U)	.20	.50
❏ 39	Metapod (U)	.20	.50
❏ 40	Nidorina (U)	.20	.50
❏ 41	Nidorino (U)	.20	.50
❏ 42	Onix (U)	.20	.50
❏ 43	Parasect (U)	.20	.50
❏ 44	Persian (U)	.20	.50
❏ 45	Pidgeotto (U)	.20	.50
❏ 46	Poliwhirl (U)	.20	.50
❏ 47	Porygon (U)	.20	.50
❏ 48	Raticate (U)	.20	.50
❏ 49	Venomoth (U)	.20	.50
❏ 50	Wartortle (U)	.20	.50
❏ 51	Weepinbell (U)	.20	.50
❏ 52	Wigglytuff (U)	.20	.50
❏ 53	Bellsprout (C)	.10	.20

#	Name		
❏ 54	Bulbasaur (C)	.10	.20
❏ 55	Bulbasaur (C)	.10	.20
❏ 56	Caterpie (C)	.10	.20
❏ 57	Charmander (C)	.10	.20
❏ 58	Charmander (C)	.10	.20
❏ 59	Clefairy (C)	.10	.20
❏ 60	Cubone (C)	.10	.20
❏ 61	Diglett (C)	.10	.20
❏ 62	Doduo (C)	.10	.20
❏ 63	Gastly (C)	.10	.20
❏ 64	Growlithe (C)	.10	.20
❏ 65	Jigglypuff (C)	.10	.20
❏ 66	Krabby (C)	.10	.20
❏ 67	Magikarp (C)	.10	.20
❏ 68	Magnemite (C)	.10	.20
❏ 69	Meowth (C)	.10	.20
❏ 70	Nidoran F (C)	.10	.20
❏ 71	Nidoran M (C)	.10	.20
❏ 72	Paras (C)	.10	.20
❏ 73	Pidgey (C)	.10	.20
❏ 74	Pikachu (C)	.10	.20
❏ 75	Poliwag (C)	.10	.20
❏ 76	Ponyta (C)	.10	.20
❏ 77	Rattata (C)	.10	.20
❏ 78	Seel (C)	.10	.20
❏ 79	Shellder (C)	.10	.20
❏ 80	Slowpoke (C)	.10	.20
❏ 81	Spearow (C)	.10	.20

TRAINER

Pokémon Reversal

Flip a coin. If heads, choose 1 of your opponent's Benched Pokémon and switch it with 1 of the Defending Pokémon. Your opponent chooses the Defending Pokémon to switch.

#	Name		
❏ 82	Squirtle (C)	.10	.20
❏ 83	Squirtle (C)	.10	.20
❏ 84	Venonat (C)	.10	.20
❏ 85	Voltorb (C)	.10	.20
❏ 86	Weedle (C)	.10	.20
❏ 87	Bill's Maintenance (U)	.20	.50
❏ 88	Celio's Network (U)	.20	.50
❏ 89	Energy Removal 2 (U)	.20	.50
❏ 90	Energy Switch (U)	.20	.50
❏ 91	EXP.ALL (U)	.20	.50
❏ 92	Great Ball (U)	.20	.50
❏ 93	Life Herb (U)	.20	.50
❏ 94	Mt. Moon (U)	.20	.50
❏ 95	Poke Ball (U)	.20	.50
❏ 96	PokeDex HANDY 909 (U)	.20	.50
❏ 97	Pokemon Reversal (U)	.20	.50
❏ 98	Professor Oak's Research (U)	.20	.50
❏ 99	Super Scoop Up (U)	.20	.50
❏ 100	VS Seeker (U)	.20	.50
❏ 101	Potion (C)	.10	.20
❏ 102	Switch (C)	.10	.20
❏ 103	Multi Energy (Holo) (R)	2.00	4.00
❏ 104	Blastoise ex (Holo) (R)	20.00	40.00

#	Name		
❏ 105	Charizard ex (Holo) (R)	75.00	125.00
❏ 106	Clefable ex (Holo) (R)	7.00	14.00
❏ 107	Electrode ex (Holo) (R)	7.00	14.00
❏ 108	Gengar ex (Holo) (R)	7.00	14.00
❏ 109	Gyarados ex (Holo) (R)	10.00	20.00
❏ 110	Mr. Mime ex (Holo) (R)	7.00	14.00
❏ 111	Mr. Mime ex (Holo) (R)	7.00	14.00
❏ 112	Venusaur ex (Holo) (R)	10.00	20.00
❏ 113	Chamander (Holo) (R)	5.00	8.00
❏ 114	Articuno ex (Holo) (R)	10.00	20.00
❏ 115	Moltres ex (Holo) (R)	10.00	20.00
❏ 116	Zapdos ex (Holo) (R)	10.00	20.00

2004 EX Fire Red Leaf Green REVERSE FOIL

COMPLETE SET (116)	200.00	275.00
Reverse Foil Cards (2x value of regular cards)		

2004 EX Team Rocket Returns

Complete Set (111)	170.00	220.00
Booster Box (36 packs)	70.00	90.00
Booster Pack (9 cards)	3.00	4.00
Common Cards (not listed) (C)	.10	.20
Uncommon Cards (not listed) (U)	.20	.50
Rare Cards (not listed) (R)	.50	1.00
Reverse Foil Cards (2x value of Regular cards)		

#	Name		
❏ 1	Azumaril (Holo) (R)	3.00	6.00
❏ 2	Dark Ampharos (Holo) (R)	3.00	6.50
❏ 3	Dark Crobat (Holo) (R)	4.00	8.00
❏ 4	Dark Electrode (Holo) (R)	6.00	8.00
❏ 5	Dark Houndoom (Holo) (R)	3.00	5.00
❏ 6	Dark Hypno (Holo) (R)	3.00	6.00
❏ 7	Dark Marowak (Holo) (R)	3.00	6.00
❏ 8	Dark Octillery (Holo) (R)	3.00	6.00
❏ 9	Dark Slowking (Holo) (R)	3.00	6.00
❏ 10	Ruckel's Scizor ex (Holo) (R)	3.00	6.00
❏ 10	Dark Steelix (Holo) (R)	5.00	8.00
❏ 11	Jumpluff (Holo) (R)	3.00	6.00
❏ 12	Kingdra (Holo) (R)	3.00	6.00
❏ 13	Piloswine (Holo) (R)	3.00	5.00
❏ 14	Togetic (Holo) (R)	3.00	5.00
❏ 15	Dark Dragonite (R)	.50	1.00
❏ 16	Dark Muk (R)	.50	1.00
❏ 17	Dark Raticate (R)	.50	1.00
❏ 18	Dark Sandslash (R)	.50	1.00
❏ 19	Dark Tyranitar (R)	.50	1.00
❏ 20	Dark Tyranitar (R)	.50	1.00
❏ 21	Delibird (R)	.50	1.00
❏ 22	Furret (R)	.50	1.00
❏ 23	Ledian (R)	.50	1.00
❏ 24	Magby (R)	.50	1.00

Azumarill   80 HP

STAGE 1

Froth
Once during your turn, when you play Azumarill from your hand to evolve 1 of your Active Pokémon, you may use this power. Each Defending Pokémon is now Paralyzed.

Water Punch   20+
Flip a coin for each ⚪ Energy attached to Azumarill. This attack does 20 damage plus 20 more damage for each heads.

Yanma   70 HP

BASIC

Quick Charge
Search your deck for up to 4 different types of basic Energy cards, show them to your opponent, and put them into your hand. Shuffle your deck afterward.

Swift   20
This attack's damage isn't affected by Weakness, Resistance, Poké-Powers, Poké-Bodies, or any other effects on the Defending Pokémon.

#	Name		
❏ 25	Misdreavus (R)	.50	1.00
❏ 26	Quagsire (R)	.50	1.00
❏ 27	Qwilfish (R)	.50	1.00
❏ 28	Yanma (R)	.50	1.00
❏ 29	Dark Arbok (U)	.20	.50
❏ 30	Dark Ariados (U)	.20	.50
❏ 31	Dark Dragonair (U)	.20	.50
❏ 32	Dark Dragonair (U)	.20	.50
❏ 33	Dark Flaafy (U)	.20	.50
❏ 34	Dark Golbat (U)	.20	.50
❏ 35	Dark Golduck (U)	.20	.50
❏ 36	Dark Gyarados (U)	.20	.50
❏ 37	Dark Houndoum (U)	.20	.50
❏ 38	Dark Magcargo (U)	.20	.50
❏ 39	Dark Magneton (U)	.20	.50
❏ 40	Dark Pupitar (U)	.20	.50
❏ 41	Dark Pupitar (U)	.20	.50
❏ 42	Dark Weezing (U)	.20	.50
❏ 43	Heracross (U)	.20	.50
❏ 44	Magmar (U)	.20	.50
❏ 45	Mantine (U)	.20	.50
❏ 46	Rocket's Meowth (U)	.20	.50
❏ 47	Rocket's Wobbuffet (U)	.20	.50
❏ 48	Seadra (U)	.20	.50
❏ 49	Skiploom (U)	.20	.50
❏ 50	Togepi (U)		
❏ 51	Cubone (C)	.10	.20
❏ 52	Dratini (C)	.10	.20
❏ 53	Dratini (C)	.10	.20
❏ 54	Drowzee (C)	.10	.20
❏ 55	Ekans (C)	.10	.20
❏ 56	Grimer (C)	.10	.20
❏ 57	Hoppip (C)	.10	.20
❏ 58	Horsea (C)	.10	.20
❏ 59	Houndour (C)	.10	.20
❏ 60	Houndour (C)	.10	.20
❏ 61	Koffing (C)	.10	.20
❏ 62	Larvitar (C)	.10	.20
❏ 63	Larvitar (C)	.10	.20
❏ 64	Ledyba (C)	.10	.20
❏ 65	Magicarp (C)	.10	.20
❏ 66	Magnemite (C)	.10	.20
❏ 67	Marrep (C)	.10	.20
❏ 68	Marril (C)	.10	.20
❏ 69	Onix (C)	.10	.20
❏ 70	Psyduck (C)	.10	.20
❏ 71	Rattata (C)	.10	.20
❏ 72	Rattata (C)	.10	.20
❏ 73	Remoraid (C)	.10	.20
❏ 74	Sandshrew (C)	.10	.20
❏ 75	Sentret (C)	.10	.20
❏ 76	Slowpoke (C)	.10	.20
❏ 77	Slugma (C)	.10	.20

❑ 78	Spinarak (C)	.10	.20
❑ 79	Swinub (C)	.10	.20
❑ 80	Voltorb (C)	.10	.20
❑ 81	Wooper (C)	.10	.20
❑ 82	Zubat (C)	.10	.20
❑ 83	Copycat (U)	.20	.50
❑ 84	Pokémon Retriever (U)	.20	.50
❑ 85	Pow! Hand Extension (U)	.20	.50
❑ 86	Rocket's Admin. (U)	.20	.50
❑ 87	Rocket's Hideout (U)	.20	.50
❑ 88	Rocket's Mission (U)	.20	.50
❑ 89	Rocket's Poke Ball (U)	.20	.50
❑ 90	Rocket's Tricky Gym (U)	.20	.50
❑ 91	Surprise! Time Machine (U)	.20	.50
❑ 92	Swoop! Teleporter (U)	.20	.50
❑ 93	Venture Bomb (U)	.20	.50
❑ 94	Dark Metal Energy (U)	.20	.50
❑ 95	R Energy (U)	.20	.50
❑ 96	Rocket's Articuno ex (Holo) (R)	7.50	15.00

❑ 97	Rocket's Entei ex (Holo) (R)	6.00	14.00
❑ 98	Rocket's Hitmonchan ex (Holo) (R)	6.00	12.00
❑ 99	Rocket's Mewtwo ex (Holo) (R)	10.00	20.00
❑ 100	Rocket's Moltres ex (Holo) (R)	10.00	20.00
❑ 101	Rocket's Scizor ex (Holo) (R)	7.50	15.00
❑ 102	Rocket's Scyther ex (Holo) (R)	5.00	10.00
❑ 103	Rocket's Sneasel ex (Holo) (R)	6.00	12.00
❑ 104	Rocket's Snorlax ex (Holo) (R)	6.00	12.00
❑ 105	Rocket's Suicune ex (Holo) (R)	7.50	15.00
❑ 106	Rocket's Zapdos ex (Holo) (R)	10.00	20.00
❑ 107	Shininy Mudkip	6.00	12.00
❑ 108	Shininy Torchic	6.00	12.00
❑ 109	Shininy Treecko	6.00	14.00
❑ 110	Charmeleon (SR)	3.00	6.00
❑ 111	Here comes Team Rocket! (SR)	6.00	14.00

2004 EX Team Rocket Returns REVERSE FOIL

COMPLETE SET (111)	200.00	300.00
Reverse Foil Cards (2x value of Regular cards)		

2004 EX Trainer Kit

Complete Set (60)	7.00	12.00
Common Cards (not listed)		
❑ 2	Latios (holo) (R)	2.00	5.00
❑ 4	Latias (holo) (R)	2.00	5.00

2005 EX Deoxys

Complete Set (108)	120.00	200.00
Booster Box (36 packs)	75.00	90.00

Booster Pack (9 cards)	3.00	4.00
Common Cards (not listed) (C)	.10	.20
Uncommon Cards (not listed) (U)	.20	.50
Rare Cards (not listed) (R)	.50	1.00
❑ 1	Altaria (Holo) (R)	2.00	4.00
❑ 2	Beautifly (Holo) (R)	3.00	6.00
❑ 3	Breloom (Holo) (R)	3.00	6.00
❑ 4	Camerupt (Holo) (R)	3.00	6.00
❑ 5	Claydol (Holo) (R)	3.00	6.00
❑ 6	Crawdaunt (Holo) (R)	3.00	6.00
❑ 7	Dusclops (Holo) (R)	3.00	6.00
❑ 8	Gyarados (Holo) (R)	4.00	8.00
❑ 9	Jirachi (Holo) (R)	3.00	6.00
❑ 10	Ludicolo (Holo) (R)	2.00	4.00
❑ 11	Metagross (Holo) (R)	5.00	10.00
❑ 12	Mightyena (Holo) (R)	3.00	6.00
❑ 13	Ninjask (Holo) (R)	3.00	6.00
❑ 14	Shedinja (Holo) (R)	3.00	6.00
❑ 15	Slaking (Holo) (R)	3.00	6.00
❑ 16	Deoxys (Normal) (R)	.50	1.00
❑ 17	Deoxys (Attack) (R)	.50	1.00
❑ 18	Deoxys (Defense) (R)	.50	1.00
❑ 19	Ludicolo (R)	.50	1.00
❑ 20	Magcargo (R)	.50	1.00
❑ 21	Pelipper (R)	.50	1.00
❑ 22	Rayquaza (R)	.50	1.00
❑ 23	Sableye (R)	.50	1.00
❑ 24	Seaking (R)	.50	1.00
❑ 25	Shiftry (R)	.50	1.00
❑ 26	Skarmory (R)	.50	1.00
❑ 27	Tropius (R)	.50	1.00
❑ 28	Whiscash (R)	.50	1.00
❑ 29	Xatu (R)	.50	1.00
❑ 96	Crobat ex (Holo) (R)	7.00	14.00

❑ 97	Deoxys ex (Normal) (Holo) (R)	7.00	14.00
❑ 98	Deoxys ex (Attack) (Holo) (R)	7.00	14.00
❑ 99	Deoxys ex (Defense) (Holo) (R)	7.00	14.00
❑ 100	Hariyama ex (Holo) (R)	7.00	14.00
❑ 101	Manectric ex (Holo) (R)	7.00	14.00
❑ 102	Rayquaza ex (Holo) (R)	12.00	20.00
❑ 103	Salamence ex (Holo) (R)	12.00	25.00
❑ 104	Sharpedo ex (Holo) (R)	10.00	20.00
❑ 105	Latias (Holo) (R)	20.00	40.00
❑ 106	Latios (Holo) (R)	20.00	40.00
❑ 107	Rayquaza (Holo) (R)	25.00	50.00
❑ 108	Rocket's Raikou ex (Holo) (R)	7.00	14.00

2005 EX Deoxys REVERSE FOIL

COMPLETE SET (108)	150.00	250.00
FOILS 2X Regular Cards		

2005 EX Emerald

Complete Set (107)	125.00	175.00
Booster Box (36 packs)	72.00	90.00
Booster Pack (9 cards)	3.25	3.75
Theme Deck	9.00	11.50
Common Cards (not listed) (C)	.10	.20
Uncommon Cards (not listed) (U)	.20	.50
Rare Cards (not listed) (R)	.50	1.00
❑ 1	Blaziken (Holo) (R)	2.00	4.00
❑ 2	Deoxys (Holo) (R)	2.00	4.00
❑ 3	Exploud (Holo) (R)	2.00	4.00
❑ 4	Gardevoir (Holo) (R)	2.00	4.00
❑ 5	Groudon (Holo) (R)	2.00	4.00
❑ 6	Kyogre (Holo) (R)	2.00	4.00
❑ 7	Manectric (Holo) (R)	2.00	4.00
❑ 8	Milotic (Holo) (R)	3.00	6.00
❑ 9	Rayquaza (Holo) (R)	3.00	6.00
❑ 10	Sceptile (Holo) (R)	2.00	4.00
❑ 11	Swampert (Holo) (R)	2.00	4.00
❑ 12	Chimecho (R)	.50	1.00
❑ 13	Glalie (R)	.50	1.00
❑ 14	Groudon (R)	.50	1.00
❑ 15	Kyogre (R)	.50	1.00
❑ 16	Manectric (R)	.50	1.00

❑ 17	Nosepass (R)	.50	1.00
❑ 18	Relicanth (R)	.50	1.00
❑ 19	Rhydon (R)	.50	1.00
❑ 20	Seviper (R)	.50	1.00
❑ 21	Zangoose (R)	.50	1.00
❑ 22	Breloom (U)	.20	.50
❑ 23	Camerupt (U)	.20	.50
❑ 24	Claydol (U)	.20	.50
❑ 25	Combusken (U)	.20	.50
❑ 26	Dodrio (U)	.20	.50
❑ 27	Electrode (U)	.20	.50
❑ 28	Grovyle (U)	.20	.50
❑ 29	Grumpig (U)	.20	.50
❑ 30	Grumpig (U)	.20	.50
❑ 31	Hariyama (U)	.20	.50
❑ 32	Illumise (U)	.20	.50
❑ 33	Kirlia (U)	.20	.50
❑ 34	Linoone (U)	.20	.50
❑ 35	Loudred (U)	.20	.50
❑ 36	Marshtomp (U)	.20	.50
❑ 37	Minun (U)	.20	.50
❑ 38	Ninetales (U)	.20	.50
❑ 39	Plusle (U)	.20	.50
❑ 40	Swalot (U)	.20	.50
❑ 41	Swellow (U)	.20	.50
❑ 42	Volbeat (U)	.20	.50

❑ 43	Baltoy (C)	.10	.20
❑ 44	Cacnea (C)	.10	.20
❑ 45	Doduo (C)	.10	.20
❑ 46	Duskull (C)	.10	.20
❑ 47	Electrike (C)	.10	.20
❑ 48	Electrike (C)	.10	.20
❑ 49	Feebas (C)	.10	.20
❑ 50	Feebas (C)	.10	.20
❑ 51	Gulpin (C)	.10	.20
❑ 52	Larvitar (C)	.10	.20
❑ 53	Luvdisc (C)	.10	.20
❑ 54	Makuhita (C)	.10	.20
❑ 55	Meditite (C)	.10	.20
❑ 56	Mudkip (C)	.10	.20
❑ 57	Numel (C)	.10	.20
❑ 58	Numel (C)	.10	.20
❑ 59	Pichu (C)	.10	.20
❑ 60	Pikachu (C)	.10	.20
❑ 61	Ralts (C)	.10	.20
❑ 62	Rhyhorn (C)	.10	.20
❑ 63	Shroomish (C)	.10	.20
❑ 64	Snorunt (C)	.10	.20
❑ 65	Spoink (C)	.10	.20
❑ 66	Spoink (C)	.10	.20
❑ 67	Swablu (C)	.10	.20
❑ 68	Taillow (C)	.10	.20
❑ 69	Torchic (C)	.10	.20
❑ 70	Treecko (C)	.10	.20

❑ 71	Voltorb (C)	.10	.20
❑ 72	Vulpix (C)	.10	.20
❑ 73	Whismur (C)	.10	.20
❑ 74	Zigzagoon (C)	.10	.20
❑ 75	Battle Frontier (U)	.20	.50
❑ 76	Double Full Heal (U)	.20	.50
❑ 77	Lanette's Net Search (U)	.20	.50
❑ 78	Lum Berry (U)	.20	.50
❑ 79	Mr. Stone's Project (U)	.20	.50
❑ 80	Oran Berry (U)	.20	.50
❑ 81	Pokenav (U)	.20	.50
❑ 82	Professor Birch (U)	.20	.50
❑ 83	Rare Candy (U)	.20	.50
❑ 84	Scott (U)	.20	.50
❑ 85	Wally's Training (U)	.20	.50
❑ 86	Darkness Energy (R)	.50	1.00
❑ 87	Double Rainbow Energy (R)	.50	1.00
❑ 88	Metal Energy (R)	.50	1.00
❑ 89	Mutli Energy (R)	.50	1.00
❑ 90	Altaria ex (Holo) (R)	6.00	12.00
❑ 91	Cacturne ex (Holo) (R)	5.00	10.00
❑ 92	Cameruptex (Holo) (R)	6.00	12.00
❑ 93	Deoxys ex (Holo) (R)	5.00	10.00

❑ 94	Dusclops ex (Holo) (R)	5.00	12.00
❑ 95	Medicham ex (Holo) (R)	10.00	18.00
❑ 96	Milotic ex (Holo) (R)	6.00	12.00
❑ 97	Raichu ex (Holo) (R)	10.00	20.00
❑ 98	Regice ex (Holo) (R)	6.00	12.00
❑ 99	Regirock (Holo) (R)	5.00	10.00
❑ 100	Registeel (Holo) (R)	7.00	16.00
❑ 101	Grass Energy (Holo)	1.00	2.00
❑ 102	Fire Energy (Holo)	1.00	2.00
❑ 103	Water Energy (Holo)	1.00	2.00
❑ 104	Lightning Energy (Holo)	1.00	2.00
❑ 105	Psychic Energy (Holo)	1.00	2.00
❑ 106	Fighting Energy (Holo)	1.00	2.00
❑ 107	Farfetch's (Holo) (R)	2.00	5.00

2005 EX Emerald REVERSE FOIL

COMPLETE SET (107)		150.00	250.00
Reverse FOILS 2X Regular cards			
❑ 54	Makuhita (C)		
❑ 67	Swablu (C)		

2005 EX Unseen Forces

Complete Set (117)		120.00	200.00
Booster Box (36 Packs)		75.00	105.00
Booster Pack (9 cards)		3.00	3.75
Common Cards (not listed) (C)		.10	.20
Uncommon Cards (not listed) (U)		.20	.50
Rare Cards (not listed) (R)		.50	1.00
❑ 1	Ampharos (Holo) (R)	3.00	5.00
❑ 2	Ariados (Holo) (R)	3.00	5.00
❑ 3	Bellossom (Holo) (R)	3.00	5.00
❑ 4	Feraligatr (Holo) (R)	3.50	5.00
❑ 5	Flareon (Holo) (R)	3.00	5.00
❑ 6	Forretress (Holo) (R)	3.00	5.00
❑ 7	Houndoom (Holo) (R)	3.00	5.00
❑ 8	Jolteon (Holo) (R)	3.00	5.00
❑ 9	Meganium (Holo) (R)	3.00	6.00
❑ 10	Octillery (Holo) (R)	3.00	5.00
❑ 11	Poliwrath (Holo) (R)	3.00	5.00
❑ 12	Porygon 2 (Holo) (R)	3.00	5.00
❑ 13	Slowbro (Holo) (R)	2.00	4.00
❑ 14	Slowking (Holo) (R)	2.00	4.00
❑ 15	Sudowoodo (Holo) (R)	3.00	5.00
❑ 16	Sunflora (Holo) (R)	3.00	5.00
❑ 17	Typhlosion (Holo) (R)	3.50	5.00
❑ 18	Ursaring (Holo) (R)	3.00	5.00

❑ 19	Vaporeon (Holo) (R)	3.00	5.00
❑ 20	Chansey (R)	.50	1.00
❑ 21	Cleffa (R)	.50	1.00
❑ 22	Electabuzz (R)	.50	1.00
❑ 23	Elekid (R)	.50	1.00

❑ 24	Hitmonchan (R)	.50	1.00
❑ 25	Hitmonlee (R)	.50	1.00
❑ 26	Hitmontop (R)	.50	1.00
❑ 27	Ho-Oh (R)	.50	1.00
❑ 28	Jynx (R)	.50	1.00
❑ 29	Lugia (R)	.50	1.00
❑ 30	Murkrow (R)	.50	1.00
❑ 31	Smoochum (R)	.50	1.00
❑ 32	Stantler (R)	.50	1.00
❑ 33	Tyrogue (R)	.50	1.00
❑ 34	Aipom (U)	.20	.50
❑ 35	Bayleef (U)	.20	.50
❑ 36	Clefable (U)	.20	.50
❑ 37	Corsola (U)	.20	.50
❑ 38	Croconaw (U)	.20	.50
❑ 39	Granbull (U)	.20	.50
❑ 40	Lanturn (U)	.20	.50
❑ 41	Magcargo (U)	.20	.50
❑ 42	Miltank (U)	.20	.50
❑ 43	Noctowl (U)	.20	.50
❑ 44	Quagsire (U)	.20	.50
❑ 45	Quilava (U)	.20	.50
❑ 46	Scyther (U)	.20	.50
❑ 47	Shuckle (U)	.20	.50
❑ 48	Smeargle (U)	.20	.50
❑ 49	Xatu (U)	.20	.50
❑ 50	Yanma (U)	.20	.50
❑ 51	Chikorita (C)	.10	.20
❑ 52	Chinchou (C)	.10	.20
❑ 53	Clefairy (C)	.10	.20

❑ 54	Cyndaquil (C)	.10	.20
❑ 55	Eevee (C)	.10	.20
❑ 56	Flaafy (C)	.10	.20
❑ 57	Gligar (C)	.10	.20
❑ 58	Gloom (C)	.10	.20
❑ 59	Hoothoot (C)	.10	.20
❑ 60	Houndour (C)	.10	.20
❑ 61	Larvitar (C)	.10	.20
❑ 62	Mareep (C)	.10	.20
❑ 63	Natu (C)	.10	.20
❑ 64	Oddish (C)	.10	.20
❑ 65	Onix (C)	.10	.20
❑ 66	Pineco (C)	.10	.20
❑ 67	Poliwag (C)	.10	.20
❑ 68	Poliwhirl (C)	.10	.20
❑ 69	Porygon (C)	.10	.20
❑ 70	Pupitar (C)	.10	.20
❑ 71	Remoraid (C)	.10	.20
❑ 72	Slowpoke (C)	.10	.20
❑ 73	Slugma (C)	.10	.20
❑ 74	Snubbull (C)	.10	.20

75	Spinarak (C)	.10	.20
76	Sunkern (C)	.10	.20
77	Teddiursa (C)	.10	.20
78	Totodile (C)	.10	.20
79	Wooper (C)	.10	.20
80	Curse Powder (U)	.20	.50
81	Energy Recycle System (U)	.20	.50
82	Energy Removal 2 (U)	.20	.50
83	Energy Root (U)	.20	.50
84	Energy Switch (U)	.20	.50
85	Fluffy Berry (U)	.20	.50
86	Mary's Request (U)	.20	.50
87	Poke Ball (U)	.20	.50
88	Pokemon Reversal (U)	.20	.50
89	Professor Elm's Training Method (U)	.20	.50
90	Protective Orb (U)	.20	.50
91	Sitrus Berry (U)	.20	.50
92	Solid Rage (U)	.20	.50
93	Warp Point (U)	.20	.50
94	Energy Search (C)	.10	.20
95	Potion (C)	.10	.20
96	Darkness Energy (R)	.50	1.00
97	Metal Energy (R)	.50	1.00
98	Boost Energy (U)	.20	.50
99	Cyclone Energy (U)	.20	.50
100	Warp Energy (U)	.20	.50
101	Blissey EX (UR) Holo	10.00	20.00
102	Espeon EX (UR) Holo	12.00	22.00
103	Feraligatr EX (UR) Holo	12.00	20.00
104	Ho-Oh EX (UR) Holo	15.00	30.00
105	Lugia EX (UR) Holo	40.00	60.00
106	Meganium EX (UR) Holo	10.00	20.00

107	Politoed EX (UR) Holo	12.00	20.00
108	Scizor EX (UR) Holo	15.00	20.00
109	Steelix EX (UR) Holo	15.00	30.00
110	Typhlosion EX (UR) Holo	10.00	20.00
111	Tyranitar EX (UR) Holo	15.00	30.00
112	Umbreon EX (UR) Holo	12.00	20.00
113	Entei Star (UR)	15.00	30.00
114	Raikou Star (UR)	15.00	25.00
115	Suicune Star (UR)	15.00	30.00
116	Rocket's Persian EX †(Box Topper)	4.00	10.00
117	Celebi EX (SCR)	15.00	30.00

2005 EX Unseen Forces REVERSE FOIL

Complete Set (117)
Reverse Foils are 2X Regular cards

2005 EX Delta Species

Complete Set (113) — 50.00 — 90.00

	Booster Box (36 packs)	60.00	80.00
	Booster Pack (9 cards)	3.00	3.50
	Common Cards (not listed) (C)	.10	.20
	Uncommon Cards (not listed) (U)	.20	.50
	Rare Cards (not listed) (R)	.50	1.00
1	Beedrill DS (Holo) (R)	3.00	6.00
2	Crobat DS (Holo) (R)	3.00	5.00

3	Dragonite DS (Holo) (R)	4.00	8.00
4	Espeon DS (Holo) (R)	3.00	6.00
5	Flareon DS (Holo) (R)	3.00	5.00
6	Gardevoir DS (Holo) (R)	3.00	5.00
7	Jolteon DS (Holo) (R)	3.00	5.00
8	Latias DS (Holo) (R)	3.00	6.00
9	Latios (holo) (R)	3.00	6.00
10	Marowak DS (Holo) (R)	2.00	5.00
11	Metagross DS (Holo) (R)	3.00	5.00
12	Mewtwo DS (Holo) (R)	4.00	7.00
13	Rayquaza DS (Holo) (R)	4.00	7.00
14	Salamence DS (Holo) (R)	3.00	5.00
15	Starmie DS (Holo) (R)	3.00	5.00
16	Tyranitar DS (Holo) (R)	3.00	6.00
17	Umbreon DS (Holo) (R)	3.00	5.00
18	Vaporeon DS (Holo) (R)	3.00	5.00
19	Azumarill DS (R)	.50	1.00
20	Azurill (R)	.50	1.00
21	Holon's Electrode (R)	.50	1.00
22	Holon's Magneton (R)	.50	1.00
23	Hypno (R)	.50	1.00
24	Mightyena DS (R)	.50	1.00
25	Porygon2 (R)	.50	1.00
26	Rain Castform (R)	.50	1.00
27	Sandslash DS (R)	.50	1.00
28	Slowking (R)	.50	1.00
29	Snow-cloud Castform (R)	.50	1.00
30	Starmie DS (R)	.50	1.00
31	Sunny Castform (R)	.50	1.00
32	Swellow (R)	.50	1.00
33	Weezing (R)	.50	1.00
34	Castform (U)	.20	.50
35	Ditto (U)	.20	.50
36	Ditto (U)	.20	.50
37	Ditto (U)	.20	.50
38	Ditto (U)	.20	.50
39	Ditto (U)	.20	.50
40	Ditto (U)	.20	.50
41	Dragonair DS (U)	.20	.50
42	Dragonair DS (U)	.20	.50
43	Golbat (U)	.20	.50
44	Hariyama (U)	.20	.50
45	Illumise (U)	.20	.50
46	Kakuna (U)	.20	.50

47	Kirlia (U)	.20	.50
48	Magneton (U)	.20	.50
49	Metang DS (U)	.20	.50
50	Persian (U)	.20	.50
51	Pupitar DS (U)	.20	.50
52	Rapidash (U)	.20	.50
53	Shelgon DS (U)	.20	.50
54	Shelgon DS (U)	.20	.50
55	Skarmory (U)	.20	.50
56	Volbeat (U)	.20	.50
57	Bagon (U)	.10	.20
58	Bagon DS (U)	.10	.20
59	Beldum DS (C)	.10	.20
60	Cubone (C)	.10	.20
61	Ditto (C)	.10	.20
62	Ditto (C)	.10	.20
63	Ditto (C)	.10	.20
64	Ditto (C)	.10	.20
65	Dratini DS (C)	.10	.20
66	Dratini DS (C)	.10	.20
67	Drowzee (C)	.10	.20
68	Eevee DS (C)	.10	.20
69	Eevee (C)	.10	.20
70	Holon's Magnemite (C)	.10	.20
71	Holon's Voltorb (C)	.10	.20

72	Koffing (C)	.10	.20
73	Larvitar DS (C)	.10	.20
74	Magnemite (C)	.10	.20
75	Makuhita (C)	.10	.20
76	Marill (C)	.10	.20
77	Meowth (C)	.10	.20
78	Ponyta (C)	.10	.20
79	Poochyena (C)	.10	.20
80	Porygon (C)	.10	.20
81	Ralts (C)	.10	.20
82	Sandshrew (C)	.10	.20
83	Slowpoke (C)	.10	.20
84	Staryu (C)	.10	.20
85	Staryu (C)	.10	.20
86	Taillow (C)	.10	.20
87	Weedle (C)	.10	.20
88	Zubat (C)	.10	.20
89	Dual Ball (U)	.20	.50
90	Great Ball (U)	.20	.50
91	Holon Farmer (U)	.20	.50
92	Holon Lass (U)	.20	.50
93	Holon Mentor (U)	.20	.50
94	Holon Research Tower (U)	.20	.50
95	Holon Researcher (U)	.20	.50
96	Holon Ruins (U)	.20	.50
97	Holon Scientist (U)	.20	.50

#	Card		
98	Holon Transceiver (U)	3.00	6.00
99	Master Ball (U)	.20	.50
100	Super Scoop Up (U)	.20	.50
101	Potion (C)	.10	.20
102	Switch (C)	.10	.20
103	Darkness Energy (R)	.50	1.00
104	Holon Energy FF (R)	.50	1.00
105	Holon Energy GL (R)	.50	1.00
106	Holon Energy WP (R)	.50	1.00
107	Metal Energy (R)	.50	1.00
108	Flareon ex (Holo) (R)	12.00	20.00
109	Jolteon ex (Holo) (R)	10.00	20.00
110	Vaporeon ex (Holo) (R)	8.00	15.00
111	Groudon [star] (Holo) (R)	12.50	25.00
112	Kyogre [star] (Holo) (R)	12.00	20.00
113	Metagross [star] (Holo) (R)	10.00	20.00
114	Azumarill (Holo) (R)	2.00	4.00

2005 EX Delta Species REVERSE FOIL

Complete Set (113)
Reverse Foils are 2X Regular cards

2006 EX Legend Maker

Complete Set (93)		100.00	150.00
Booster Box (36 packs)		75.00	100.00
Booster Pack (9 cards)		3.00	3.50
Common Cards (not listed) (C)		.10	.20
Uncommon Cards (not listed) (U)		.20	.50
Rare Cards (not listed) (R)		.50	1.00

#	Card		
1	Aerodactyl (Holo) (R)	2.00	4.00
2	Aggron (Holo) (R)	2.00	4.00
3	Cradily (Holo) (R)	2.00	4.00
4	Delcatty (Holo) (R)	2.00	4.00
5	Gengar (Holo) (R)	2.00	4.00
6	Golem (Holo) (R)	2.00	4.00
7	Kabutops (Holo) (R)	2.00	4.00
8	Lapras (Holo) (R)	2.00	4.00
9	Machamp (Holo) (R)	2.00	4.00
10	Mew (Holo) (R)	4.00	8.00
11	Muk (Holo) (R)	2.00	4.00
12	Shiftry (Holo) (R)	2.00	4.00
13	Victreebel (Holo) (R)	2.00	4.00
14	Wailord (Holo) (R)	4.00	8.00
15	Absol (R)	.50	1.00
16	Girafarig (R)	.50	1.00
17	Gorebyss (R)	.50	1.00
18	Huntail (R)	.50	1.00
19	Lanturn (R)	.50	1.00
20	Lunatone (R)	.50	1.00
21	Magmar (R)	.50	1.00
22	Magneton (R)	.50	1.00
23	Omastar (R)	.50	1.00
24	Pinsir (R)	.50	1.00
25	Solrock (R)	.50	1.00
26	Spinda (R)	.50	1.00
27	Torkoal (R)	.50	1.00
28	Wobbuffet (R)	.50	1.00
29	Anorith (U)	.20	.50
30	Cascoon (U)	.20	.50
31	Dunsparce (U)	.20	.50
32	Electrode (U)	.20	.50
33	Furret (U)	.20	.50
34	Graveler (U)	.20	.50
35	Haunter (U)	.20	.50
36	Kabuto (U)	.20	.50
37	Kecleon (U)	.20	.50
38	Lairon (U)	.20	.50
39	Machoke (U)	.20	.50
40	Misdreavus (U)	.20	.50
41	Nuzleaf (U)	.20	.50
42	Roselia (U)	.20	.50
43	Sealeo (U)	.20	.50
44	Tangela (U)	.20	.50
45	Tentacruel (U)	.20	.50
46	Vibrava (U)	.20	.50
47	Weepinbell (U)	.20	.50
48	Aron (C)	.10	.20
49	Bellsprout (C)	.10	.20
50	Chinchou (C)	.10	.20
51	Clamperl (C)	.10	.20
52	Gastly (C)	.10	.20
53	Geodude (C)	.10	.20
54	Grimer (C)	.10	.20
55	Growlithe (C)	.10	.20
56	Lileep (C)	.10	.20
57	Machop (C)	.10	.20
58	Magby (C)	.10	.20
59	Magnemite (C)	.10	.20
60	Omanyte (C)	.10	.20
61	Seedot (C)	.10	.20
62	Sentret (C)	.10	.20
63	Shuppet (C)	.10	.20
64	Skitty (C)	.10	.20
65	Spheal (C)	.10	.20
66	Tentacool (C)	.10	.20
67	Trapinch (C)	.10	.20
68	Voltorb (C)	.10	.20

#	Card		
69	Wailmer (C)	.10	.20
70	Wurmple (C)	.10	.20
71	Wynaut (C)	.10	.20
72	Cursed Stone (U)	.20	.50
73	Fieldworker (U)	.20	.50

#	Card		
74	Full Flame (U)	.20	.50
75	Giant Stump (U)	.20	.50
76	Power Tree (U)	.20	.50
77	Strange Cave (U)	.20	.50
78	Claw Fossil (C)	.10	.20
79	Mysterious Fossil (C)	.10	.20
80	Root Fossil (C)	.10	.20
81	Rainbow Energy (R)	.50	1.00
82	React Energy (U)	.20	.50
83	Arcanine ex (Holo) (R)	12.50	25.00
84	Armaldo ex (Holo) (R)	12.50	25.00
85	Banette ex (Holo) (R)	15.00	30.00
86	Dustox ex (Holo) (R)	10.00	20.00
87	Flygon ex (Holo) (R)	15.00	30.00
88	Mew ex (Holo) (R)	15.00	30.00
89	Walrein ex (Holo) (R)	7.00	14.00
90	Regice [star] (Holo) (R)	18.00	25.00
91	Regirock [star] (Holo) (R)	15.00	30.00
92	Registeel [star] (Holo) (R)	10.00	20.00
93	Pikachu (Holo) (R)	3.00	5.00

2006 EX Legend Maker REVERSE FOIL

Complete Set (93)   125.00   225.00
Reverse Foils are 2X Regular cards

2006 EX Holon Phantoms

Complete Set (111)		200.00	250.00
Booster Box (36 packs)		70.00	85.00
Booster Pack (9 cards)		3.75	4.00
Common Cards (not listed)		.10	.20
Uncommon Cards (not listed)		.20	.50
Rare Cards (not listed)		.50	1.00
Theme Decks		7.00	10.00

#	Card		
1	Armaldo (Holo) (R)	2.00	4.00
2	Cradily (Holo) (R)	2.00	4.00
3	Deoxys (Attack) (Holo) (R)	2.00	4.00
4	Deoxys (Defense) (Holo) (R)	2.00	4.00
5	Deoxys (Normal) (Holo) (R)	3.00	6.00
6	Deoxys (Speed) (Holo) (R)	2.00	4.00
7	Flygon (Holo) (R)	2.00	4.00
8	Gyarados (Holo) (R)	4.00	8.00
9	Kabutops (Holo) (R)	2.00	4.00
10	Kingdra (Holo) (R)	2.00	4.00
11	Latias (Holo) (R)	3.00	5.00
12	Latios (Holo) (R)	3.00	5.00
13	Omastar (Holo) (R)	2.00	4.00
14	Pidgeot (Holo) (R)	2.00	4.00
15	Raichu (Holo) (R)	3.00	5.00
16	Rayquaza (Holo) (R)	3.00	5.00
17	Vileplume (Holo) (R)	2.00	4.00
18	Absol (R)	.50	1.00
19	Bellossom (R)	.50	1.00

No.	Name	Lo	Hi
20	Blaziken (R)	.50	1.00
21	Latias (R)	.50	1.00
22	Latios (R)	.50	1.00
23	Mawile (R)	.50	1.00
24	Mewtwo (R)	.50	1.00
25	Nosepass (R)	.50	1.00
26	Rayquaza (R)	1.00	2.00
27	Regice (R)	.50	1.00
28	Regirock (R)	1.00	2.00
29	Registeel (R)	1.00	2.00
30	Relicanth (R)	.50	1.00
31	Sableye (R)	.50	1.00
32	Seviper (R)	.50	1.00
33	Torkoal (R)	.50	1.00
34	Zangoose (R)	.50	1.00
35	Aerodactyl (U)	.20	.50
36	Camerupt (U)	.20	.50
37	Chimecho (U)	.20	.50
38	Claydol (U)	.20	.50
39	Combusken (U)	.20	.50
40	Donphan (U)	.20	.50
41	Exeggutor (U)	.20	.50
42	Gloom (U)	.20	.50
43	Golduck (U)	.20	.50
44	Holon's Castform (U)	.20	.50
45	Lairon (U)	.20	.50
46	Manectric (U)	.20	.50
47	Masquerain (U)	.20	.50
48	Persian (U)	.20	.50
49	Pidgeotto (U)	.20	.50
50	Primeape (U)	.20	.50
51	Raichu (U)	.20	.50

No.	Name	Lo	Hi
52	Seadra (U)	.20	.50
53	Sharpedo (U)	.20	.50
54	Vibrava (U)	.20	.50
55	Whiscash (U)	.20	.50
56	Wobbuffet (U)	.20	.50
57	Anorith (C)	.10	.20
58	Aron (C)	.10	.20
59	Baltoy (C)	.10	.20
60	Barboach (C)	.10	.20
61	Carvanha (C)	.10	.20
62	Corphish (C)	.10	.20
63	Corphish (C)	.10	.20
64	Electrike (C)	.10	.20
65	Exeggcute (C)	.10	.20
66	Horsea (C)	.10	.20
67	Kabuto (C)	.10	.20
68	Lileep (C)	.10	.20
69	Magikarp (C)	.10	.20
70	Mankey (C)	.10	.20

No.	Name	Lo	Hi
71	Meowth (C)	.10	.20
72	Numel (C)	.10	.20
73	Oddish (C)	.10	.20
74	Omanyte (C)	.10	.20
75	Phanpy (C)	.10	.20
76	Pichu (C)	.20	.50
77	Pidgey (C)	.10	.20
78	Pikachu (C)	.20	.50
79	Pikachu (C)	.20	.50
80	Poochyena (C)	.10	.20
81	Psyduck (C)	.10	.20
82	Surskit (C)	.10	.20
83	Torchic (C)	.10	.20
84	Trapinch (C)	.10	.20
85	Holon Adventurer (U)	.20	.50
86	Holon Fossil (U)	.20	.50
87	Holon Lake (U)	.20	.50
88	Mr. Stone's Project (U)	.20	.50
89	Professor Cozmo's Discovery (U)	.20	.50
90	Rare Candy (C)	1.00	2.00
91	Claw Fossil (C)	.10	.20
92	Mysterious Fossil (C)	.10	.20
93	Root Fossil (C)	.10	.20
94	Darkness Energy (R)	.50	1.00
95	Metal Energy (R)	.50	1.00
96	Multi Energy (R)	.50	1.00
97	Dark Metal Energy (U)	.20	.50
98	d Rainbow Energy (U)	.20	.50
99	Crawdaunt ex (Holo) (R)	10.00	20.00
100	Mew ex (Holo) (R)	15.00	30.00
101	Mightyena ex (Holo) (R)	10.00	20.00

ENERGY

Dark Metal Energy Special Energy Card

No.	Name	Lo	Hi
102	Gyarados (Shining Holo)	25.00	50.00
103	Mewtwo (Shining Holo)	20.00	40.00
104	Pikachu (Shining Holo)	2.00	40.00
105	Grass Energy	.10	.20
106	Fire Energy	.10	.20
107	Water Energy	.10	.20
108	Lightning Energy	.10	.20
109	Psychic Energy	.10	.20
110	Fighting Energy	.10	.20
111	Mew (Holo) (R)	2.00	4.00

2006 EX Holon Phantoms REVERSE FOIL

Complete Set (111)
Reverse Foils 2X Regular Cards

2006 EX Crystal Guardians

	Lo	Hi
Complete Set (100)	250.00	300.00
Booster Box (36 packs)	70.00	100.00
Booster Pack (9 cards)	3.75	4.00
Theme Decks		
Common Cards (not listed)	.10	.20
Uncommon Cards (not listed)	.20	.50
Rare Cards (not listed)	.50	1.00

No.	Name	Lo	Hi
1	Banette (Holo) (R)	3.00	6.00
2	Blastoise DS (Holo) (R)	4.00	12.00
3	Camerupt (Holo) (R)	3.00	6.00
4	Charizard DS (Holo) (R)	12.50	23.00
5	Dugtrio (Holo) (R)	3.00	6.00

No.	Name	Lo	Hi
6	Ludicolo DS (Holo) (R)	3.00	6.00
7	Luvdisc (Holo) (R)	3.00	6.00
8	Manectric (Holo) (R)	3.00	6.00
9	Mawile (Holo) (R)	3.00	6.00
10	Sableye (Holo) (R)	3.00	6.00
11	Swalot (Holo) (R)	3.00	6.00
12	Tauros (Holo) (R)	3.00	6.00
13	Wigglytuff (Holo) (R)	3.00	6.00
14	Blastoise (R)	1.00	2.00
15	Cacturne DS (R)	.50	1.00
16	Combusken (R)	.50	1.00
17	Dusclops (R)	.50	1.00
18	Fearow DS (R)	.50	1.00
19	Grovyle DS (R)	.50	1.00
20	Grumpig (R)	.50	1.00
21	Igglybuff (R)	.50	1.00
22	Kingler DS (R)	.50	1.00
23	Loudred (R)	.50	1.00
24	Marshtomp (R)	.50	1.00
25	Medicham (R)	.50	1.00
26	Pelipper DS (R)	.50	1.00
27	Swampert (R)	.50	1.00
28	Venusaur (R)	.20	.50

#	Card		
29	Charmeleon (U)	.20	.50
30	Charmeleon DS (U)	.20	.50
31	Combusken (U)	.20	.50
32	Grovyle (U)	.20	.50
33	Gulpin (U)	.20	.50
34	Ivysaur (U)	.20	.50
35	Ivysaur (U)	.20	.50
36	Lairon (U)	.20	.50
37	Lombre (U)	.20	.50
38	Marshtomp (U)	.20	.50
39	Nuzleaf (U)	.20	.50
40	Shuppet (U)	.20	.50
41	Skitty (U)	.20	.50
42	Wartortle (U)	.20	.50
43	Wartortle (U)	.20	.50
44	Aron (C)	.10	.20
45	Bulbasaur (C)	.10	.20
46	Bulbasaur (C)	.10	.20
47	Cacnea (C)	.10	.20
48	Charmander (C)	.10	.20
49	Charmander DS (C)	.10	.20
50	Diglett (C)	.10	.20
51	Duskull (C)	.10	.20
52	Electrike (C)	.10	.20
53	Jigglypuff (C)	.10	.20
54	Krabby (C)	.10	.20
55	Lotad (C)	.10	.20
56	Meditite (C)	.10	.20

#	Card		
57	Mudkip (C)	.10	.20
58	Mudkip (C)	.10	.20
59	Numel (C)	.10	.20
60	Seedot (C)	.10	.20
61	Spearow (C)	.10	.20
62	Spoink (C)	.10	.20
63	Squirtle (C)	.10	.20
64	Squirtle (C)	.10	.20
65	Torchic (C)	.10	.20
66	Torchic (C)	.10	.20
67	Treecko (C)	.10	.20
68	Treecko (C)	.10	.20
69	Whismur (C)	.10	.20
70	Wingull (C)	.10	.20
71	Bill's Maintenance (U)	.20	.50
72	Castaway (U)	.20	.50
73	Celio's Network (U)	.20	.50
74	Cessation Crystal (U)	.20	.50
75	Crystal Beach (U)	.20	.50
76	Crystal Shard (U)	.20	.50
77	Double Full Heal (U)	.20	.50
78	Dual Ball (U)	.20	.50
79	Holon Circle (U)	.20	.50

#	Card		
80	Memory Berry (U)	.20	.50
81	Mysterious Shard (U)	.20	.50
82	Poke Ball (U)	.20	.50
83	PokeNav (U)	.20	.50
84	Warp Point (U)	.20	.50
85	Windstorm (U)	.20	.50
86	Energy Search (C)	.10	.20
87	Potion (C)	.10	.20
88	Double Rainbow Energy (R)	.50	1.00
89	Aggron ex (Holo) (R)	15.00	20.00
90	Blaziken ex (Holo) (R)	18.00	27.00
91	Delcatty ex (Holo) (R)	12.00	20.00
92	Exploud ex (Holo) (R)	12.00	15.00
93	Groudon ex (Holo) (R)	12.00	20.00
94	Jirachi ex (Holo) (R)	12.00	20.00
95	Kyogre ex (Holo) (R)	10.00	15.00
96	Sceptile ex DS (Holo) (R)	15.00	22.00
97	Shiftry ex (Holo) (R)	12.00	20.00
98	Swampert ex (Holo) (R)	12.00	20.00
99	Alakazam Shining (Holo) (R)	15.00	25.00
100	Celebi Shining (Holo) (R)	23.00	35.00

2006 EX Dragon Frontiers

	Complete Set (101)	70.00	120.00
	Booster Box (36 packs)	75.00	100.00
	Booster Packs (9 cards)	3.00	4.00
	Theme Decks	10.00	14.00
1	Ampharos DS (Holo) (R)	3.00	6.00
2	Feraligatr DS (Holo) (R)	3.00	6.00
3	Heracross DS (Holo) (R)	3.00	6.00
4	Meganium DS (Holo) (R)	3.00	6.00
5	Milotic DS (Holo) (R)	4.00	8.00
6	Nidoking DS (Holo) (R)	3.00	6.00
7	Nidoqueen DS (Holo) (R)	3.00	6.00
8	Ninetales DS (Holo) (R)	3.00	6.00
9	Pinsir DS (Holo) (R)	3.00	6.00
10	Snorlax DS (Holo) (R)	3.00	6.00
11	Togetic DS (Holo) (H)	3.00	6.00
12	Typhlosion DS (Holo) (R)	3.00	6.00
13	Arbok DS (R)	.50	1.00
14	Cloyster DS (R)	.50	1.00
15	Dewgong DS (R)	.50	1.00
16	Gligar DS (R)	.50	1.00
17	Jynx DS (R)	.50	1.00
18	Ledian DS (R)	.50	1.00
19	Lickitung DS (R)	.50	1.00

#	Card		
20	Mantine DS (R)	.50	1.00
21	Quagsire DS (R)	.50	1.00
22	Seadra DS (R)	.50	1.00
23	Tropius DS (R)	.50	1.00

#	Card		
24	Vibrava DS (R)	.50	1.00
25	Xatu DS (R)	.50	1.00
26	Bayleef DS (U)	.20	.50
27	Croconaw DS (U)	.20	.50
28	Dragonair DS (U)	.20	.50
29	Electabuzz DS (U)	.20	.50
30	Flaaffy DS (U)	.20	.50
31	Horsea DS (U)	.20	.50
32	Kirlia (U)	.20	.50
33	Kirlia DS (U)	.20	.50
34	Nidorina DS (U)	.20	.50
35	Nidorino DS (U)	.20	.50
36	Quilava DS (U)	.20	.50
37	Seadra DS (U)	.20	.50
38	Shelgon DS (U)	.20	.50
39	Smeargle DS (U)	.20	.50
40	Swellow DS (U)	.20	.50
41	Togepi DS (U)	.20	.50
42	Vibrava DS (U)	.20	.50
43	Bagon DS (C)	.10	.20
44	Chikorita DS (C)	.10	.20
45	Cyndaquil DS (C)	.10	.20
46	Dratini DS (C)	.10	.20
47	Ekans DS (C)	.10	.20
48	Elekid DS (C)	.10	.20
49	Feebas DS (C)	.10	.20
50	Horsea DS (C)	.10	.20
51	Lavitar (C)	.10	.20
52	Lavitar DS (C)	.10	.20
53	Ledyba DS (C)	.10	.20

#	Card		
54	Mareep DS (C)	.10	.20
55	Natu DS (C)	.10	.20
56	Nidoran DS (C)	.10	.20
57	Nidoran DS (C)	.10	.20
58	Pupitar (C)	.10	.20
59	Pupitar DS	.10	.20
60	Ralts (C)	.10	.20
61	Ralts DS (C)	.10	.20
62	Seel DS (C)	.10	.20
63	Shellder DS (C)	.10	.20
64	Smoochum DS (C)	.10	.20
65	Swablu DS (C)	.10	.20
66	Tailow DS (C)	.10	.20
67	Totodile DS (C)	.10	.20
68	Trapinch DS (C)	.10	.20
69	Trapinch DS (C)	.10	.20
70	Vulpix DS (C)	.10	.20
71	Wooper DS (C)	.10	.20
72	Buffer Piece (U)	.20	.50
73	Copycat (U)	.20	.50
74	Holon Legacy (U)	.20	.50

75 Holon Mentor (U)	.20	.50
76 Island Hermit (U)	.20	.50
77 Mr. Stone's Project (II)	.20	.60
78 Old Rod (U)	.20	.50
79 Professor Elm's Training Method (U)	.20	.50
80 Professor Oak's Research (U)	.20	.50
81 Strength Charm (U)	.20	.50
82 TV Reporter (U)	.20	.50
83 Switch (C)	.10	.20
84 Holon Energy FF (R)	.50	1.00
85 Holon Energy GL (R)	.50	1.00
86 Holon Energy WP (R)	.50	1.00
87 Boost Energy (U)	.20	.50
88 Rainbow Energy (U)	.20	.50
89 Scramble Energy (U)	.20	.50
90 Altaria ex DS (Holo) (R)	8.00	16.00
91 Dragonite ex DS (R)	10.00	20.00
92 Flygon ex DS (R)	15.00	25.00
93 Gardevoir cx DS (II)	10.00	20.00
94 Kingdra ex DS (R)	10.00	16.00
95 Latias ex DS (R)	12.00	18.00
96 Latios ex DS (R)	12.50	25.00
97 Rayquaza ex DS (R)	18.00	25.00
98 Salamence ex DS (R)	15.00	30.00
99 Tyranitar ex DS (R)	15.00	30.00
100 Charizard DS (Holo) (R)	35.00	60.00
101 Mew DS (Holo) (R)	20.00	30.00

2007 EX Power Keepers

Complete Set (108)	70.00	120.00
Booster Box (36 packs)	65.00	85.00
Booster Packs (9 cards)	3.00	3.75

1 Aggron Holo (R)	3.00	6.00
2 Altaria Holo (R)	2.00	4.00
3 Armaldo Holo (R)	3.00	6.00
4 Banette Holo (R)	3.00	6.00
5 Blaziken Holo (R)	3.00	6.00
6 Charizard Holo (R)	8.00	15.00
7 Cradily Holo (R)	2.00	4.00
8 Delcatty Holo (R)	2.00	4.00
9 Gardevoir Holo (R)	3.00	6.00
10 Kabutops Holo (R)	2.00	4.00
11 Machamp Holo (R)	2.00	4.00
12 Raichu Holo (R)	2.00	4.00
13 Slaking Holo (R)	1.00	4.00
14 Dusclops (R)	.50	1.00
15 Lantum (R)	.50	1.00
16 Magneton (R)	.50	1.00
17 Mawile (R)	.50	1.00
18 Mightyena (R)	.50	1.00

19 Ninetales (R)	.50	1.00
20 Omastar (R)	.50	1.00
21 Pichu (R)	.50	1.00
22 Sableye (R)	.50	1.00
23 Seviper (R)	.50	1.00
24 Wobbuffet (R)	.50	1.00
25 Zangoose (R)	.50	1.00

26 Anorith (U)	.20	.50
27 Cacturne (U)	.20	.50
28 Charmeleon (U)	.20	.50
29 Combusken (U)	.20	.50
30 Glalie (U)	.20	.50
31 Kirlia (U)	.20	.50
32 Lairon (U)	.20	.50
33 Machoke (U)	.20	.50
34 Medicham (U)	.20	.50
35 Metang (U)	.20	.50
36 Nuzleaf (U)	.20	.50
37 Sealeo (U)	.20	.50
38 Sharpedo (U)	.20	.50
39 Shelgon (U)	.20	.50
40 Vibrava (U)	.20	.50
41 Vigoroth (U)	.20	.50
42 Aron (C)	.10	.20
43 Bagon (C)	.10	.20
44 Baltoy (C)	.10	.20
45 Beldum (C)	.10	.20
46 Cacnea (C)	.10	.20
47 Carvanha (C)	.10	.20
48 Charmander (C)	.10	.20
49 Chinchou (C)	.10	.20
50 Duskull (C)	.10	.20
51 Kabuto (C)	.10	.20
52 Lileep (C)	.10	.20
53 Machop (C)	.10	.20
54 Magnemite (C)	.10	.20
55 Meditite (C)	.10	.20
56 Omanyte (C)	.10	.20
57 Pikachu (C)	.10	.20
58 Poochyena (C)	.10	.20
59 Ralts (C)	.10	.20
60 Seedot (C)	.10	.20
61 Shuppet (C)	.10	.20
62 Skitty (C)	.10	.20
63 Slakoth (C)	.10	.20
64 Snorunt (C)	.10	.20
65 Spheal (C)	.10	.20
66 Swablu (C)	.10	.20
67 Torchic (C)	.10	.20
68 Trapinch (C)	.10	.20
69 Vulpix (C)	.10	.20

70 Wynaut (C)	.10	.20
71 Battle Frontier (U)	.20	.50
72 Drake's Stadium (U)	.20	.50
73 Energy Recycle System (U)	.20	.50
74 Energy Removal 2 (U)	.20	.50
75 Energy Switch (U)	.20	.50
76 Glacia's Stadium (U)	.20	.50
77 Great Ball (U)	.20	.50
78 Master Ball (U)	.20	.50
79 Phoebe's Stadium (U)	.20	.50
80 Professor Birch (U)	.20	.50
81 Scott (U)	.20	.50
82 Sidney's Stadium (U)	.20	.50
83 Steven's Advice (U)	.20	.50
84 Claw Fossil (C)	.10	.20
85 Mysterious Fossil (C)	.10	.20
86 Root Fossil (C)	.10	.20
87 Darkness Energy (R)	.50	1.00
88 Metal Energy (R)	.50	1.00
89 Multi Energy (R)	.50	1.00
90 Cyclone Energy (U)	.20	.50
91 Warp Energy (U)	.20	.50
92 Absol ex (Holo) (R)	10.00	20.00
93 Claydol ex (Holo) (R)	12.00	15.00
94 Flygon ex (Holo) (R)	8.00	20.00

95 Metagross ex (Holo) (R)	10.00	18.00
96 Salamence ex (Holo) (R)	20.00	30.00
97 Shiftry ex (Holo) (R)	10.00	18.00
98 Skarmory ex (Holo) (R)	8.00	16.00
99 Walrein ex (Holo) (R)	7.00	15.00

❏ 100	Flareon [star] (Holo) (R)	12.00	25.00	
❏ 101	Jolteon [star] (Holo) (R)	18.00	30.00	
❏ 102	Vaporeon [star] (Holo) (R)	20.00	30.00	
❏ 103	Grass Energy Holo (R)	.50	1.00	
❏ 104	Fire Energy Holo (R)	.50	1.00	
❏ 105	Water Energy Holo (R)	.50	1.00	
❏ 106	Lightning Energy Holo (R)	.50	1.00	
❏ 107	Psychic Energy Holo (R)	.50	1.00	
❏ 108	Fighting Energy Holo (R)	.50	1.00	

2007 Diamond & Pearl

	Complete Set (130)	120.00	200.00
	Booster Box (36 packs)	80.00	110.00
	Booster Pack (9 cards)	3.50	4.00
❏ 1	Dialga (Holo) (R)	10.00	15.00
❏ 2	Dusknoir (Holo) (R)	2.00	5.00
❏ 3	Electivire (Holo) (R)	5.00	11.00
❏ 4	Empoleon (Holo) (R)	5.00	11.00
❏ 5	Infernape (Holo) (R)	6.00	12.00
❏ 6	Lucario (Holo) (R)	10.00	20.00
❏ 7	Luxray (Holo) (R)	2.00	6.00
❏ 8	Magnezone (Holo) (R)	4.00	8.00
❏ 9	Manaphy (Holo) (R)	2.00	6.00
❏ 10	Mismagius (Holo) (R)	2.00	5.00
❏ 11	Palkia (Holo) (R)	10.00	20.00
❏ 12	Rhyperior (Holo) (R)	6.00	12.00
❏ 13	Roserade (Holo) (R)	2.00	4.00
❏ 14	Shiftry (Holo) (R)	2.00	5.00
❏ 15	Skuntank (Holo) (R)	2.00	4.00
❏ 16	Staraptor (Holo) (R)	5.00	10.00
❏ 17	Torterra (Holo) (R)	4.00	8.00
❏ 18	Azumarill (R)	.50	1.00
❏ 19	Beautifuly (R)	.50	1.00
❏ 20	Bibarel (R)	.50	1.00
❏ 21	Carnivine (R)	.50	1.00
❏ 22	Clefable (R)	.50	1.00
❏ 23	Drapion (R)	.50	1.00
❏ 24	Drifblim (R)	.50	1.00
❏ 25	Dustox (R)	.50	1.00
❏ 26	Floatzel (R)	.50	1.00
❏ 27	Gengar (R)	.50	1.00
❏ 28	Heracross (R)	.50	1.00
❏ 29	Hippowdon (R)	.50	1.00
❏ 30	Lopunny (R)	.50	1.00
❏ 31	Machamp (R)	.50	1.00
❏ 32	Medicham (R)	.50	1.00

❏ 33	Munchlax (R)	.50	1.00
❏ 34	Noctowl (R)	.50	1.00
❏ 35	Pachirisu (R)	1.00	2.00
❏ 36	Purugly (R)	.50	1.00

❏ 37	Snorlax (R)	.50	1.00
❏ 38	Steelix (R)	.50	1.00
❏ 39	Vespiquen (R)	.50	1.00

❏ 40	Weavile (R)	.50	1.00
❏ 41	Wobbuffet (R)	.50	1.50
❏ 42	Wynaut (R)	.50	1.00
❏ 43	Budew (U)	.10	.20
❏ 44	Cascoon (U)	.20	.50
❏ 45	Cherrim (U)	.20	.50
❏ 46	Drifloon (U)	.20	.50
❏ 47	Dusclops (U)	.20	.50
❏ 48	Elekid (U)	.20	.50
❏ 49	Grotle (U)	.20	.50
❏ 50	Haunter (U)	.20	.50
❏ 51	Hippopotas (U)	.20	.50
❏ 52	Luxio (U)	.20	.50
❏ 53	Machoke (U)	.20	.50
❏ 54	Magneton (U)	.20	.50
❏ 55	Mantyke (U)	.20	.50
❏ 56	Monferno (U)	.20	.50
❏ 57	Nuzleaf (U)	.20	.50
❏ 58	Prinplup (U)	.20	.50
❏ 59	Rapidash (U)	.20	.50
❏ 60	Rhydon (U)	.20	.50
❏ 61	Riolu (U)	.20	.50
❏ 62	Seaking (U)	.20	.50
❏ 63	Silcoon (U)	.20	.50
❏ 64	Staravia (U)	.20	.50
❏ 65	Unown A (U)	.20	.50
❏ 66	Unown B (U)	.20	.50
❏ 67	Unown C (U)	.20	.50
❏ 68	Unown D (U)	.20	.50
❏ 69	Azurill (C)	.10	.20
❏ 70	Bidoof (C)	.10	.20
❏ 71	Bonsly (C)	.10	.20
❏ 72	Buizel (C)	.10	.20
❏ 73	Buneary (C)	.10	.20
❏ 74	Chatot (C)	.10	.20
❏ 75	Cherubi (C)	.10	.20
❏ 76	Chimchar (C)	.10	.50
❏ 77	Clefairy (C)	.10	.20
❏ 78	Cleffa (C)	.10	.20
❏ 79	Combee (C)	.10	.20
❏ 80	Duskull (C)	.10	.20
❏ 81	Electabuzz (C)	.10	.20
❏ 82	Gastly (C)	.10	.20
❏ 83	Glameow (C)	.10	.20
❏ 84	Goldeen (C)	.10	.20
❏ 85	Hoothoot (C)	.10	.20
❏ 86	Machop (C)	.10	.20
❏ 87	Magnemite (C)	.10	.20

❏ 88	Marill (C)	.10	.20
❏ 89	Meditite (C)	.10	.20
❏ 90	Mime Jr. (C)	.10	.20
❏ 91	Misdreavus (C)	.10	.20
❏ 92	Onix (C)	.10	.20
❏ 93	Piplup (C)	.10	.50
❏ 94	Ponyta (C)	.10	.20
❏ 95	Rhyhorn (C)	.10	.20
❏ 96	Roselia (C)	.10	.20
❏ 97	Seedot (C)	.10	.20
❏ 98	Shinx (C)	.10	.20
❏ 99	Skorupi (C)	.10	.20
❏ 100	Sneasel (C)	.10	.20
❏ 101	Starly (C)	.10	.20
❏ 102	Stunky (C)	.10	.20
❏ 103	Turtwig (C)	.10	.50
❏ 104	Wurmple (C)	.10	.20
❏ 105	Double Full Heal (U)	.20	.50
❏ 106	Energy Restore (U)	.20	.50
❏ 107	Energy Switch (U)	.20	.50
❏ 108	Night Pokemon Center (U)	.20	.50
❏ 109	PlusPower (U)	.20	.50
❏ 110	Poke Ball (U)	.20	.50
❏ 111	Pokedex HANDY910s (U)	.20	.50
❏ 112	Professor Rowan (U)	.20	.50
❏ 113	Rival (U)	.20	.50
❏ 114	Speed Stadium (U)	.20	.50
❏ 115	Super Scoop Up (U)	.20	.50
❏ 116	Warp Point (U)	.20	.50
❏ 117	Enery Search (C)	.10	.20

❏ 118	Potion (C)	.10	.20
❏ 119	Switch (C)	.10	.20
❏ 120	Empoleon Lv.X (Holo) (R)	20.00	35.00
❏ 121	Infernape Lv.X (Holo) (R)	20.00	35.00
❏ 122	Torterra Lv.X (Holo) (R)	18.00	33.00
❏ 123	Grass Energy	.10	.20
❏ 124	Fire Energy	.10	.20
❏ 125	Water Energy	.10	.20
❏ 126	Lightning Energy	.10	.20
❏ 127	Fighting Energy	.10	.20
❏ 128	Psychic Energy	.10	.20
❏ 129	Darkness Energy	.10	.20
❏ 130	Metal Energy	.10	.20

2007 DP Mysterious Treasures

	Complete Set	120.00	200.00
	Booster Pack (9 cards)	80.00	110.00
	Booster Box (36 packs)	3.50	4.00
❏ 1	Aggron (Holo) (R)	2.00	5.00
❏ 2	Alakazam (Holo) (R)	2.00	5.00

☐ 3	Ambipom (Holo) (R)	3.00	6.00
☐ 4	Azelf (Holo) (R)	5.00	8.00
☐ 5	Blissey (Holo) (R)	5.00	10.00
☐ 6	Bronzong (Holo) (R)	3.00	6.00
☐ 7	Celebi (Holo) (R)	5.00	10.00
☐ 8	Feraligatr (Holo) (R)	3.00	6.00
☐ 9	Garchomp (Holo) (R)	8.00	16.00
☐ 10	Honchkron (Holo) (R)	3.00	6.00
☐ 11	Lumineon (Holo) (R)	2.00	4.00
☐ 12	Magmortar (Holo) (R)	4.00	8.00
☐ 13	Meganium (Holo) (R)	4.00	8.00
☐ 14	Mesprint (Holo) (R)	3.00	6.00
☐ 15	Raichu (Holo) (R)	3.00	7.00
☐ 16	Typholosion (Holo) (R)	3.00	6.00
☐ 17	Tyranitar (Holo) (R)	3.00	6.00
☐ 18	Uxie (Holo) (R)	2.00	5.00
☐ 19	Abomasnow (R)	.50	1.00
☐ 20	Ariados (R)	.50	1.00
☐ 21	Bastiodon (R)	.50	1.00
☐ 22	Chimecho (R)	.50	1.00
☐ 23	Crobat (R)	.50	1.00
☐ 24	Exeggutor (R)	.50	1.00
☐ 25	Glalie (R)	.50	1.00
☐ 26	Gyarados (R)	.50	1.00
☐ 27	Kricketune (R)	.50	1.00
☐ 28	Manectric (R)	.50	1.00
☐ 29	Mantine (R)	.50	1.00
☐ 30	Mr. Mime (R)	.50	1.00
☐ 31	Nidoqueen (R)	.50	1.00
☐ 32	Ninetales (R)	.50	1.00
☐ 33	Rampardos (R)	.50	1.00
☐ 34	Slaking (R)	.50	1.00

☐ 35	Sudowoodo (R)	.50	1.00
☐ 36	Toxicroak (R)	.50	1.00
☐ 37	Unown (R)	.50	1.00
☐ 38	Ursaring (R)	.50	1.00
☐ 39	Walrein (R)	.50	1.00
☐ 40	Whiscash (R)	.50	1.00
☐ 41	Bayleef (U)	.20	.50
☐ 42	Chingling (U)	.20	.50
☐ 43	Cranidos (U)	.20	.50
☐ 44	Croconaw (U)	.20	.50
☐ 45	Dewgong (U)	.20	.50
☐ 46	Dodrio (U)	.20	.50
☐ 47	Dunsparce (U)	.20	.50
☐ 48	Gabite (U)	.20	.50
☐ 49	Girafarig (U)	.20	.50
☐ 50	Golbat (U)	.20	.50
☐ 51	Graveler (U)	.20	.50
☐ 52	Happiny (U)	.20	.50
☐ 53	Lairon (U)	.20	.50

☐ 54	Magmar (U)	.20	.50
☐ 55	Macquorain (U)	.20	.50
☐ 56	Nidorina (U)	.20	.50
☐ 57	Octillery (U)	.20	.50
☐ 58	Parasect (U)	.20	.50
☐ 59	Pupitar (U)	.20	.50
☐ 60	Quilava (U)	.20	.50

☐ 61	Sandslash (U)	.20	.50
☐ 62	Sealeo (U)	.20	.50
☐ 63	Shieldon (U)	.20	.50
☐ 64	Tropius (U)	.20	.50
☐ 65	Unown E (U)	.20	.50
☐ 66	Unown M (U)	.20	.50
☐ 67	Unown T (U)	.20	.50
☐ 68	Vigoroth (U)	.20	.50
☐ 69	Abra (C)	.10	.20
☐ 70	Aipom (C)	.10	.20
☐ 71	Aron (C)	.10	.20
☐ 72	Barboach (C)	.10	.20
☐ 73	Bidoof (C)	.10	.20
☐ 74	Bronzor (C)	.10	.20
☐ 75	Buizel (C)	.10	.20
☐ 76	Chansey (C)	.10	.20
☐ 77	Chikorita (C)	.10	.20
☐ 78	Croagunk (C)	.10	.20
☐ 79	Cyndaquil (C)	.10	.20
☐ 80	Doduo (C)	.10	.20
☐ 81	Electrike (C)	.10	.20
☐ 82	Exeggcute (C)	.10	.20
☐ 83	Finneon (C)	.10	.20
☐ 84	Geodude (C)	.10	.20
☐ 85	Gible (C)	.10	.20
☐ 86	Kricketot (C)	.10	.20
☐ 87	Larvitar (C)	.10	.20
☐ 88	Magby (C)	.10	.20
☐ 89	Magikarp (C)	.10	.20
☐ 90	Murkrow (C)	.10	.20
☐ 91	Nidoran (C)	.10	.20
☐ 92	Paras (C)	.10	.20
☐ 93	Pichu (C)	.10	.20
☐ 94	Pickahu (C)	.10	.20
☐ 95	Remoriad (C)	.10	.20
☐ 96	Sanshrew (C)	.10	.20
☐ 97	Seel (C)	.10	.20
☐ 98	Shinx (C)	.10	.20
☐ 99	Slakoth (C)	.10	.20
☐ 100	Snorunt (C)	.10	.20
☐ 101	Snover (C)	.10	.20
☐ 102	Spheal (C)	.10	.20
☐ 103	Spinarak (C)	.10	.20
☐ 104	Surskit (C)	.10	.20

☐ 105	Teddiursa (C)	.10	.20
☐ 100	Totodile (C)	.10	.20
☐ 107	Vulpix (C)	.10	.20
☐ 108	Zubat (C)	.10	.20
☐ 109	Bebe's Search (U)	.20	.50
☐ 110	Dusk Ball (U)	.20	.50
☐ 111	Fossil Excavator (U)	.20	.50
☐ 112	Lake Boundary (U)	.20	.50
☐ 113	Night Maintenance (U)	.20	.50
☐ 114	Quick Ball (U)	.20	.50
☐ 115	Team Galactic's Wager (U)	.20	.50
☐ 116	Armor Fossil (C)	.10	.20
☐ 117	Skull Fossil (C)	.10	.20
☐ 118	Multi Energy (U)	.50	1.00
☐ 119	Darkness Energy (U)	.20	.50
☐ 120	Metal Energy (U)	.20	.50
☐ 121	Electivire Lv.X (Holo) (R)	25.00	40.00
☐ 122	Lucario Lv.X (Holo) (R)	20.00	30.00
☐ 123	Magmortar Lv.X (Holo) (R)	25.00	35.00
☐ 124	Time Space Distortion (Holo)(SCR)	35.00	60.00

JAPANESE & FOREIGN SETS
Japanese Base (Series 1)

	Complete Set (102)	60.00	85.00
	Booster Box (60 ct)	40.00	80.00
	Booster Pack (10 cards)	2.00	4.00
	Common Card (not listed)	.10	.25
	Uncommon Card (not listed)	.50	1.00
	Starter Set (60 cards)	15.00	20.00
☐ 3	Venusaur (holo) (R)	6.00	12.00
☐ 5	Charmeleon (U)	1.00	2.00
☐ 6	Charizard (holo) (R)	12.00	20.00
☐ 8	Wartortle (U)	1.00	2.00
☐ 9	Blastoise (holo) (R)	6.00	10.00
☐ 15	Beedrill (R)	3.00	5.00
☐ 17	Pidgeotto (R)	2.00	4.00

☐ 25	Pikachu (C)	.50	1.50
☐ 26	Raichu (holo) (R)	4.00	8.00
☐ 34	Nidoking (holo) (R)	3.00	6.00
☐ 35	Clefairy (holo) (R)	4.00	8.00
☐ 38	Ninetales (holo) (R)	4.00	8.00
☐ 51	Dugtrio (R)	3.00	5.00
☐ 62	Poliwrath (holo) (R)	2.00	4.00
☐ 65	Alakazam (holo) (R)	4.00	8.00
☐ 68	Machamp (holo) (R)	4.00	7.00
☐ 82	Magneton (holo) (R)	3.00	6.00
☐ 101	Electrode (R)	2.00	5.00
☐ 107	Hitmonchan (holo) (R)	4.00	8.00
☐ 113	Chansey (holo) (R)	5.00	8.00
☐ 125	Electabuzz (R)	3.00	5.00

☐ 71	Victreebel (holo) (R)	2.00	4.00
☐ 101	Electrode (holo) (R)	2.00	4.00
☐ 115	Kangaskhan (holo) (R)	2.00	4.00
☐ 122	Mr Mime (holo) (R)	2.00	4.00
☐ 123	Scyther (holo) (R)	2.00	5.00
☐ 127	Pinsir (holo) (R)	2.00	4.00
☐ 134	Vaporeon (holo) (R)	2.00	4.00
☐ 135	Jolteon (holo) (R)	2.00	4.00
☐ 136	Flareon (holo) (R)	2.00	4.00
☐ 143	Snorlax (holo) (R)	2.00	4.00

Japanese Fossil (Series 3)

Complete Set (48)		50.00	65.00
Booster Box (60 ct)		75.00	100.00
Booster Pack (10 cards)		2.25	4.00
Common Card (not listed)		.10	.25
Uncommon Card (not listed)		.25	.50
☐ 26	Raichu (holo) (R)	2.00	4.00
☐ 82	Magneton (holo) (R)	2.00	4.00
☐ 89	Muk (holo) (R)	2.00	4.00
☐ 93	Haunter (holo) (R)	2.00	4.00
☐ 94	Gengar (holo) (R)	2.00	4.00
☐ 97	Hypno (holo) (R)	2.00	4.00
☐ 106	Hitmonlee (holo) (R)	2.00	4.00
☐ 131	Lapras (holo) (R)	2.00	4.00
☐ 132	Ditto (holo) (R)	2.00	4.00
☐ 141	Kabutops (holo) (R)	2.00	4.00

☐ 142	Aerodactyl (holo) (R)	2.00	4.00
☐ 144	Articuno (holo) (R)	2.00	5.00
☐ 145	Zapdos (holo) (R)	2.00	5.00
☐ 146	Moltres (holo) (R)	2.00	5.00
☐ 149	Dragonite (holo) (R)	2.00	5.00
☐ 151	Mew (holo) (R)	7.00	15.00

Japanese Team Rocket (Series 4)

Complete Set (65)		40.00	65.00
Booster Box (60 ct.)		50.00	90.00
Booster Pack (10 cards)		1.00	3.00
Common Card (not listed)		.10	.25
Uncommon Card (not listed)		.25	.50
☐ 5	Charmeleon (U)	.50	1.00
☐ 6	Evil Charizard (holo) (R)	5.00	10.00
☐ 8	Evil Wartortle (U)	.50	1.00
☐ 9	Evil Blastoise (holo) (R)	3.00	6.00
☐ 24	Evil Arbok (holo) (R)	2.00	4.00
☐ 42	Evil Golbat (holo) (R)	2.00	4.00
☐ 45	Evil Vileplume (holo) (R)	2.00	4.00
☐ 51	Evil Dugtrio (holo) (R)	2.00	4.00
☐ 65	Evil Alakazam (holo) (R)	2.00	4.00
☐ 68	Evil Machamp (holo) (R)	2.00	4.00

☐ 130	Gyarados (holo) (R)	4.00	8.00
☐ 145	Zapdos (holo) (R)	4.00	8.00
☐ 148	Dragonair (R)	3.00	5.00
☐ 150	Mewtwo (holo) (R)	4.00	8.00
☐ NNO	Trainer: Super Energy Removal (R)	1.00	3.00
☐ NNO	Trainer: Lass (R)	1.00	3.00
☐ NNO	Trainer: Scoop Up (R)	1.00	3.00
☐ NNO	Trainer: Pokemon Breeder (R)	1.00	3.00
☐ NNO	Trainer: Item Finder (R)	1.00	3.00
☐ NNO	Trainer: Imposter Prof. Oak (R)	1.00	3.00
☐ NNO	Trainer: Devolution Spray (R)	1.00	3.00
☐ NNO	Trainer: Computer Search (R)	1.00	3.00
☐ NNO	Trainer: Clefairy Doll (R)	2.00	4.00
☐ NNO	Trainer: Pokemon Trader (R)	2.00	4.00

Japanese Jungle (Series 2)

Complete Set (48)		40.00	65.00
Booster Box (60 ct)		50.00	90.00
Booster Pack (10 cards)		2.00	3.00
Common Card (not listed)		.10	.25
Uncommon Card (not listed)		.25	.50
☐ 12	Butterfree (U)	.50	1.00
☐ 18	Pidgeot (holo) (R)	2.00	4.00
☐ 25	Pikachu (C)	.75	1.50
☐ 31	Nidoqueen (holo) (R)	2.00	4.00
☐ 36	Clefable (holo) (R)	2.00	4.00
☐ 40	Wigglytuff (holo) (R)	2.00	4.00
☐ 45	Vileplume (holo) (R)	2.00	4.00
☐ 49	Venomoth (holo) (R)	2.00	4.00
☐ 57	Primeape (U)	.50	1.00

☐ 80	Evil Slowbro (holo) (R)	2.00	4.00
☐ 82	Evil Magneton (holo) (R)	2.00	4.00
☐ 97	Evil Hypno (holo) (R)	2.00	4.00
☐ 110	Evil Weezing (holo) (R)	2.00	4.00
☐ 130	Evil Gyarados (holo) (R)	4.00	5.00
☐ 149	Evil Dragonite (holo) (R)	2.00	5.00
☐ NNO	Energy: Rainbow (holo) (R)	2.00	4.00
☐ NNO	Trainer: TR's Little Sister (holo.) (R)	3.00	6.00

Japanese Gym Leaders 1 (Series 5)

Complete set (96)		40.00	80.00
Booster Box (60 ct.)		60.00	95.00
Booster Pack (10 cards)		2.00	4.00
Common Card (not listed)		.10	.25
Uncommon Card (not listed)		.50	1.00
Nivi City Gym Deck #1 (Brock)		10.00	20.00
Hanada Gym Deck #2 (Misty)		8.00	16.00
Kuchiba Gym Deck #3 (Lt.Surge)		10.00	20.00
Tamamushi Gym Deck #4 (Erika)		10.00	20.00
Yamabuki Gym Deck #5 (Sabrina)		8.00	16.00
Gume Gym Deck #6 (Blaine)		10.00	20.00
☐ 1	Bulbasaur (U)	1.00	2.00
☐ 22	Fearow (holo) (R)	2.00	4.00
☐ 36	Clefable (R)	2.00	4.00
☐ 38	Ninetales (holo) (R)	2.00	4.00
☐ 45	Vileplume (holo) (R)	2.00	4.00
☐ 55	Golduck (holo) (R)	2.00	4.00
☐ 71	Victreebel (R)	1.00	2.00
☐ 73	Tentacruel (holo) (R)	2.00	4.00
☐ 76	Golem (holo) (R)	1.00	2.00
☐ 82	Magneton (holo) (R)	2.00	4.00

❏ 107	Hitmonchan (holo) (R)	2.00	5.00
❏ 112	Rhydon (holo) (R)	2.00	4.00
❏ 117	Seadra (holo) (R)	2.00	4.00
❏ 123	Scyther (holo) (R)	3.00	6.00
❏ 125	Electabuzz (holo) (R)	2.00	4.00
❏ 130	Gyarados (holo) (R)	2.00	4.00
❏ 135	Jolteon (R)	1.00	2.00
❏ 146	Moltres (holo) (R)	2.00	4.00
❏ 148	Dragonair (holo) (R)	2.00	5.00
❏ NNO	Trainer: Brock Fighting Badge (R)	2.00	4.00
❏ NNO	Trainer: Brock's Number One (R)	1.00	2.00
❏ NNO	Trainer: Erika w/Grass Badge (R)	1.00	2.00
❏ NNO	Trainer: Erika Thinking (R)	1.00	2.00
❏ NNO	Trainer: Erika's Umbrella (R)	1.00	2.00
❏ NNO	Trainer: Flare (R)	1.00	2.00
❏ NNO	Trainer: Lt.Surge's Aim (R)	1.00	2.00
❏ NNO	Trainer: Lt.Surge w/Lightning (R)	1.00	2.00
❏ NNO	Trainer: Misty's Love w/hearts (R)	1.00	2.00
❏ NNO	Trainer: Misty w/Water Badge (R)	1.00	2.00
❏ NNO	Trainer: No Energy Removal (R)	1.00	2.00
❏ NNO	Trainer: Prison (R)	1.00	2.00
❏ NNO	Trainer: Stadium Psychedelic (R)	1.00	2.00
❏ NNO	Trainer: Rocket Girl Pointing (holo.) (R)	1.00	2.00

Japanese Gym Leaders 2 (Series 6)

	Complete set (98)	40.00	60.00
	Booster Box (60)	55.00	85.00
	Booster Pack (10)	2.00	3.00
	Common Card (not listed)	.10	.25
	Uncommon Card (not listed)	.50	1.00
❏ 2	Ivysaur (U)	1.00	2.00
❏ 3	Venusaur (holo) (R)	3.00	6.00
❏ 5	Charmeleon (U)	1.00	2.00
❏ 6	Charizard (holo) (R)	6.00	12.00

❏ 15	Beedrill (holo) (R)	2.00	4.00
❏ 17	Pidgeotto (R)	1.00	2.00
❏ 24	Arbok (R)	1.00	2.00
❏ 26	Raichu (holo) (R)	2.00	5.00
❏ 31	Nidoqueen (R)	1.00	2.00
❏ 34	Nidoking (holo) (R)	2.00	4.00
❏ 38	Ninetales (R)	1.00	2.00
❏ 49	Venomoth (R)	1.00	2.00
❏ 51	Dugtrio (R)	1.00	2.00
❏ 53	Persian (holo) (R)	2.00	4.00
❏ 55	Golduck (R)	1.00	2.00
❏ 59	Arcanine (holo) (R)	2.00	4.00
❏ 62	Poliwrath (R)	1.00	2.00
❏ 65	Alakazam (holo) (R)	2.00	4.00
❏ 68	Machamp (holo) (R)	2.00	4.00
❏ 84	Doduo Level 15 (R)(White Star)	5.00	12.00

❏ 89	Muk (R)	2.00	4.00
❏ 94	Gengar (holo) (R)	2.00	4.00
❏ 113	Chansey (U) (White Diamond)	5.00	12.00
❏ 127	Pinsir (R)	1.00	2.00
❏ 130	Gyarados (holo) (R)	2.00	4.00
❏ 132	Ditto (holo) (R)	2.00	4.00
❏ 143	Snorlax (R)	2.00	4.00
❏ 145	Zapdos (holo) (R)	3.00	6.00
❏ 146	Moltres (holo) (R)	3.00	6.00
❏ 150	Mewtwo (holo) (R)	4.00	8.00
❏ NNO	Trainer: Blaine's Fire Badge (R)	1.00	2.00
❏ NNO	Trainer: Contract Golbat/Koga's Skill (U)	8.00	20.00
❏ NNO	Trainer: Giovanni (holo) (R)	2.00	4.00
❏ NNO	Trainer: Giovanni's Trump/Nidoking (R)	1.00	2.00
❏ NNO	Trainer: Koga Badge (R)	1.00	2.00
❏ NNO	Trainer: Rocket's Test Potion (U)	.50	1.00
❏ NNO	Trainer: Sabrina (R)	1.00	2.00

❏ NNO	Trainer: Sabrina's Psychic Control (U)	.50	1.00
❏ NNO	Trainer: Saffron City Gym (U)	.50	1.00
❏ NNO	Trainer: Team Rocket Member (U)	.50	1.00
❏ NNO	Trainer: TR's Exploding Gym (U)	.50	1.00
❏ NNO	Trainer: Viridian City (R)	1.00	2.00

Japanese Neo (Series 7)

	Complete Set (96)	60.00	100.00
	Booster Box (60 ct)	50.00	75.00
	Booster Pack (10 cards)	3.00	4.00
	Common Card (not listed)	.10	.25
	Uncommon Card (not listed)	.25	.50

	Starter Set (60)	20.00	25.00
❏ 25	Pikachu (C)	.50	1.25
❏ 154	Meganium (holo) (R)	2.00	4.00
❏ 157	Typhlosion (holo) (R)	3.00	6.00
❏ 160	Feraligatr (holo) (R)	3.00	6.00
❏ 172	Pichu (holo) (R)	4.00	8.00
❏ 173	Cleffa (holo) (R)	2.00	4.00
❏ 175	Togepi (U)	1.00	2.00

❏ 176	Togetic (holo) (R)	2.00	4.00
❏ 181	Ampharos (holo) (R)	2.00	4.00
❏ 182	Bellossom (holo) (R)	2.00	4.00
❏ 184	Azumarill (holo) (R)	2.00	4.00
❏ 189	Jumpluff (holo) (R)	2.00	4.00
❏ 198	Murkrow (R)	2.00	4.00
❏ 199	Slowking (holo) (R)	2.00	4.00
❏ 208	Steelix (holo) (R)	2.00	4.00
❏ 214	Heracross (holo) (R)	2.00	4.00
❏ 215	Sneasel (R)	2.00	4.00
❏ 227	Skarmory (holo) (R)	2.00	4.00
❏ 230	Kingdra (holo) (R)	2.00	4.00
❏ 232	Donphan (R)	1.00	2.00
❏ 239	Elekid (R)	1.00	2.00
❏ 240	Magby (R)	1.00	2.00
❏ 249	Lugia (holo) (R)	6.00	12.00
❏ NNO	Evil Energy (R)	1.00	2.00
❏ NNO	Recycle Energy (R)	1.00	2.00
❏ NNO	Steel Energy (holo) (R)	2.00	4.00
❏ NNO	Trainer: Ekoro Gym (R)	1.00	2.00
❏ NNO	Trainer: Energy Charge (R)	1.00	2.00

NNO	T: Fighting Spirit Headband (R)	1.00	2.00
NNO	Trainer: Kurumi (radio) (R)	1.00	2.00
NNO	Trainer: Poke Gear (R)	1.00	2.00
NNO	Trainer: Slot Machine (R)	1.00	2.00
NNO	T: Super Energy Retrieval (R)	1.00	2.00
NNO	Trainer: Time Capsule (R)	1.00	2.00

Japanese Neo 2 (Series 8)

	Complete Set (57)	30.00	50.00
	Unopened Box (60 ct)	40.00	60.00
	Unopened Pack (10 cards)	2.00	4.00
	Common Card (not listed)	.10	.25
	Uncommon Card (not listed)	.25	.50
12	Butterfree (holo) (R)	2.00	4.00
15	Beedrill (holo) (R)	2.00	4.00
26	Dark Raichu (holo) (R)	3.00	6.00
62	Poliwrath (holo) (R)	2.00	4.00
81	Magnemite (holo) (R)	2.00	4.00
141	Kabutops (holo) (R)	2.00	4.00
186	Politoed (holo) (R)	2.00	4.00
193	Yanma (holo) (R)	2.00	4.00
196	Espeon (holo) (R)	3.00	6.00
197	Umbreon (holo) (R)	2.00	4.00
201	Unown A (holo) (R)	2.00	4.00
202	Wobbuffet (holo) (R)	2.00	4.00
205	Forretress (holo) (R)	2.00	4.00
212	Scizor (holo) (R)	3.00	6.00
217	Ursaring (holo) (R)	2.00	4.00

228	Houndour (holo) (R)	3.00	6.00
229	Houndoom (holo) (R)	3.00	6.00
235	Smeargle (holo) (R)	2.00	4.00
237	Hitmontop (holo) (R)	2.00	4.00
248	Tyranitar (holo) (R)	3.00	6.00
NNO	Trainer: Ruin Wall Pikachu (U)	1.00	2.00
NNO	Trainer: Ruin Wall Raichu (U)	.75	1.50

Japanese Neo 3 (Series 9)

	Complete Set (57)	35.00	60.00
	Unopened Box (60 ct)	40.00	60.00
	Unopened Pack (10 cards)	1.00	2.00
	Common Card (not listed)	.10	.25
	Uncommon Card (not listed)	.25	.50
26	Raichu (U)	.50	1.25
41	Zubat (C)	.25	.50
82	Magneton (holo) (R)	2.00	4.00
121	Starmie (holo) (R)	2.00	4.00
129	Magikarp (holo) (UR)	6.00	12.00
130	Gyarados (holo) (UR)	6.00	12.00
142	Aerodactyl (holo) (R)	2.00	4.00
169	Crobat (holo) (R)	2.00	4.00

181	Ampharos (holo) (R)	2.00	4.00
189	Jumpluff (holo) (R)	2.00	4.00
200	Misdreavus (holo) (R)	2.00	4.00
225	Delibird (holo) (R)	2.00	4.00
229	Houndoom (holo) (R)	3.00	6.00
230	Kingdra (holo) (R)	2.00	4.00
233	Porygon2 (holo) (R)	2.00	4.00
242	Blissey (holo) (R)	2.00	4.00
243	Raikou (holo) (R)	2.00	4.00
244	Entei (holo) (R)	2.00	4.00
245	Suicune (holo) (R)	3.00	5.00
250	Ho-oh (holo) (R)	3.00	5.00
251	Celebi (holo) (R)	3.00	5.00
NNO	Trainer: Rocket's Gengar "R" (U)	.50	1.00

Japanese Neo 4 (Series 10)

	Complete Set (113)	100.00	200.00
	Unopened Box (60 ct)	75.00	125.00
	Unopened Pack (10 cards)	2.00	4.00
	Common Card (not listed)	.10	.25
	Uncommon Card (not listed)	.25	.75

6	Charizard (foil) (UR)	10.00	20.00
26	Raichu (foil) (UR)	5.00	10.00
59	Arcanine (holo) (R)	3.00	6.00
68	Machamp (R)	1.00	2.00
94	Gengar (holo) (R)	3.00	6.00
139	Omastar (R)	1.00	2.00
141	Kabutops (foil) (UR)	5.00	10.00
148	Dragonair (R)	1.00	2.00

149	Dragonite (holo) (R)	3.00	6.00
150	Mewtwo (foil) (UR)	8.00	12.00
157	Typhlosion (holo) (R)	3.00	5.00
160	Feraligatr (holo) (R)	3.00	5.00
164	Noctowl (foil) (UR)	8.00	12.00
166	Ledian (R)	1.00	2.00
168	Ariados (R)	1.00	2.00
169	Crobat (holo) (R)	2.00	5.00
171	Lanturn (R)	.50	1.00
175	Togepi (C)	.25	.50
176	Togetic (holo) (R)	2.00	5.00
181	Ampharos (holo) (R)	2.00	5.00
184	Azumarill (holo) (R)	2.00	4.00
196	Espeon (holo) (R)	3.00	6.00
199	Slowking (R)	1.00	2.00
201	Unown X (R)	1.00	2.00
201	Unown S (R)	1.00	2.00
201	Unown G (R)	1.00	2.00
201	Unown T (R)	1.00	2.00
201	Unown H (R)	1.00	2.00
201	Unown W (R)	2.00	4.00
208	Steelix (foil) (UR)	3.00	6.00
212	Scizor (foil) (UR)	3.00	7.00
217	Ursaring (R)	1.00	2.00
219	Magcargo (R)	1.00	2.00
221	Piloswine (R)	1.00	2.00
229	Houndoom (holo) (R)	3.00	6.00
232	Donphan (R)	3.00	6.00
233	Porygon2 (R)	3.00	6.00
248	Tyranitar (foil) (UR)	6.00	10.00

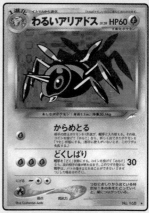

248	Tyranitar (holo) (R)	4.00	8.00
251	Celebi (foil) (UR)	5.00	10.00
NNO	Trainer: Radio Tower (R)	1.00	2.00
NNO	Trainer: Bumpy Gym (R)	1.00	2.00
NNO	Trainer: Impostor Oak's Invention (R)	1.00	2.00
NNO	Miracle Energy (holo) (R)	2.00	4.00
NNO	Trainer: Lucky Stadium (U)	.50	1.00
NNO	Trainer: Determine Personality (U)	1.00	2.00
NNO	Trainer: Rocket's Secret Machine (R)	1.00	2.00
NNO	Trainer: Experience Share (R)	1.00	2.00

Japanese Pokemon VS 1st Edition

Complete Set (144)	150.00	300.00
Fire/Water Booster Box (10 ct.)	60.00	100.00
Grass/Lightning Booster Box (10 ct.)	60.00	100.00
Psychic/Fighting Booster Box (10 ct.)	60.00	100.00
Fire/Water Pack (30 cards)	8.00	12.00
Grass/Lightning Pack (30 cards)	8.00	12.00
Psychic/Fighting Pack (30 cards)	8.00	12.00
Common Card (not listed)	.10	.25

#	Card		
	Uncommon Card (not listed)	.50	1.00
7	Skarmory (holo) (R)	3.00	6.00
13	Scizor (holo) (R)	3.00	6.00
25	Murkrow (holo) (R)	3.00	6.00
43	Sneasel (holo) (R)	3.00	6.00
84	Steelix (holo) (R)	3.00	6.00
90	Tyranitar (holo) (R)	4.00	8.00
91	Umbreon (holo) (R)	2.00	5.00
93	Wobbuffet (holo) (R)	2.00	4.00
94	Raikou (holo) (R)	2.00	4.00
95	Entei (holo) (R)	3.00	7.00
96	Suicune (holo) (R)	3.00	6.00
97	Charizard (C)	2.00	4.00
107	Trainer: Whitney's TM 01 (U)	1.00	2.00
108	Trainer: Whitney's TM 02 (U)	2.00	4.00
113	Trainer: Chuck's TM 01 (U)	1.00	2.00
119	Trainer: Janine's TM 01 (U)	1.00	2.00
120	Trainer: Janine's TM 02 (U)	1.00	2.00
124	Trainer: Bruno's TM 02 (U)	1.00	2.00
125	Trainer: Karen's TM 01 (U)	1.00	2.00
128	Trainer: Lance's TM 01 (U)	1.00	2.00
NNO	Dark Energy (holo)	2.00	4.00
NNO	Metal Energy (holo)	2.00	4.00
NNO	Rainbow Energy (holo)	2.00	4.00

Japanese Pokemon E Cards Series 1

#	Card		
	Complete Set (128)	125.00	180.00
	Booster Box (40 ct)	75.00	120.00
	Booster Pack (5 cards)	3.00	6.00
	Common Cards (not listed)	.25	.50
	Uncommon Card (not listed)	.50	1.00
16	Pikachu (C)	.50	1.00
65	Venusaur (R)	1.00	3.00
66	Butterfree (R)	1.00	3.00
67	Arbok (R)	1.00	2.00
68	Vileplume (R)	1.00	2.00
69	Weezing (R)	1.00	2.00
70	Meganium (R)	1.00	3.00
71	Charizard (R)	2.00	5.00
72	Ninetales (R)	1.00	2.00
73	Rapidash (R)	1.00	2.00
74	Typhlosion (R)	1.50	3.00
75	Magby (R)	1.00	2.00
76	Blastoise (R)	1.50	3.00

#	Card		
77	Poliwrath (R)	1.00	2.00
78	Cloyster (R)	1.00	2.00
79	Kingler (R)	1.00	2.00
80	Feraligatr (R)	1.50	3.00
81	Raichu (R)	1.50	3.00
82	Pichu (R)	1.50	4.00

#	Card		
83	Ampharos (R)	1.00	2.00
84	Alakazam (R)	1.00	2.00
85	Gengar (R)	1.00	2.00
86	Mewtwo (R)	1.50	3.00
87	Mew (R)	1.50	3.50
88	Dugtrio (R)	1.00	2.00
89	Machamp (R)	1.00	2.00
90	Golem (R)	1.00	2.00
91	Pidgeot (R)	1.00	2.00
92	Fearow (R)	1.00	2.00

#	Card		
93	Clefable (R)	1.00	2.00
94	Dragonite (R)	1.00	2.00
95	Tyranitar (R)	1.50	3.00
96	Skarmory (R)	1.00	2.00
97	Venusaur (holo) (R)	3.00	6.00
98	Butterfree (holo) (R)	2.00	4.00
99	Arbok (holo) (R)	2.00	4.00
100	Vileplume (holo) (R)	2.00	4.00
101	Weezing (holo) (R)	2.00	4.00
102	Meganium (holo) (R)	2.00	4.00
103	Charizard (holo) (R)	10.00	18.00
104	Ninetales (holo) (R)	2.00	4.00
105	Rapidash (holo) (R)	2.00	4.00
106	Typhlosion (holo) (R)	2.00	5.00
107	Magby (holo) (R)	2.00	4.00
108	Blastoise (holo) (R)	4.00	8.00
109	Poliwrath (holo) (R)	2.00	4.00
110	Cloyster (holo) (R)	2.00	4.00
111	Kingler (holo) (R)	2.00	4.00

#	Card		
112	Feraligatr (holo) (R)	2.00	5.00
113	Raikou (holo) (R)	2.00	4.00
114	Pichu (holo) (R)	3.00	6.00
115	Ampharos (holo) (R)	2.00	4.00
116	Alakazam (holo) (R)	2.00	4.00
117	Gengar (holo) (R)	2.00	4.00
118	Mewtwo (holo) (R)	4.00	8.00
119	Mew (holo) (R)	4.00	8.00
120	Dugtrio (holo) (R)	2.00	4.00
121	Machamp (holo) (R)	2.00	4.00
122	Golem (holo) (R)	2.00	4.00
123	Pidgeot (holo) (R)	2.00	4.00
124	Fearow (holo) (R)	2.00	4.00
125	Clefable (holo) (R)	2.00	4.00
126	Dragonite (holo) (R)	2.00	5.00
127	Tyranitar (holo) (R)	2.00	5.00
128	Skarmory (holo) (R)	2.00	4.00

Japanese Pokemon E Series 2

Complete set (92)	75.00	100.00
Booster Box (40 packs)	65.00	80.00
Booster Pack (5 cards)	2.00	3.50

Japanese Pokemon E Series 3

Card		
Complete Set (90)	150.00	225.00
Booster Box (40 packs)	50.00	70.00
Booster Pack (5 cards)	2.00	4.00

Japanese Pokemon E Series 4

Card		
Booster Box (40 packs)	45.00	75.00
Golem (UR)	10.00	20.00
Booster Pack (5 cards)	3.00	4.00
Ho-oh (UR)	10.00	25.00
Raikou (UR)	5.00	10.00

Japanese Pokemon Web Set

#	Card		
	Complete Set (48)	40.00	75.00
	Sealed Pack	3.00	7.00
	Common cards (not listed)	.25	.50
17	Dark Ivysaur (U)	.50	1.00
18	Nidorino (U)	.50	1.00
19	Venomoth (U)	.50	1.00
20	Exeggutor (U)	.50	1.00
21	Dark Weezing (U)	.50	1.00
22	Dark Charmeleon (U)	.75	1.50

#	Card		
23	Arcanine (U)	1.00	2.00
24	Dark Wartortle (U)	.75	1.50
25	Pikachu (U)	.75	1.50
26	Electrode (U)	.50	1.00

❏ 27	Dark Kadabra (U)	.50	1.00
❏ 28	Dark Slowbro (U)	.50	1.00
❏ 29	Dugtrio (U)	1.00	2.00
❏ 30	Trainer: Crystal (U)	.75	1.50
❏ 31	Trainer: Hyper Devolution Spray (U)	.50	1.00
❏ 32	Trainer: Primeape Poke Ball (U)	.50	1.00
❏ 33	Nidoking (R)	1.00	2.00
❏ 34	Ninetails (R)	1.00	2.00
❏ 35	Magikarp (R)	2.00	4.00
❏ 36	Raichu (R)	2.00	4.00
❏ 37	Dark Alakazam (R)	2.00	4.00
❏ 38	Dragonite (R)	2.00	4.00
❏ 39	Meowth (R)	1.00	2.00
❏ 40	Trainer: Rocket's Sneak Attack (R)	1.00	2.00
❏ 41	Dark Venusaur (holo) (R)	3.00	6.00
❏ 42	Dark Charizard (holo) (R)	10.00	20.00
❏ 43	Moltres (holo) (R)	3.00	6.00

❏ 44	Dark Blastoise (holo) (R)	4.00	8.00
❏ 45	Articuno (holo) (R)	3.00	6.00
❏ 46	Zapdos (holo) (R)	3.00	6.00
❏ 47	Gengar (holo) (R)	3.00	6.00
❏ 48	Machamp (holo) (R)	3.00	6.00

2004 Japanese Crash of the Blue Sky

Complete Set		
Booster Box (20 packs)	60.00	75.00
Booster Pack	3.00	4.00
Released July 2004		

Chinese Base 1st Edition Wizards of the Coast

Complete Set (102)	75.00	150.00
Booster Box (36 ct.)	75.00	100.00
Booster Pack (11 cards)	3.00	5.00

French Base 1st Edition Wizards of the Coast

Complete Set (102)	75.00	100.00
Booster Box (36 ct)	40.00	80.00
Booster Pack (10 cards)	3.00	6.00
Starter Set (60 cards)	12.00	20.00
Single Cards are valued at 25% of American Base 1st Edition		

German Base 1st Edition Wizards of the Coast

Complete Set (102)	75.00	100.00
Booster Box (36 ct)	50.00	80.00
Booster Pack (11 cards)	3.00	6.00
Starter Set (60 cards)	12.00	20.00
Single Cards are valued at 25% of American Base 1st Edition		

Italian Base 1st Edition Wizards of the Coast

Complete Set (102)	75.00	150.00
Booster Box (36 ct)	75.00	100.00
Booster Pack (11 cards)	2.00	4.00
Single Cards are valued at 25% of American Base 1st Edition		

Italian Jungle 1st Edition Wizards of the Coast

Complete Set (64)	75.00	150.00
Booster Box (36 ct.)	75.00	100.00
Booster Pack (11 cards)	2.00	4.00

Spanish Base 1st Edition Wizards of the Coast

Complete Set	75.00	150.00
Booster Box (36 ct)	75.00	125.00
Booster Pack (11 cards)	3.00	6.00
Single Cards are valued at 25% of American Base 1st Edition		

PROMO SETS

Japanese Coro Coro Comics

Note: Also spelled as Koro Koro.

❏	Abra	5.00	10.00
❏	Blastoise	5.00	10.00
❏	Celebi (Jumbo VS)	25.00	40.00
❏	Charizard (Jumbo size)	20.00	35.00
❏	Cubone	5.00	10.00
❏	Dratini	5.00	10.00
❏	Entei (Jumbo)	5.00	10.00
❏	Electabuzz	5.00	10.00
❏	Farfetch'd	5.00	10.00
❏	Growlithe	6.00	12.00
❏	Ho-oh	5.00	10.00
❏	Jigglypuff	25.00	50.00
❏	Jolteon	5.00	10.00
❏	Legendary Birds (Jumbo Size)	20.00	30.00
❏	Mankey	5.00	10.00
❏	Marill (also known as Pikablu)	5.00	10.00
❏	Meowth (Team Rocket)	5.00	10.00
❏	Meowth GB	5.00	10.00
❏	Mew on Lily Pad (Glossy)	10.00	20.00
❏	Mew (Shiny)(holo)	8.00	16.00
❏	Mewtwo	20.00	40.00
❏	Mewtwo vs. Mew (Jumbo size)	25.00	50.00
❏	Nidoking	5.00	10.00
❏	Onix	5.00	10.00
❏	Cleffa	5.00	10.00
❏	Pichu, Pikachu (Jumbo)	10.00	20.00
❏	Pikachu Flying Balloons	15.00	30.00
❏	Pikachu In Ivy	20.00	40.00
❏	Pikachu, Jigglypuff, Clefairy (Jumbo)	20.00	40.00
❏	Pikachu Surfing	15.00	30.00
❏	Pikachu swimming (Jumbo)	20.00	40.00
❏	Scizor	5.00	10.00
❏	Slowking	5.00	10.00
❏	Staryu	5.00	10.00
❏	Smoochum	5.00	10.00
❏	Togepi	10.00	20.00
❏	Unown R	5.00	10.00
❏	Wooper	5.00	10.00
❏	Trainer: Imakuni	5.00	10.00
❏	Trainer: Koffing	5.00	10.00
❏	Trainer: Legendary birds (Jumbo size)	10.00	20.00
❏	Trainer: Pikachu and friends	35.00	50.00
❏	Trainer: Pokemon Island	10.00	20.00

Japanese CD Promos

	Complete set (10)	15.00	30.00
❏ 3	Venusaur (holo) (lightning bolt)	3.00	6.00
❏ 6	Charizard (holo) (lightning bolt)	6.00	12.00
❏ 9	Blastoise (holo) (lightning bolt)	4.00	8.00
❏ 59	Arcanine	1.00	2.00
❏ 137	Porygon (holo)	3.00	6.00
❏ 143	Snorlax (holo)	1.00	3.00
❏ 150	Mewtwo (glossy) (Poke Ball)	5.00	10.00
❏ 151	Mew (glossy) (Poke Ball)	4.00	8.00
❏ NNO	Trainer Card	.75	2.00
❏ NNO	Trainer Card with Onix	1.00	3.00

Japanese Meiji Set 1997

❏	Ash	60.00	100.00
❏	Pokemon Cards (not listed)	5.00	10.00
❏	Blastoise	20.00	40.00
❏	Brock	40.00	70.00
❏	Charizard	50.00	100.00
❏	Charmander	12.00	25.00
❏	Dragonair	5.00	12.00
❏	Ekans	25.00	50.00
❏	Giovanni	35.00	70.00
❏	James	50.00	75.00
❏	Jesse	40.00	70.00

❏	Jolteon	5.00	12.00
❏	Mew	15.00	35.00
❏	Mewtwo	50.00	80.00
❏	Nidoqueen	12.00	20.00
❏	Persian	20.00	30.00

❏	Pikachu	50.00	90.00
❏	Prof. Oak	20.00	30.00
❏	Squirtle	15.00	25.00
❏	Weezing	20.00	30.00
❏	Zapdos	15.00	30.00

Japanese Meiji Set 1998

Complete Set (48)		450.00	600.00
Pokemon Cards (not listed)		2.00	5.00

❏ 1	Mewtwo		20.00	40.00
❏ 3	Ancient Mew		100.00	200.00
❏ 4	Mewtwo in armor		25.00	40.00
❏ 5	Mewtwo close-up		25.00	35.00
❏ 7	Dragonite		10.00	22.00
❏ 8	Nurse Joy holograph		3.00	7.00
❏ 9	Officer Jenny		4.00	10.00
❏ 10	Pidgeot		3.00	7.00
❏ 12	Nurse Joy		4.00	8.00
❏ 13	Brock		5.00	10.00
❏ 14	Mew flying		18.00	30.00
❏ 18	Team Rocket		10.00	20.00
❏ 19	Meowth and James		5.00	11.00
❏ 20	Venusaur		12.00	20.00

❏ 21	Charizard & Blastoise		15.00	30.00
❏ 22	Mewtwo & Evil Pokemon		20.00	40.00
❏ 23	Charizard battle		20.00	30.00
❏ 24	Mewtwo		25.00	35.00
❏ 25	Psyducks		10.00	15.00
❏ 26	Pikachu		20.00	30.00
❏ 27	Meowth		10.00	18.00
❏ 28	Sad Pikachu		10.00	17.00
❏ 29	Misty and Brock		12.00	20.00
❏ 30	Mew		22.00	40.00
❏ 31	Gyarados battle		10.00	20.00
❏ 32	Happy Mew		25.00	60.00
❏ 34	Charizard and others		15.00	22.00
❏ 35	Togepi		20.00	30.00
❏ 36	Togepi crying		18.00	35.00
❏ 37	Funny face Pikachu		15.00	25.00
❏ 38	Pikachu, Squirtle and Bulbasaur		10.00	20.00
❏ 39	Pikachu & Togepi		10.00	20.00
❏ 40	Pikachu & Raichu battle		15.00	30.00
❏ 41	Pikachu & Raichu Cheek to cheek		25.00	40.00
❏ 42	Pikachu & Raichu Cheek to cheek		18.00	30.00
❏ 43	Pikachu & Raichu get squashed		10.00	20.00
❏ 44	Pikachu and others		25.00	45.00
❏ 45	Charizard & Squirtle		20.00	30.00
❏ 46	Swinging Pikachu		30.00	50.00
❏ 47	Togepi & Vulpix		15.00	25.00
❏ 48	Happy Pikachu		20.00	40.00

Japanese Meiji Set 1999

Complete Set (24)			30.00	60.00
Pokemon Cards (not listed)			1.00	2.00
❏ NNO	Articuno (Freezer)		3.00	6.00
❏ NNO	Blastoise (Kamex)		4.00	7.00
❏ NNO	Bulbasaur (Fushigidane)		3.00	5.00
❏ NNO	Charizard (Lizardon)		10.00	20.00
❏ NNO	Dragonite (Kairyu)		3.00	5.00
❏ NNO	Jigglypuff (Purin)		3.00	5.00
❏ NNO	Mew		5.00	10.00
❏ NNO	Mewtwo		3.00	5.00
❏ NNO	Pikachu		3.00	5.00
❏ NNO	Raichu		3.00	5.00
❏ NNO	Squirtle (Zenigame)		3.00	5.00
❏ NNO	Togepi (Togepy)		3.00	6.00
❏ NNO	Ash & Misty (Satoshi & Kasumi)		3.00	5.00

Japanese Meiji Set 2000

Complete Set (16)			20.00	40.00
Pokemon Cards (not listed)			2.00	4.00
❏ NNO	Pikachu		4.00	8.00
❏ NNO	Marill		5.00	10.00
❏ NNO	Lugia		5.00	12.00
❏ NNO	Togepi		4.00	8.00

Japanese Meiji Blue Set 2000

Complete Set (16)			10.00	20.00
Pokemon Card (not listed)			1.00	3.00
❏	Entei		2.00	4.00
❏	Ho-oh		2.00	4.00
❏	Pichu		2.00	4.00
❏	Pikachu		3.00	6.00

Japanese Meiji Silver Set 2001

Complete Set (18)			12.00	25.00
Pokemon Cards (not listed)			1.00	3.00
❏	Bayleaf		2.00	4.00
❏	Celebi		3.00	6.00
❏	Entei		2.00	4.00
❏	Ho-oh		2.00	4.00
❏	Lugia		4.00	8.00
❏	Marill		2.00	4.00
❏	Pichu		2.00	4.00
❏	Pikachu		4.00	8.00

Japanese Meiji Set 2002

Complete Set (16)			20.00	35.00
❏	Charizard vs. Lugia		5.00	10.00

Japanese Neo Promos

Complete Set (9)			10.00	15.00
❏ 152	Chikorita		1.00	2.00
❏ 153	Bayleef		1.00	2.00
❏ 154	Meganium (holo)		2.00	4.00
❏ 155	Cyndaquil		1.00	2.00
❏ 156	Quilava		1.00	2.00
❏ 157	Typhlosion (holo)		2.00	4.00
❏ 158	Totodile		1.00	2.00
❏ 159	Croconaw		1.00	2.00
❏ 160	Feraligatr (holo)		2.00	4.00

Japanese Neo 2 Promo Set

Complete Set (9)			15.00	30.00
❏ 6	Charizard (holo)		8.00	15.00
❏ 133	Eevee		1.00	2.00
❏ 172	Pichu (holo)		3.00	6.00
❏ 196	Espeon		1.00	2.00
❏ 197	Umbreon		1.00	2.00
❏ 201	Unown N		.75	1.50
❏ 201	Unown E		.75	1.50
❏ 201	Unown O		.75	1.50
❏ 244	Entei (holo)		3.00	6.00

Japanese Neo 3 Promo Set

Complete Set (9)			15.00	30.00
❏ 185	Sudowoodo		1.00	3.00
❏ 215	Sneasel		1.00	3.00
❏ 227	Skarmory		1.00	3.00
❏ 243	Raikou		3.00	6.00

❏ 244	Entei		3.00	6.00
❏ 245	Suicune		3.00	6.00
❏ 249	Lugia		6.00	10.00
❏ 250	Ho-oh		3.00	6.00
❏ 251	Celebi (holo)		6.00	12.00

Japanese Neo 4 Intro Set

Complete Set (80 cards)		30.00	60.00

Japanese Quick Starters

Boxed Set (Green, Red, Promos)			100.00	175.00
❏ 50	Diglett (packaged with booklet)		5.00	10.00
❏ 51	Dugtrio (packaged with booklet)		5.00	10.00

Japanese Quick Starters Green

	Green (Olive) Set (60)		35.00	75.00
	Pokemon cards (not listed)		1.00	2.00
❑ 1	Bulbasaur		2.00	4.00
❑ 4	Charmander		2.00	4.00
❑ 35	Clefairy		2.00	4.00
❑ 64	Kadabra		6.00	10.00
❑ 113	Chansey		2.00	4.00
❑ 115	Kangaskhan		2.00	4.00

❑ 122	Mr Mime		2.00	4.00
❑ 123	Scyther (holo)		12.00	20.00
❑ 144	Articuno (holn)		10.00	20.00
❑ 150	Mewtwo		4.00	8.00
❑ NNO	Trainer: Poke Ball (holo)		4.00	8.00
❑ NNO	Trainers or Energies		.10	.25

Japanese Quick Starters Red

	Red (Pink) Set (60)		60.00	100.00
	Pokemon cards (not listed)		2.00	4.00
❑ 7	Squirtle		2.00	4.00
❑ 25	Pikachu (Level 5)		10.00	20.00
❑ 25	Pikachu (Level13)		10.00	20.00
❑ 26	Raichu		2.00	5.00
❑ 107	Hitmonlee		2.00	5.00
❑ 131	Lapras		2.00	5.00
❑ 143	Snorlax		2.00	5.00
❑ 145	Zapdos (holo)		12.00	20.00
❑ 146	Moltres (holo)		10.00	20.00
❑ NNO	Trainer: Poke Ball (holo)		4.00	8.00
❑ NNO	Trainers or Energies		.10	.25

Japanese Southern Islands

	Complete set (18)		12.00	20.00
	Rainbow Collection (9)		6.00	10.00
	Tropical Island Collection (9)		6.00	10.00
	Pokemon cards (not listed)		2.00	4.00
❑ 45	Vileplume (holo) (Tropical)		3.00	6.00
❑ 151	Mew (holo) (Rainbow)		3.00	6.00
❑ NNO	Marill (holo) (Tropical)		3.00	6.00
❑ NNO	Ledyba (holo) (Rainbow)		4.00	8.00
❑ NNO	Togepi (holo) (Rainbow)		3.00	6.00
❑ NNO	Slowking (holo) (Tropical)		3.00	6.00

Japanese Sweepstakes

	Complete Set 1 (3)		25.00	50.00
	Complete Set 2 (3)		25.00	50.00
❑	Blastoise (set 1)		12.00	20.00
❑	Charizard (set 1)		15.00	30.00

❑	Venusaur (set 1)		5.00	10.00
❑	Feraligatr (set 2)		10.00	20.00
❑	Meganium (set 2)		10.00	20.00
❑	Typhlosion (set 2)		10.00	20.00

Japanese Vending Series One

	Series One set (36)		40.00	60.00
	Vending Sheets		5.00	15.00
	Pokemon cards (not listed)		2.00	4.00
❑ 1	Bulbasaur		5.00	8.00
❑ 4	Charmander		5.00	8.00
❑ 7	Squirtle		4.00	8.00
❑ 25	Pikachu		8.00	16.00
❑ 35	Clefairy		5.00	8.00
❑ 113	Chansey		4.00	7.00
❑ 122	Mr Mime		4.00	7.00
❑ 150	Mewtwo		8.00	15.00

Japanese Vending Series Two

	Series Two set (36)		35.00	60.00
	Vending Sheets		10.00	20.00
	Pokemon cards (not listed)		2.00	4.00
❑ 26	Raichu		5.00	10.00
❑ 125	Electabuzz		3.00	6.00
❑ 142	Aerodactyl		5.00	10.00
❑ 144	Articuno		5.00	10.00
❑ 145	Zapdos		5.00	10.00
❑ 146	Moltres		4.00	8.00

Japanese Vending Series Three

	Series Three set (45)		30.00	60.00
	Vending Sheets		5.00	15.00
	Pokemon cards (not listed)		2.00	4.00
	White Back cards (not listed)		1.00	2.00
❑ 115	Kangaskhan		3.00	6.00
❑ 123	Scyther		4.00	8.00
❑ 150	Mewtwo		6.00	12.00
❑ NNO	WB Extra Rule: 6 Decks		3.00	6.00
❑ NNO	WB Extra Rule: 6 Players		4.00	8.00
❑ NNO	WB Extra Rule: Deck Swap		3.00	6.00
❑ NNO	WB Extra Rule: Girl & Boy		4.00	8.00
❑ NNO	WB Extra Rule: Meowth		4.00	7.00
❑ NNO	WB Pikachu		10.00	15.00

Japanese Vending Series Three Mail-in

	Complete Set (5)		50.00	100.00
❑	Alakazam (holo)		15.00	30.00
❑	Gengar (holo)		15.00	30.00
❑	Golem (holo)		15.00	30.00
❑	Machamp (holo)		15.00	30.00

❑	Omastar (holo)		15.00	30.00

Japanese Vending Series Double Zero

	Complete Set (3)		30.00	50.00
❑	Mew (with bubbles)		10.00	20.00
❑	Mewtwo		10.00	20.00
❑	Pikachu (lightning bolt)		10.00	20.00

Japanese Video Starter Set

	Complete Set (82)		14.00	30.00
	Energy Cards (not listed)		.20	.50
	Trainer Cards (not listed)		.20	.50
	Pokemon Cards (not listed)		1.00	2.00
❑	Blastoise (holo) (SD)		8.00	12.00
❑	Venusaur (holo) (BD)		8.00	12.00
❑ 3	Raichu (BD)		1.50	3.00
❑ 13	Pikachu (BD)		2.00	5.00
❑ 16	Squirtle (SD)		2.00	4.00

❑ 18	Squirtle (SD)		2.00	4.00
❑ 37	Squirtle (SD)		2.00	4.00
❑ 40	Squirtle (SD)		2.00	4.00
❑ 40	Pikachu (BD)		3.00	6.00

Promo Star Wizards of the Coast

❑ 1	Pikachu 1st Edition (Jungle packs)		60.00	120.00
❑ 1	Pikachu (Pokemon League)		4.00	8.00
❑ 2	Electabuzz (First Movie)		2.00	4.00
❑ 3	Mewtwo (First Movie)		3.00	6.00

❑ 4	Pikachu (First Movie)	5.00	10.00
❑ 5	Dragonite (First Movie)	3.00	6.00
❑ 6	Arcanine (Pokemon League)	4.50	8.00

❑ 7	Jigglypuff (Cassette Mail-in)	2.00	4.00
❑ 8	Mew (Pokemon League)	.50	2.00
❑ 9	Mew (holo) (Pokemon League)	2.00	4.00
❑ 10	Meowth (holo) (TCG Game Boy)	6.00	10.00
❑ 11	Eevee (Pokemon League)	1.00	3.00
❑ 12	Mewtwo (Nintendo Magazine)	15.00	25.00

❑ 13	Venusaur (Strategy Guide)	4.00	10.00
❑ 14	Mewtwo (Movie Video)	2.00	4.00
❑ 15	Cool Porygon (Stadium Bundle)	5.00	10.00
❑ 16	Computer Error (Pokemon League)	1.00	3.00
❑ 17	Dark Persian (Nintendo Mag.)(Err)	40.00	75.00
❑ 17	Dark Persian (Nintendo Mag.)	5.00	10.00
❑ 18	TR's Meowth (Pokemon League)	1.00	3.00
❑ 19	Sabrina's Abra (Nintendo Mag.)	4.00	8.00
❑ 20	Psyduck (Pokemon League)	1.00	3.00
❑ 21	Moltres (Movie 2000)	2.00	5.00
❑ 22	Articuno (Movie 2000)	1.00	3.00
❑ 23	Zapdos (Movie 2000)	2.00	5.00
❑ 24	Birthday Pikachu (holo) (Pokemon League)	8.00	12.00
❑ 25	Flying Pikachu	2.00	4.00
❑ 26	Pikachu (Snap)	4.00	8.00
❑ 27	Pikachu (Movie 2000 Video)	8.00	16.00
❑ 28	Surfing Pikachu	3.00	7.00
❑ 29	Marill (Neo Genesis)	3.00	6.00
❑ 30	Togepi	3.00	7.00

❑ 31	Cleffa	1.00	2.00
❑ 32	Smeargle	1.00	3.00
❑ 33	Scizor (holo)	1.00	2.00
❑ 34	Entei (holo) (Movie 2001)	3.00	6.00
❑ 35	Pichu (holo) (Pokemon Lea.)	5.00	10.00
❑ 36	Igglybuff	2.00	4.00
❑ 37	Hitmontop	.50	1.00
❑ 38	Unown J	3.00	6.00
❑ 39	Misdreavus	1.00	2.00
❑ 40	Trainer: Pokemon Center	5.00	10.00
❑ 41	Trainer: Lucky Stadium	3.00	6.00
❑ 42	Trainer: Pokemon Tower	3.00	6.00
❑ 43	Machamp	1.00	2.00
❑ 44	Magmar	1.00	2.00
❑ 45	Scyther	1.00	3.00
❑ 46	Electabuzz	1.00	3.00
❑ 47	Mew (Lilypad)	1.00	3.00
❑ 48	Articuno	4.00	8.00
❑ 49	Snorlax	2.00	5.00
❑ 50	Celebi (movie promo)	3.00	6.00
❑ 51	Rapidash	3.00	6.00
❑ 52	Ho-oh	8.00	12.00
❑ 53	Suicune	3.00	7.00

MISCELLANEOUS PROMO CARDS

American Promo

❑	Aerodactyl (Fossil) (Pre-release)	6.00	10.00
❑	Ancient Mew (holo) (Movie 2000)	1.00	2.00
❑	Articuno,Moltres,Zapdos (Jumbo)	8.00	20.00
❑	Brock's Vulpix W gold	2.00	4.00
❑	Clefable (Jungle) (Pre-release)	14.00	27.00
❑	Dark Arbok W gold stamp	2.00	4.00

❑	Dark Charmeleon W gold stamp	5.00	10.00
❑	Dark Gyarados (holo) (Pre-rel.)	3.00	6.00
❑	Exeggutor (Bilingual)	10.00	25.00
❑	Kabuto W gold stamped (TopDeck)	2.00	4.00
❑	Meowth gold border	8.00	15.00
❑	Misty's Psyduck W gold stamped (TopDeck)	6.00	9.00
❑	Misty's Seadra (Pre-release)	1.00	3.00
❑	Pikachu E3 gold stamped	5.00	12.00
❑	Pikachu E3 gold (Red Cheeks)	50.00	100.00
❑	Pikachu Jumbo Size (TopDeck)	3.00	6.00
❑	Pikachu PokeTour 1999 gold stamped	20.00	30.00
❑	Pikachu W gold stamped (Duelist)	8.00	12.00
❑	Wartortle W gold (TopDeck)	4.00	8.00
❑	Gyarados (Pre-release)	3.00	6.00
❑	Wartortle (Pre-release)	4.00	8.00

American EX Promo Cards

❑	Bagon (Gencon)	10.00	20.00
❑	Bagon (Inquest Magazine)	4.00	8.00
❑	Bagon (Scrye Magazine)	4.00	8.00
❑	Blastoise (Nat.Chmpship)	15.00	30.00
❑	Chansey (ERR)	20.00	40.00
❑	Gastly	30.00	60.00
❑	Hoppip (2002 E3)	20.00	40.00
❑	Pichu (2002 E3)	20.00	40.00
❑	Chadow Lugia (jumhn)	10.00	20.00
❑ 1	Kyogre ex (Promo Star)	10.00	20.00
❑ 2	Groudon ex (Promo Star)	10.00	20.00
❑ 3	Treecko	4.00	10.00
❑ 4	Grovyle	4.00	8.00
❑ 8	Torchic	4.00	9.00
❑ 9	Combusken	8.00	16.00
❑ 10	Mudkip	4.00	10.00
❑ 11	Marshtomp	4.00	10.00
❑ 12	Pikachu	8.00	12.00
❑ 13	Meowth	2.00	5.00
❑ 14	Latias	3.00	7.00
❑ 15	Latios	3.00	7.00

BECKETT® POKÉMON® MARKETPLACE

A. Gaming Back Pack
PDYG9010 ....$35.99

B. Gaming Album
PDYG9009 ....$19.99

C. Card & Magazine Pages
PDYG6020 (25 Card pages) $4.99
PDYG6021P (25 Mag. pages)$4.99

D. Gaming Case
PDYG9008 ....$18.99

E. Deck Boxes
Gold - PDYG6022 ....$2.99
Blue - PDYG6023 ....$2.99
Red - PDYG6028 ....$2.99
Cranberry Ice - PDYG6030 ..$2.99
Green - PDYG6031 ....$2.99
Orange - PDYG6033 ....$2.99
Black - PDYG6035..............$2.99

F. Deck Protector Sleeves
Gold - PDYG6025 ....$3.99
Blue - PDYG6027 ....$3.99
Red - PDYG6029.................$3.99
Green - PDYG6032..............$3.99
Yellow - PDYG6037.............$3.99

G. Pokémon EX Power Keepers
(3 Packs)
PDPK010 ....$12.99

H. Pokémon 4 Pocket Album
(Holds up to 80 cards)
PDPK007 ....$6.99

I. Pokémon Ex Crystal Guardians
Booster Packs (3 Packs)
PDPK008 ....$12.99

J. Pokémon Legend Maker Booster
Packs (3 Packs)
PDPK004 ....$9.99

K. Pokémon EX-Delta Species
Booster Packs (3 Packs)
PDPK005 ....$9.99

L. Pokémon EX Holon Phantoms
Booster Packs (3 Packs)
PDPK006 ....$12.99

M. Pokémon EX Dragon Frontiers
Booster Packs (3 Packs)
PDPK009 ....$12.99

N. Pokémon Diamond & Pearl
Booster Packs (3 Packs)
PDPK011 ....$12.99

O. Pokémon Diamond & Pearl ➤NEW!
Mysterious Treasures (3 Packs)
PDPK012 ....$12.99

P. Beckett Pokémon Back Issues; NEW!
Indicate issue # on order form.
MGPK 1 - 46.......................$3.00
PK 1 - 3.............................$6.99
PK 89 - 94.........................$6.99

A

B

Items are not included

C

D   Items are not included

P   Go To www.beckettpokemon.com for complete back issue list

Issue #1   Issue #2   Issue #3   Issue #4   Issue #5   Issue #8   Issue #9   Issue #10   Issue #11

Issue #12   Issue #13   Issue #14   Issue #15   Issue #16   Issue #17   Issue #27   Issue #28   Issue #3

Issue #35   Issue #36   Issue #37   Issue #46   PK1 - Oct '06   PK2 - Dec '06   PK3 - Feb '07   Issue #89   Issue #9

Issue #91   Issue #92   Issue #93   Issue #94

254 2008 Beckett Pokémon Price Guide Book

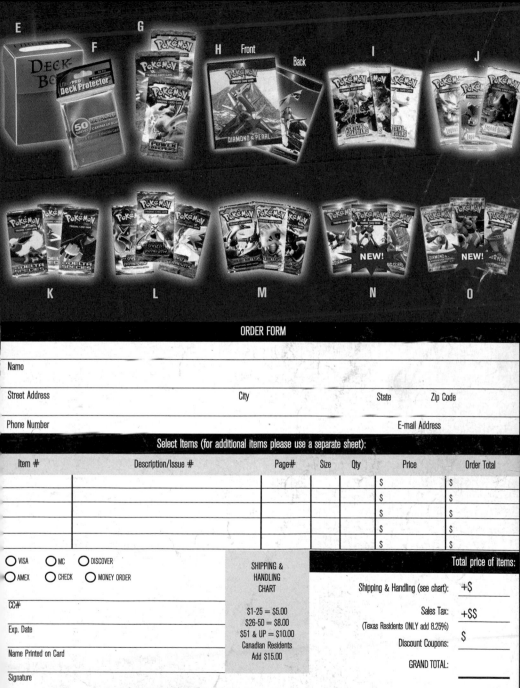

ORDER FORM

Name

Street Address   City   State   Zip Code

Phone Number   E-mail Address

Select Items (for additional items please use a separate sheet):

Item #	Description/Issue #	Page#	Size	Qty	Price	Order Total
					$	$
					$	$
					$	$
					$	$
					$	$

○ VISA   ○ MC   ○ DISCOVER

○ AMEX   ○ CHECK   ○ MONEY ORDER

CC#

Exp. Date

Name Printed on Card

Signature

SHIPPING & HANDLING CHART

$1-25 = $5.00
$26-50 = $8.00
$51 & UP = $10.00
Canadian Residents
Add $15.00

Total price of items:

Shipping & Handling (see chart): +$

Sales Tax: +$$
(Texas Residents ONLY add 8.25%)

Discount Coupons: $

GRAND TOTAL:

SORRY, NO INTERNATIONAL ORDERS. Payable in US Funds. Payable to: *Beckett Spotlight on Pokemon*
Mail to: *Beckett Spotlight on Pokemon Products*, 4635 McEwen Drive, Dallas, TX 75244-5308
FOR FASTER CREDIT CARD SERVICE CALL 972-991-6657 OR FAX YOUR ORDER TO 972-448-9078.
www.beckettpokémon.com

PKBKCAT03